A-Level Sociology

CloudLearn Ltd

Specification code: 7192

First Teaching: 2015

First Assessment: 2017

A Level Sociology

Published and distributed by: OSC Ltd.

First published in July 2015

Edition Number: 2015/01

© OSC Ltd.

Printed under license by CloudLearn Ltd

Disclaimer

The authors of this text believe the contents of this course to be accurate and correct. While all possible care has been taken in producing this work, no guarantee can be given.

Contents

Introduction

You have chosen to study A-Level Sociology. In order to successfully complete the A-Level Sociology course from AQA, you will need to pass the three A-Level written examinations. You can register to sit these at any examination centre that will accept you as an external candidate, and we remind you that it is your responsibility to find an examination centre and to book your exams.

3A Tutors Ltd.
1A High Street
Staple Hill
Bristol
BS16 5HA
www.3at.org.uk
Tel: 0117 9109931

English Maths Science Tuition and Educational Centre
40 Showell Green Lane
Sparkhill
Birmingham
B11 4JP
Tel: 0121 771 1298
Fax: 0872 110 7502
e-mail: info@englishandmaths.com
Website: www.englishandmaths.com

London Brookes College
40/42 The Burroughs
Hendon
London
NW4 4AP
Tel: 020 8202 2007
E-mail: info@londonbrookescollege.co.uk
Website: http://www.londonbrookescollege.co.uk/

Assessment

In this course, at the end of certain topics, you will find a series of TMAs (Tutor Marked Assignments). The answers should be types onto a word document and e-mailed to your tutor for marking when you reach the appropriate place.

Throughout the course there are a number of activities and self-assessment questions: these are not to be returned to your tutor. They are there to get you thinking about key concepts and ideas and to encourage you to do some on-going revision and additional research as and when needed.

In order to sit your exams you will need to contact an examination centre and organise this for yourselves.

Details of the written exams can be found on the following page.

A-level Sociology: an overview

Each subject content section will provide you with a choice of topics; but they are organised differently. In the examination, certain units will include compulsory questions regarding theory and methodology. Details regarding what you will be examined on will follow. Be sure to read this outline carefully so that you fully understand what will be required of you.

Integral Elements and Core Themes

Throughout the entire course, we invite you to consider some basic elements and themes that you will incorporate in your investigation of each individual topic. You should always consider the general sociological theories, perspectives and methods when examining specific topics (for example, Education and Crime and Deviance. You should be applying research methods by focusing on how sociologists obtain data that you are considering as well as the strengths and weaknesses of their approaches.

Further, you should consider the following core themes:

- Socialisation, culture and identity
- Social differentiation, power and stratification

These themes should not be considered as discrete topics but rather should be interpreted broadly as threads that run through many areas of social life.

A-level Sociology is designed to bring about all of the following gains in knowledge and skills for those students willing to study and learn independently:

- To promote an awareness, knowledge and understanding of human societies, especially comparisons between modern and traditional ones.
- To develop an understanding of sociological method, including the collection, analysis and interpretation of data.
- To provide an introduction to sociological concepts, theories and research findings.
- To stimulate awareness of the range and limitations of sociological theory and research.
- To promote an understanding of continuity and change in social life.
- To encourage a critical awareness of social, economic and political processes, and their effects.
- To develop the capacity for the critical evaluation of different forms of information and evidence.
- To promote an appreciation and understanding of individual, social and cultural diversity.
- To enhance candidates' ability to apply sociological knowledge and understanding to their own lives and participation within society.

A Level

For the A-Level you will develop a greater depth and range of knowledge than at the AS level. As such you will engage in sociological enquiry and the nature of sociological thought in greater range and depth, while demonstrating more advanced application, analysis, interpretation and evaluation than at the AS level.

Through this area of study and the various topics within this section, you will be looking the following:

- Structural, social action, consensus and conflict theories.
- The concepts of modernity and post-modernity in relation to sociological theory.
- The nature of science and to what extent Sociology can be considered 'scientific'.
- Relationships between theory and method.
- Debates about objectivity, subjectivity and value freedom.
- The relationship between Sociology and social policy.

Core Content

The A-Level Sociology consists of 3 Examinations:

Paper 1 – Education with Theory and Methods

Paper 2 – Topics in Sociology

Paper 3 – Crime and Deviance with Theory and Methods

The formal assessment for A-Level Sociology is as follows:

Paper 1: Education with Theory and Methods	Paper 2: Topics in Sociology	Paper 3: Crime and Deviance with Theory and Methods
What's assessed	**What's assessed**	**What's assessed**
Compulsory content 4.1.1, 4.1.2, 4.1.3	Section A: one from option 1: 4.2.1, 4.2.2, 4.2.3 or 4.2.4 Section B: one from option 2: 4.2.5, 4.2.6, 4.2.7 or 4.2.8	Compulsory content 4.3.1, 4.3.2
Assessed	**Assessed**	**Assessed**
• 2 hour written exam • 80 marks • 33.3% of A-level	• 2 hour written exam • 80 marks • 33.3% of A-level	• 2 hour written exam • 80 marks • 33.3% of A-level
Questions	**Questions**	**Questions**
• Education: short answer and extended writing, 50 marks • Methods in Context: extended writing, 20 marks • Theory and Methods: extended writing, 10 marks	Section A: extended writing, 40 marks Section B: extended writing, 40 marks	Crime and Deviance: short answer and extended writing, 50 marks Theory and Methods: extended writing, 30 marks

Timescales

The written exams for the A-Level are held in May/June every year (starting in 2017).

You need to confirm the specific dates with your chosen examination centre, and we always recommend you book early for the written examinations.

Students must take all written exams in the same year; it is not permissible to take some exams one year and some the following year.

Course structure

The course is written systematically to cover the AQA specification, and, as a result, there are times when a particular issue or subject is discussed in more than one section. This is not an error but reflects the specification which also does this. This should not in any way harm your learning but should actually enhance it as it gives you the opportunity to learn/revise a key issue in several different areas of the course.

A-level Assessment (AQA 7192)

The A-Level exam consists of three papers.

Paper 1 and Paper 3 consist of compulsory content, so all questions must be answered (see below).

Paper 2 has two sections: Section A which consists of optional content in which you will be required to answer one question selected from your preferred option and Section B, in which, as with Section A, you will need to respond to a question from one of your chosen options (see the table below).

A-Level Paper 1: Education with Theory and Methods (4.1)	What is Assessed
Compulsory content	4.1.1 – Education
	4.1.2 – Methods in Context
	4.1.3 – Theory and Methods

The 4.1 (Education with Theory and Methods) units cover in more depth, some of the units covered as part of the AS (3.1.1; 3.1.2; 3.2.1)

A-Level Paper 3: Crime and Deviance with Theory and Methods (4.3)	What is Assessed
Compulsory Content	4.3.1 – Crime and Deviance
	4.3.2 – Theory and Methods

A-Level Paper 2: Topics in Sociology (4.2)	What is Assessed
Section A: Option 1 unit – choose one topic	4.2.1 – Culture and Identity 4.2.2 – Families and Households 4.2.3 – Health 4.2.4 – Work, Poverty and Welfare
Section B: Option 2 unit – choose one topic	4.2.5 – Beliefs in Society 4.2.6 – Global Development 4.2.7 – The Media 4.2.8 – Stratification and Differentiation

You should continue to draw links between these topics and other topics already studied. In addition, you should try to apply examples from your own experience with small-scale social research throughout the following sections. You must also examine both evidence of, and sociological explanations for, the content listed in the topic that follow.

A-Level Compulsory Content – Paper 1

4.1.1 Education

- The role and functions of the education system
- Differential educations achievement of social groups
- Relationships and process within schools
- The significance of education policy

4.1.2 Methods in Context

- Applying sociological research methods to the study of education

4.1.3 Theory and Methods

- Quantitative and qualitative methods of research
- Sources of data
- Primary and secondary data
- Positivism, Interpretivism and sociological methods
- Theoretical, practical and ethical considerations
- Modernity and Post-Modernity in relation to sociological theory
- Science and Sociology
- Subjectivity, Objectivity and Value Freedom
- The relationship between Sociology and social policy

A-Level Compulsory Content – Paper 3

4.3.1 Crime and Deviance

- Theories of crime, deviance, social control and social order
- Patterns in crime distribution—how crime is socially distributed by age, ethnicity, gender, locality, and social class
- Special topics: mass media and crime, globalization and crime in contemporary society, green crime, human rights and state crime
- Crime control, surveillance, prevention, punishment, and the CJS and other agencies
- Connecting theory to method in studies of crime and deviance

4.3.2 Theory and Methods

For the final section, you should study the following areas:

- Assessing qualitative and quantitative research methods (strengths and limitations and research designs of each)
- Different sources of data: questionnaires, interviews, participant observation, non-participant observation, experiments, documents, and official statistics (strengths, limitations of these sources)
- Distinctions between primary/secondary data and between quantitative/qualitative data
- The relationship between Positivism, Interpretivism and sociological methods, as well as the nature of 'social facts'
- Selection of research topics and methods: theoretical, practical and ethical considerations
- Understanding the concepts of modernity and post-modernity in relation to sociological theory
- The relationship between Science and Sociology in terms of theory and methodology
- The link and connections between Sociology and Social Policy
- Subjectivity, objectivity and value freedom in Sociology

As you work through this portion of your studies, the aim is for you to be able to approach each topic using sociological theory and research methods and, as always, you will be expected to relate each topic back to the two core themes listed above (socialisation, culture and identity and social differentiation, power and stratification). You will be expected to recognise evidence of, and sociological explanations for, the content that follows.

A-Level Optional Content – Paper 2 - Section A – Option 1 (choose one)

4.2.1 – Culture and Identity

For this unit you will examine sociological explanations of identity looking at the following areas:

- What is meant by the terms culture and conceptions of culture
- Difference categories of culture – sub-culture; mass culture; high culture; low culture; popular culture and global culture
- Socialisation and the process of socialisation; primary and secondary socialisation; agencies of socialisation
- What is identity; socially constructed identities; identity and choice
- Identity and age, disability, ethnicity, gender, nationality, sexuality, social class
- The relationship of identity to production, consumption and globalisation

4.2.2 – Families and Households

For this topic, you will look at:

- The relationship of the family to social structures, social change, the economy and state policies
- The diversity of the contemporary family; patterns of marriage; cohabitation; separation and divorce; household structures; personal life; children; the course of life
- Gender roles; division of labour within the family; power relationships
- Childhood and the status of children in the family and society over the years
- Demographic trends in the UK since 1900; birth rates; mortality rates; family size; life expectancy; ageing population; migration and globalisation

4.2.3 Health

For this topic, you will look at:

- The social construction of health, illness, disability and the body.
- Models of health and illness
- The unequal distribution of health chances in the UK based on social class, gender, ethnicity and region.
- Inequalities in terms of the provision of and access to health care
- The nature and social distribution of mental illness
- The role of medicine, the health professions and the globalised health industry

4.2.4 Work, Poverty and Welfare

For this topic, you will look at:

- Definitions of poverty; the nature, existence and persistence of poverty in contemporary society
- How different social groups are affected by the distribution of poverty, wealth and income
- The state's response to poverty; solutions by the state and private agencies, voluntary and informal welfare providers to poverty in contemporary society
- The organisation and control of the labour process; division of labour; the role of technology; skill and de-skilling
- The impact of work and worklessness on people's lives and life chances; the effect of globalisation

A-Level Optional Content – Section B – Option 2 (choose one)

4.2.5 Beliefs in Society

- Theories of ideology, science and religion (Christian and non-Christian)
- The relationship between religious beliefs, practices and organisations in relation to social stability and social change
- Various religious organisations: sects, cults, denominations, New Age movements and their relationships to religious/spiritual beliefs and practice
- How different social groups may engage in differing religious/spiritual organisations, movements, beliefs, and practices
- Contemporary perspectives on religion and religiosity; the nature and extent of secularisation in terms of global perspectives; globalisation and the spread of religion

4.2.6 Global Development

- Theories of development, underdevelopment, and global inequality
- Globalisation's influence on culture, politics and economics; the global relationship between societies
- How global aid and trade impacts on political, economic and cultural relationships between societies
- Development in relation to industrialisation, urbanisation, the environment, war and conflict
- Local and global strategies of development through non-governmental agencies, transnational corporations and international agencies
- How employment, education, health, demographic shifts and gender can be considered as aspects of development

4.2.7 The Media

- The new media and its significance; the role of the media in contemporary society
- The relationship between ownership and control of the mass media
- The mass media, globalisation and popular culture
- The processes of selection and presentation of the content of the news
- Media representations of age, social class, ethnicity, gender, sexuality and disability
- The relationship between the mass media, media content and presentation, and audiences

4.2.8 Stratification and Differentiation

- Theories of stratification and differentiation by social class, gender, ethnicity and age
- Dimensions of inequality (class, status, and power) and studies of life chances, as varied according to class, gender, ethnicity, age and disability
- Problems of defining and measuring social class; studies of occupation, gender and social class, age and disability
- Defining and measuring social class; occupation and gender
- Structures of inequality—changes and implications in terms of globalisation and transnational capitalist class
- Patterns of social mobility—nature and significance
- Applying sociological theory and methods to studies of stratification and differentiation

Assessment Summary

A-Level Assessment (AQA 7192)

The A-Level exam consists of three papers.

Paper 1 and Paper 3 consists of compulsory content, so all questions must be answered.

Paper 1: Education with Theory and Methods (4.1)	What is Assessed	Questions	Assessed
Compulsory content	4.1.1 – Education	Short answer and extended writing (50 marks)	2 hour written exam
	4.1.2 – Methods in Context	Extended writing (20 marks)	80 marks
	4.1.3 – Theory and Methods	Extended writing (10 marks)	33.3% of the A level

Paper 3: Crime and Deviance with Theory and Methods (4.3)	What is Assessed	Questions	Assessed
Compulsory content	4.3.1 – Crime and Deviance	Short answer and extended writing (50 marks)	2 hour written exam
			80 marks
	4.3.2 – Theory and Methods	Extended writing (30 marks)	33.3 of the A level

Paper 2 has two sections. Section, A which consists of optional content in which you will be required to answer one question selected from your preferred option and Section B, which, as with Section A you will need to respond to a question from one of your chosen options (see the table below)

Paper 2: Topics in Sociology (4.2)	What is Assessed	Questions	Assessed
Section A: Option 1 unit – choose one topic	4.2.1 – Culture and Identity 4.2.2 – Families and Households 4.2.3 – Health 4.2.4 – Work, Poverty and Welfare	Extended writing (40 marks)	2 hour written exam 80 marks 33.3% of the AS level
Section B: Option 2 unit – choose one topic	4.2.5 – Beliefs in Society 4.2.6 – Global Development 4.2.7 – The Media 4.2.8 – Stratification and Differentiation	Extended writing (40 marks)	

Assessment Objectives (AOs)

When you sit your examination, you will acquire marks by demonstrating that you are able to meet the skills requirements for what is referred to as Assessment Objectives (AOs).

In terms of how you are assessed for both the AS and A level, you are not only being assessed on how much you know about a particular subject, but you are also being assessed on associated skills you are expected to demonstrate. Therefore, the marks you acquire will be based upon how effectively you have met the requisite skills.

The three Assessment Objectives (AOs) are:

- AO1 – Knowledge and understanding.
- Demonstrate knowledge and understanding of sociological theories, concepts and evidence studied on the course
- AO2 – Application
- Apply sociological theories, concepts and evidence and research methods to a range of issues
- AO3 – Analysis and Evaluation
- Analyse and Evaluate sociological theories, concepts, evidence and research methods in order to, present arguments, make judgements and draw conclusions

Suggested Reading

Although there is no required textbook or reading for this course. However, here are some suggested suitable textbooks and reference works if you wish to continue your studies further.

Abercrombie, N., Hill., S and Turner B.	The Penguin Dictionary of Sociology 5th edition 2006
Bilton, A., *et al*	Introductory Sociology 4th edition 2002
Browning, G., Haleli, A. and Webster, F.	Understanding Contemporary Society 1999
Bruce, S.	Sociology: A Very Short Introduction 2000
Fulcher, J., and Scott, J.	Sociology 3rd edition 2007
Macionis, J.	Sociology 15th (international) edition 2013
Macionis, J., and Plummer, K.	Sociology: A global introduction 5th edition 2011
Haralambos, M	Sociology Themes and Perspectives, 2004

The following AQA-approved A-level Sociology textbooks are also available:

http://www.aqa.org.uk/subjects/sociology/as-and-a-level-sociology-textbooks2

And if you would like to keep up-to-date with contemporary research into how society works, the Radio 4 programme 'Thinking Allowed' is highly recommended. This weekly 30 minute programme features interviews with Sociologists (and Anthropologists) about their recent research. You will find that you can listen to past episodes using the BBC iplayer:

http://www.bbc.co.uk/programmes/b006qy05

Introduction: What is Sociology?

Sociology is the study of people in society. It examines people as social beings on the individual, group and societal level. It can be defined as: 'the scientific study of human social life, groups and societies'. Sociologists consider how social and socially-influenced factors, such as family, education, ethnicity, social class and gender can play a part in shaping individual identities.

Sociologists also consider group behaviour. For example, a sociologist may study how an office team works together, and how people's behaviour is affected by those of their colleagues or work associates. They may also question how factors such as gender or class influence our behaviours as individuals and in group contexts.

Sociologists also study society-at-large, and may consider the correlations between factors such as ethnicity or class, for example, and an individual's participation in wider social structures such as government or education.

Sociologists therefore often study wider social trends or patterns: these wider social trends or patterns, which could be as wide and diverse as rates of marriage, divorce or birth, unemployment, suicide, levels of university education or consumption of the mass media. All these wider trends and patterns point to something that sociologist often call social norms.

Social norms are thus the 'rules of behaviour which reflect or embody a culture's values' (in the words of the modern and highly influential British sociologist Anthony Giddens). What is clear to the sociologist is that these social norms can vary from place to place, from human society to society. Sociology thus reminds us not to take for granted what we know in our own human society and in our own lives as 'normal' because it reminds us to study society at large, and the many different examples of human society that there have been.

In order to do this effectively you will need to learn how to exercise your sociological imagination. Your sociologist imagination is the ability to think or imagine yourself into another person's shoes, and to start to recognise how individual and small-scale or personal behaviours also serve to reflect the social norms that are embedded within social structures (such as family, education, work, government and commerce).

As the sociologist Anthony Giddens emphasises, 'the sociological imagination requires us to "think ourselves away" from the routines of our daily lives in order to look at them anew' and further 'allows us to see that many events that seem to concern only the individual reflect larger issues.'

In conclusion, sociologists dedicate much of their time to analysing how society influences individual identity. They examine how people respond to cultural values: rejecting them, accepting them, and ultimately, passing along knowledge to their children. Both cultural values and the relationships between individuals and these values are changing every day; this creates cultural diversity, a concept which lies at the centre of sociological study.

An example would be the institution of marriage. Whereas marriages were once, almost unanimously, considered lifelong agreements and were nearly impossible to terminate (certainly this was the case in the nineteenth century), now, approximately 40 per cent of all marriages in the UK end in divorce. Cultural changes such as the modern women's movement, using feminist ideas (which deconstructed marriage as a patriarchal institution), secularisation, and the introduction of specific laws, have caused people to value their lives, and thus interact with one another, in culturally diverse ways that differ from the historical norm.

Integral Elements and Core Themes

Throughout the entire course, we invite you to consider some basic elements and themes that you will incorporate in your investigation of each individual topic. You should always consider the general sociological theories, perspectives and methods when examining specific topics, such as Families and Households or Global Development. You should be applying research methods by focusing on how sociologists obtain data; you should also understand the strengths and weaknesses of the different research approaches. Theories (e.g. functionalism, feminism) and methods (e.g. participant observation) were introduced in the IGCSE course, and will be discussed throughout this course. Further, you should keep in mind the core themes of socialization, culture and identity; social differentiation, power and stratification. You will find that these core themes run throughout all the topics you will study at A-level.

What is the relationship between sociology and the other social sciences?

Sociology is a social science (like psychology or anthropology), rather than a physical one (such as physics, chemistry or biology). It is the task of the sociologist to unravel how 'nurture' or 'social' factors, rather than 'nature' (or genetic, biological or inherited and innate factors, as in the study of biology) influence people at the level of the individual, group or wider society.

We know that Sociology is a social science (like Psychology) and that Biology is a physical one. Nevertheless, all three of these disciplines (Sociology, Psychology and Biology) are concerned with the study of humans. However, they all take very different approaches and often reach very different conclusions.

Biology

A biologist is a scientist concerned with human biology, the human organism, human genetics or inheritance. When it comes to human behaviour, a biologist focuses on the importance of nature as an explanation. For example, a biologist might examine a person's genetic inheritance as a means of explaining their character or their behaviour. They may also look at the human organism and its normal or typical behaviours (such as speaking, eating, procreating or sleeping) and think about how these work within the context of human anatomy or physiology, genetics or biological processes.

Psychology

Like many biologists, a psychologist is also concerned with human behaviour. However, in contrast to the biologist, a psychologist is concerned with the behaviour of an individual from the perspective of their own thoughts or 'psyche' (from the Greek word for 'soul', and often used to mean 'character'). For example, a psychologist might think about an individual's upbringing or early childhood experiences and how these have made an impact on the behaviour of an individual in the present.

A psychologist may also treat individuals for their mental health problems, and this would be based on analysis of that individual's thoughts, experiences, typical patterns of behaviour or ways of interacting with other people. All of these areas for discussion would be drawn out of conversation or therapy between that individual and the psychologist. The psychologist would ask the individual questions and this would open up discussion about all those things that might be causing a problem or creating difficulties for the individual in their life.

Anthropology

Anthropologists are well-known for their ethnographies (studies of a particular social grouping or culture) which serve as the primary sources of information from which they draw general, theoretical conclusions. Anthropology is different from sociology in that the foundational studies in anthropology are of non-western, marginalised cultures, though today contemporary anthropologists operate in a variety of western and non-western environments and contexts.

The research of an anthropologist is often presented as a cross-cultural comparison. Traditionally or typically, an anthropologist will go to live in a small, remote community for an extended period of time in order to conduct thorough participant observation research (this is usually after an extended period of preparatory research and, when necessary, language immersion). Good ethnography can require a very long immersion period.

Sociology

Like the anthropologist, psychologist and some biologists, a sociologist is also concerned with human behaviour. However, in contrast to the biologist, a sociologist looks at the importance human culture (rather than human nature) has on human behaviour. Most sociologists reject the view that human behaviour is determined by biology (this position is usually called biological determinism), and as evidence of this they point to the vast differences in human culture and behaviour both over time and over place.

If human behaviour were determined by human nature, then we would expect human societies to be very similar (given that as humans, we all have the same or very similar innate human biology and we are all human organisms). In reality, we find things are rather different, and for the sociologist the explanation is to be found in human culture, in human society and in social behaviour.

In contrast to the psychologist, the sociologist is less concerned with individual behaviour (although individuals can still be very useful case studies for sociologists). What sociologists are more concerned with is social behaviour; this is how people behave in groups and in society at large. This is why sociologists so often look at social institutions, such as the family, education or government, and at subsections of society, such as looking at groups of people of the same class, age, ethnicity or gender and then comparing and contrasting their actions and behaviours across that group. This is very distinct to the psychologist. Whereas the psychologist is often concerned to alleviate mental distress in an individual, a sociologist looks at an individual's behaviour only as a way to gain sociological evidence for a wider societal trend. An individual thus tells the sociologist something about society at large.

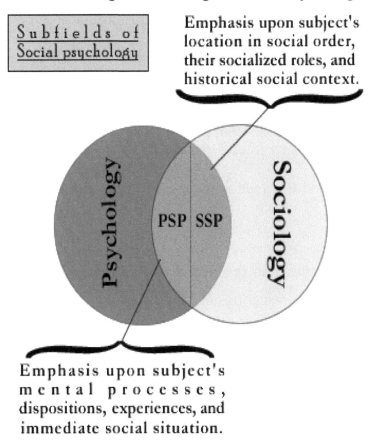

Whereas psychology is the study of the mind, sociology is the study of the small group in society, though both disciplines have overlaps as this diagram shows.

What are the biological, psychological and social elements of human behaviour?

We have already examined a little of the nature of Biology, Psychology, Anthropology and Sociology and how they intersect. However, we have yet to look at a specific example of human behaviour and to think about its biological, psychological and social aspects. Let's do that now, with one particular example: sex.

Sex: the biological, psychological and social elements of human behaviour

Human sexuality is a good case study to use in thinking about the biological, psychological and social elements of human behaviour.

Clearly, sexuality has a biological element: men and women differ anatomically, and sex as a means for reproduction is an important biological process and biological imperative. Thus, the science and study of sex and reproduction form an important part of the discipline of biology.

However, human sexuality (unlike animal sexual behaviour) also has significant psychological and social elements. Unlike other animals, and in contrast to animal sexual behaviour, for the human animal sex is something that has a cultural or symbolic meaning attached to it, and this meaning can vary greatly cross-culturally and from individual to individual.

The psychological aspect of human sexuality, therefore, at the level of the individual, relates to a person's personal sexual desires and preferences, their thoughts, feelings and assumptions about sex, and how they feel about their current sexual relationship/s, or lack of the same. These feelings will all inevitably be conditioned by the individual's childhood, personal experiences and character, and can therefore vary enormously from person to person. The social or cultural aspect of human sexuality refers to how society views human sexual behaviour. In all human societies, there are sexual behaviours which are viewed as normal, usual or desirable, and then there are those which are not, perhaps even being viewed as unlawful or immoral. These norms of human sexual behaviours vary massively from culture to culture, time and place, including what is viewed as physically or sexually attractive in both men and women, and what is not.

To what extent is human behaviour determined by social factors?

To continue with the theme of human sexuality as a case study: the area of human sexual orientation (the direction of an individual's sexual attraction) highlights the extent to which human behaviour is determined by social factors.

Heterosexuality is the most common of all human sexual orientations, and it is the sexual attraction towards the opposite sex, whereas homosexuality is the attraction towards others of the same sex.

Since human sexual behaviour and sexual orientation are typically such an important part of an individual's personal identity, and since most humans seem to be heterosexual, studying the reasons why some people are homosexual has been an area of sociological, psychological and biological study. For this reason, the results have much to say about the nature of human sexual orientation, and the extent to which it is determined by social factors. There are some key points outlined below.

The extent to which human sexual orientation is biological:

For the reason that heterosexuality is more common, it has been argued that there is a biological basis for homosexuality, which gives an individual a predisposition for homosexuality. For example, biological factors such as exposure of the foetus to different hormone levels have been suggested as an explanation for homosexuality.

Studies of identical twins (who, since they share the same genes, should also typically have the same sexual orientation if human sexual behaviour is biologically based) also suggested that is it far more likely that identical twins will both be homosexual than it is for both non-identical twins and for adopted siblings. This again suggests that there is a biological component to homosexuality. If there were not, we would expect the incidence of homosexuality to bear no relation to one's genes, meaning that it would be no more likely that identical twins would both be homosexual than it would for adopted siblings (who are not genetically related).

However, roughly half of those pairs of identical twins studied did not have a twin who was also homosexual, suggesting that there is still a strong social or psychological aspect to human sexual behaviour. If human sexual behaviour were entirely based on biology, then we would have to expect every single identical twin who had a homosexual twin to also be homosexual themselves: and this is also not the case.

In conclusion, it seems that as with so much of human behaviour, there is a complex mix of factors at work: biological and social, psychological and cultural. To ignore either the biological or the social at the expense of the other would certainly be a mistake, but for the sociologist the answer is still clear that the social or cultural underpinnings of human behaviour are real and are worthy of study.

How diverse are human behaviour and cultural variation?

It has already been assumed that human behaviour and cultural variation are diverse: that this is so is typical to the thinking of sociologists since researching cultural variation and diversity are part of what sociologists do. However, like any theoretical assumption, it is necessary to question it for its validity. Perhaps, in fact, human societies are rather similar than different?

How similar or how different you think human societies ultimately are is another of the questions a sociologist needs to answer for her or himself, so to start to think about this now, we can use one approach: the lessons of history.

For example, it is very clear that the changes to human behaviour and culture over time have been vast. Even if we only look at our immediate history from the last 4,500 years or so, those comprise only the most recent chapter in the story of human development, which begins as early as 50,000 BCE, when the first hunting and gathering societies appeared around the world. Needless to say, these hunting and gathering societies were very different to our own; members of these societies survived by hunting, fishing, and gathering nuts, seeds and plants from their natural surroundings. Although there are still a few types of hunter-gatherer societies in existence, this way of life is increasingly rare in the modern world.

However, even more changes took place. Circa 12,000 BCE, several hunting and gathering societies resorted to new sources of livelihood; some began to cultivate fixed plots of land, and others started to domesticate animals. Agrarian societies were the first societies to practise agriculture (often in addition to hunting and gathering methods). These societies remained small but were marked by increased social inequalities and were ruled by chiefs in many cases.

In contrast, pastoral societies also developed. They were dependent on domesticated livestock for food, clothing and trade. These highly mobile groups could vary in size (anywhere from a hundred to thousands), were marked by distinct social inequalities and were ruled by chiefs or warrior kings.

And then from roughly 6,000 BCE, we finally see the first of the non-industrial civilisations. These included the complex civilisations of the Middle East (such as Mesopotamia or Egypt) as well as the civilisations of Mexico and Latin America (such as the Incas, the Aztecs or the Mayans). These societies were very large (some numbering millions), produced an agricultural surplus and were usually characterised by major social and economic inequalities, which were headed by a king or emperor. Large cities existed in these societies, where trade and manufacture were concentrated.

To conclude: we can see that human society and culture has varied enormously over time; people in the past did not live the way we live now. They also did not think or act in the way that we do. This shows us that human culture and behaviour are capable of being incredibly diverse, and that we therefore must be very careful not to assume that our societal norms and cultures should or ought to be the same for everyone else.

This completes your introduction to the study of Sociology as a field distinct to Biology, Psychology or Anthropology. The first topic you will be covering next is education, where you will be invited to think about how socially ascribed characteristics (such as gender, class, ethnicity or age) affect education.

4.1.1: Education with Methods in Context

A Level – 4.1.1

For this part of the course, you will be examining topics addressing various aspects of education in society. The themes discussed in this section relate to Paper 1 of the examination.

By the end of this unit you should have a sound understanding of the following:

- The education system as an important institution in our society.
- There are a number of forces that affect the shape that the education system takes in a society: political, ideological, economic and traditional
- The UK education system and some of the factors that have shaped it.

Why do sociologists study education?

The study of education is an examination and understanding of, as well as providing an insight into, how educational institutions are structured, how education plays a part in the process of socialisation and operate in terms of social interaction.

Key Areas:

- The role and function of the education system, including vocational education and training, in contemporary society
- Theoretical perspectives that aim to explain the role and purpose of education.
- Differentiation in education of social groups according to social class, gender and ethnicity
- Interaction in education, with particular reference to teacher/pupil relationships, pupil subcultures, the hidden curriculum, and the organisation of teaching and learning
- The significance of educational policies, including selection, comprehensivisation and marketisation, for an understanding of the structure, role, impact and experience of education
- The impact of globalisation on education and educational policy
- The application of sociological research methods to the study of education

The core themes of this unit are:	
Socialisation, Culture and Identity	**Social Differentiation, Power and Stratification**
The role and function of the education system	Education's relationship to the economy
Interaction - Teacher/Pupil relationships	Education's relationship to class structure
Interaction – Classroom interaction, pupil to pupil	Educational Differentiation and achievement – Class, Gender and Ethnicity
Interaction – Identity formation	School structures and hierarchical structures – power relationships between teachers and students
Interaction – Subcultures	Educational policies
Secondary Socialisation – hidden curriculum	Equality in education; access to education
	Selection processes and policy
	Globalisation's impact on education
	Marketisation and privatisation in education

Activity 1 - Before we start, if you were asked by someone who had never heard the term 'education' before, how would you define it or explain it to them?

Definitions:

Oxford English Dictionary

"Education: the process of receiving or giving systematic instruction, especially at school or university."

Collins New English Dictionary

"Instruction and training as imparted in schools, colleges and universities: the theory and practice of teaching."

Dictionaries can give us a starting point in terms of gaining a provisional understanding of what we mean by education. Sociology, however, enables us to look into this more deeply, uncovering the workings of education and how this impacts upon society.

Sociological Explanations of Education

As you work through this section, try to make connections between educational issues and other social factors such as:

- Culture and identity (think secondary socialisation)
- The family (think about how, for example, divorce could affect a child's educational performance)
- Wealth, poverty and welfare (think about private versus stated funded education, or how a lack of resources due to financial issues can affect education achievement)

Activity 2 - It is said that your school days are the best days of your life. Would you agree?

Thinking back to your own school or educational experience:

What kind of school did you go to?

What kind of education did you receive?

Was your schooling experience conventional/mainstream or alternative, e.g. homeschooling or Summer Hill (see page www.summerhillschool.co.uk)

Did you enjoy school? If so, why; if not, why not?

In terms of the social factors that contributed to your school experience, to what extent do you think your ethnicity, class, gender or disability had a part to play in how you experienced school – positively or negatively?

The role and purpose of education

Education is a social institution that plays a significant role in society, which is why most sociologists would agree that education serves a central purpose in society. Some form of education exists in most societies and can be categorised as both formal and informal.

Informal Education	Formal Education
Occurs outside of a classroom setting and can come from family, friends, religious organisations etc.	Associated with an established publicly recognised and accepted institution, such as a school, college or training centre with a structured or institutionalised approach to education.

Sociologists who investigate education think that it has several aims and functions within society. However, they may disagree about which are the most important. Some of these aims/functions are:

3 aims of education:

Secondary socialisation - it is through this process of socialisation that a child continues to learn and have reinforced, the acceptable norms and values of adult society. They can then enter adult society with confidence.

Education in key skills, such as literacy and numeracy, as well as science and foreign languages, are important for many modern careers. Teaching history, for example, provides a child with a deeper understanding of their own society. Without these skills, a child would find it hard to function in adult society or to successfully undertake most modern careers (most of which usually require at least literacy and numeracy).

A process of individualisation - a child learns about her or himself through education. She or he learns what they like and dislike, what their talents are and what they are good or not so good at. This is an important part of the process of working towards the adult role, and finding out how a child will fit into adult society.

Those who criticise modern formal education say that the real aim is to make sure that through a process of hierarchy, inequalities in society stay the same. This sort of socialisation really teaches the child about unfairness, as well as where they are 'supposed to be' in terms of their position in society as an adult without questioning this in the first place.

In the light of the above points, we have established that whilst sociologists would agree that education serves a significant purpose in society, what that purpose and function is and the extent of it will vary according to which sociological school of thought is being offered as an explanation of this.

In recent years, a school of thought that moves away from any formality in terms of education is known as 'Unschooling'. Unschooling is an alternative philosophy of education to formal schools and to homeschooling and as such would fall under the category of informal education. Unschooling is unstructured learning; therefore, instead of set lessons, books and teachers (whether at home or in school) children are taught in a more 'natural' style, through interaction with their environment in their day-to-day lives. For example, a parent may explain to a child the names of some common plants or animals while out shopping together, when they see a Siamese cat in the street and a sycamore growing by the road on the way to the shops. When they are doing the shopping, the parent might ask the child to add up the cost of what they have in the basket before they go and pay. In this way, the child is being taught basic biology and mathematics, but they are both in a real-life context, and it is through a more spontaneous interaction rather than through strict lessons and timetables as is the case in school. (For example, a lesson in Mathematics every Tuesday at 9am; a lesson in Biology every Friday afternoon at 2pm).

This example should help to remind us that not all forms of education are the same. There are some, which have a very different ethos and educational philosophy. An example of this is Summer Hill.

Activity 3 - What do you think about unschooling as an educational philosophy?

Research the famous and unconventional school of Summer Hill. You may like to visit their website to do this:

http://www.summerhillschool.co.uk/

What are the rules of this school?

What is taught there?

What is the relationship between staff and pupils?

Do you think this is a good educational ethos or not? Why, or why not?

⮡ lessons, GCSE opphional
+ rules made by the students
∴ more equal relationship
between teachers and students.

I think having students govern school rules is beneficial as it creates an environment of independence promoting socialisation. Whilst there may be fears that the children will not to leave with qualifications, i believe it is possible to learn through life experiences. Furthermore, giving students the autonomy to choose, means they are more likely to be passionate about their learning as they can pursue what genuinely interests them.

I do think the summerhill method might disadvantage students that ~~assesses to require~~ ata want to pursue

Sociological Theories

There are various perspectives and schools of thought within Sociology that try to explain the role and function of education in society. What follows is an overview of two of the core theories in this area of discussion, the Structuralist Approach and the Interactionist Approach.

Structuralist Approach (Structuralism)

Structuralism broadly refers to the belief that it is social structures or wider frameworks and systems that have priority over the actions of an individual or individuals. Sociologists who subscribe to a structuralist perspective would see people primarily as the outcome or product of social factors and groupings (such as gender, class, ethnic, family, work or social relationships). Therefore, an individual's actions are because of social factors/groupings rather than as a result of free agency and choice over their own actions. At its extreme, a structuralist sociologist might see society as 'telling' people what to do and how to act. In other words, the wider systems and structures of society dictate who each of us is and what we do; it is not we who make society, but rather the pre-existing social frameworks and systems that 'make' us. This school of thought sees the education process of formal schooling as an agent of social control, which some see as a positive thing that benefits society as a whole, whilst other schools of thought see as a form of exploitation. Formal education through schools implement a code of conduct and discipline which teaches a child what is acceptable behaviour and what is not in that society. They also help to teach the norms and values and social expectations of a given society. Therefore, social factors such as gender roles and appropriate gender behaviour, as well as authority and power relations and how to relate to and interact with others according to their status, authority etc. is also reinforced through the process of formal education. Some theories that would come under this heading see structure and social order as a positive thing that ensures the smooth running of society (such as the Functionalists).[1] Others see this as a mode of oppression and control that allows one group to exert power over another in order to keep some in their place (such as the Marxist perspective).[2]

Interactionist Approach

---

[1] To be discussed later.
[2] To be discussed later.

This approach stresses the importance of social interaction. This viewpoint, as its name suggests, is more concerned with looking at the interaction or relationship between people and how that conditions behaviour. It rests on the thinking that people act towards things and other people based on the meanings that those things or people have for them. These meanings come from social groups and from relationships.

With this approach, education can have either a positive or a negative impact, depending on the type of interaction that is experienced by an individual. For example, negative interaction through bullying is invariably going to have a detrimental impact on an individual's learning experience, and as such affect how they experience the world outside of a school environment.

Conversely, a positive experience could be had by having an encouraging and motivating interaction with a teacher who reinforces an individual's self-belief in their abilities, resulting in that individual doing well at school.

Seen in a positive light, a school can be an agent of social stability (like the family) rather than strict social control. A good school especially can provide a haven for the child and a place where their minds are challenged and their talents and abilities are developed and expressed. It can also provide a child with positive personal relationships (friends their own age) and positive adult role models.

The Role and Function of Education

Structuralist versus Interactionist

As discussed previously, sociological approaches to education can, at the broadest level, be divided into two schools of thoughts: structuralist and interactionist.

Structuralist sociologists think that education is a necessity in that it serves important purposes, or functions, for the individual and for society (we will expand upon this in the section on Functionalism below).

Interactionists, on the other hand, focus on small-scale social processes: what goes on in the classroom and how students relate to teachers, other students and to their curricula.

Both groups of sociologists note the importance of the 'hidden curriculum', which consists of school rules and regulations that, in addition to the official curriculum of scholastic subjects, play an important role in the socialisation process.

Overall, sociologists are concerned with how education can facilitate, or detract from, social mobility and equality of opportunity.

Activity 4 - Briefly summarise the differences between structuralist and interactionist sociologists.
Looking at these two ideological positions, which one appeals to you the most and why?
Which approach do you think provides a good explanation of the role of education?

Summary:

- Education is part of the process of socialisation (Secondary socialisation)
- An individual need not receive their schooling at school
- An individual can experience education in many ways
- Education can be informal as well as formal and can take place over the life course (not just when an individual is young)
- Education can be seen as a form of social control (positively or negatively)
- Education can be seen as a means to maintain social order (either positively or negatively)
- Education allows for social interaction and the development of an individual's personality and individuality, as well as the means by which an individual learns skills such as literacy or numeracy.

Sociological Theories in Depth

Sociology as a discipline contributes to our understanding of order and patterns in the social world; as such, some theoretical perspectives can fall into one of two groups.

Consensus Theory	Conflict Theory
Social order is based on agreement and a shared sense of mutual order. The focus is on collaboration. In education, therefore, the emphasis is on maintaining order through reinforcing the norms and values of mainstream society through the education system itself. Perspectives such as the Functionalists would come under this group.	Social order operates via a dominant group controlling or manipulating a subordinate or less powerful group. Education plays a part in maintaining and reinforcing social hierarchy. Perspectives such as the Marxist and Feminists would come under this group.

Functionalist (consensus) perspective

Functionalism is a consensus perspective in that it evaluates how society functions for the 'common good' of people. Functionalists believe that education serves to instil key cultural values and socially acceptable modes of behaviour in children so that they will ultimately function in society as adults. According to Emile Durkheim, education prevents anomie,[3] or social chaos within which there are no norms or values. When people live in anomie, they do not experience a sense of purpose or belonging.

Children who are educated are able to formulate instrumental relationships with members of society (thus reaching beyond the affective relationships of their families). According to Talcott Persons, education liberates children from ascribed statuses imposed upon them by their family structures as they enter a meritocratic system. In school, students are assessed based on universal standards of hard work and achievement and thus may strive for achieved statuses. Education also teaches values of competition and individualism that are not necessarily taught within the family.

What are ascribed and achieved status?

Although we all have a social and cultural identity by virtue of factors such as our class, sex and age, there is also scope for movement and change. For example, through the social institution of education, individuals are given the opportunity to break out of their ascribed status.

This technical term refers to the status of an individual which has been determined by social factors such as: age, sex, class, ethnicity and so on, and over which the individual has little control (we do not choose our sex, for example). This is why they are 'ascribed' – they are given to the individual by society, in accordance with how society views a particular gender, ethnicity, social class or age group.

---

[3] A condition where there is little consensus, a lack of certainty in terms of values and goals

However, by means such as education and through achievement derived from academic success (for example, by gaining a prestigious job) an individual can have an achieved status. As the name suggests, this term refers to the status and successes that an individual has achieved based on their own personal merit, hard work, skills, talents and commitment. This is usually viewed as separate to the social roles each individual has by virtue of their gender, age, ethnicity, sexual orientation, dis/ability and class.

Activity 5 -
What is the difference between ascribed and achieved status?
Can you think of some examples of ascribed and achieved status from your own life?

Functionalists, such as Emile Durkheim, note education's essential purposes in society not only to produce skilled and able workers but also to instil values of punctuality and hard work. Educated workers, who are also disciplined, will be more employable and will keep the economy healthy and stable.

Talcott Parsons takes this a step further by arguing that the meritocratic education system challenges and 'filters' individuals so that the most talented and hard working are able to accelerate into more challenging, specialised careers. Education ensures that people are dispersed correctly and keeping the work force balanced.

Activity 6 - Summarise the consensus or functionalist perspectives on the role of education in society.

Marxist and Feminist (conflict) perspectives

Conflict theorists agree that education performs a key 'sorting' function, but in doing so, education can also perpetuate inequality. Education serves to maintain our already stratified society. Marxists would say that the proletariat (the majority of the population, which is not of the ruling class) are placed in low pay/working class jobs, whereas the prestigious jobs are still reserved for ruling/upper class students.

Marxists are critical of education's role in society, believing that the education system perpetuates social and class inequalities by effectively brainwashing the proletariat into passively accepting inequalities in society as normative and legitimate. For example, children learn about history or about modern government from the official curriculum, yet are even more influenced by the hidden curriculum, which communicates values such as respect for authority. For example, Bowles and Gintis (1976) conducted an interesting study in America, which demonstrated how the American educational system embodies capitalist values and socialises children into accepting this unequal system.

The Hidden curriculum ← things never currently used to pass exams e.g. political beliefs

It might seem that the most important things we learn in school are the contents of our lessons. We are taught information and we use this to pass exams, to gain qualifications and to enter adult society. In a sense, this is true: if we had a good education, then we left it with the skills and qualifications necessary to choose a good career for ourselves. This kind of education, the one of lessons, exams and qualifications, is often called by sociologists: formal education. This means, the education that is clear and obvious, the stated aim of lessons (to teach children maths or reading and writing, for example).

However, sociologists who research education have also pointed to another kind of education that happens at school. Not only do we learn things and pass exams, but we also get taught a great deal about people, about relationships, about the way society works, about rules, structures, hierarchy, communication and adult behaviour. This is the education that is hidden; it is not clear or obvious. It is often called by sociologists: the hidden curriculum.

For example, children spend hundreds of hours in lessons. They might learn Maths, Science or Geography but they also learn a great deal, about how adults behave, and about interaction with them. They watch their teachers, and they know which ones are good and which ones are not. They know about their teachers' behaviour and their own particular characteristics and habits, how to annoy their teachers and how to please them. They learn about good and bad behaviour, and they learn about the hidden rules and systems of their school and about society as a whole, such as how adults present themselves and how they view others of a particular social class, ethnicity, gender (etc.). In other words, school is a place where you lean social roles, as well as learning the formal curriculum.

A good case study of the hidden curriculum might be the teacher who always expects the girls (but not the boys) to tidy the classroom at the end of the lesson. Not only is this teacher teaching these children the formal curriculum of the lesson, but s/he is also teaching them gender roles in the form of the hidden curriculum. That is, the implicit message here is that cleaning and tidying is a role proper to girls, but not boys. This is a good example of a socially constructed role: there is nothing inherently 'natural' or biological about the performance of cleaning by one gender rather than the other, so the fact that in this instance girls (but not boys) are expected to do the tidying has been determined by society or culture. Other examples can include teaching children about acceptable forms of address to adults of different status, the wearing of uniforms to cancel out individuality etc.

gender roles in society (handwritten margin note)

Activity 7 –
How does the hidden curriculum influence students' experiences?
Reflect on your own schooling again. Can you think of any examples of the hidden curriculum at work from your own school days?

In fact, some Feminists argue that education reproduces gender inequalities as it is seen to promote and reinforce male domination through engendered language, stereotyping, and the hidden curriculum generating 'boy' and 'girl' subjects, thereby reinforcing gender differences; informally, girls and boys are encouraged to pursue different types of careers. Indeed, it is certainly the case that the top levels of many prestigious careers are still dominated by men (despite the fact that girls now outperform boys at school and that there are now more female graduates than male), and the lower paid and lower status jobs (such as the 5 Cs) are still heavily female dominated. Even within the education system itself in terms of the staff profile of schools, men are seen to dominate the top positions.

improvement

Drawing on the example given above, feminists would also argue that education exacerbates power inequalities and legitimises patriarchy: boys and girls are socialised into unequal gender roles at school through the social stereotypes perpetuated by their teachers and by society at large as they are filtered through the school.

Activity 8 -

Summarise the conflict, Marxist and feminist perspectives on the role and purpose of education.

Which one do you favour the most, and why is this?

marx marxist and feminist
both agree that our education
system that has education
creates inequalities.
marxist believe it and promotes
capitalist ideologie whilst feminist
focus on the the aspect
of the reproduction patriarchy
being pushed onto students

Another important theoretical approach/perspective

Symbolic interactionism

As social beings we all interact or communicate every day with other people and social structures (such as institutions like the state, the police, the health service, education and so on), as well as with the things and objects around us (in the form of resources we use), and it is through that interaction that we are able to establish and reinforce meanings (purposes, motives, beliefs reasons etc.) for our social interaction in any social context. As such every day we remake those meanings through that interaction, so nothing is fixed or permanent. There is always scope to create new forms of social interaction, though largely social interaction is governed by rules and codes of conduct. Therefore, the study of how we interact with those things, and how we make those interactions meaningful, is the starting point for the symbolic interactionist sociologist. In terms of education, this perspective focuses on the interaction that occurs in the classroom in terms of pupil/pupil and teacher/pupil interaction, as well as any other forms of meaningful interaction that can influence the processes that occur within education and how this affects an individual's development.

Influence on social policy

The impact of social policy on the structure of education has been significant since the inception of a formal education system. For example, the socialising function of education has influenced the National Curriculum, which saw the introduction of Citizenship Studies as a required subject.[4] In addition, the liberal education movement has recognised the need to expose students to a wide variety of subjects so that they may function in society as well-rounded individuals. Another significant factor that has resulted in changes in education over the years has been the relationship between education and the economy which has definitely influenced social policy. For example, in the 1980s, the government began to match educational curricula to society's economic needs through a movement known as New Vocationalism. Both the conservative and the following New Labour governments re-branded vocational programmes to give them a higher status, and integrated work-based learning into required educational curricula.

---

[4] https://www.gov.uk/government/publications/national-curriculum-in-england-citizenship-programmes-of-study

Educational Policy

As a social institution, the education system is one of the most influential in terms of the social development of an individual, as well as providing the basis for the understanding of wider social structures. It is through education and the process of secondary socialisation that an individual learns acceptable modes of behaviour, norms and values.

Before examining further some of the core sociological perspectives in relation to education in terms of social groups such as social class, gender and ethnicity, we need to look at educational policies that have been instrumental in the development of the education system we have in place today.

The development of the structure of the British Education system can be best summarised in terms of the significant educational reforms that have occurred over the past several decades.

History of English Education

1870: Prior to the twentieth century, education was reserved for wealthy people that could afford private tuition. State schools did not exist, though some poorer students would receive schooling through churches. The Forster Act 1870 required the establishment of non-denominational elementary schools nationwide for children aged 5 to 13. Schools could charge parents no more than nine pence a week to educate a child.

1880: Attendance was made compulsory until the age of 10.

1891: Elementary education effectively became free.

1918: Leaving age was raised to 14.

1944: Prior to 1944, the majority of British children had access to free elementary education until the age of fourteen; though secondary schools existed, they charged for tuition and thus exacerbated social class divisions, as only children with adequate financial resources could attend secondary school. The Education Act 1944 allowed free secondary education for all, raising the school leaving age to fifteen.[5] Local governments became responsible for supporting these initiatives, adopting selection methods as a way to place children (from age eleven) in appropriate secondary schools, which they felt were suited to differing individual needs. The aim was to encourage the "spiritual, mental and physical" well-being of the community. This Act created a "tripartite", hierarchical system of grammar, technical and secondary modern schools. Students were to take an 'eleven-plus' examination, which would determine whether they would be placed in a secondary grammar school, which focussed primarily on academic learning, or a secondary modern school, which focussed on a mix of vocational training and general academic learning. Other students with talents in mechanical engineering attended secondary technical schools. This tripartite system approach proved unsuccessful as, by the 1960s, researchers found that only 12 per cent of students were staying in school until age seventeen.

1951: General Certificate of Education (GCE) O-levels and A-levels were introduced, replacing the School Certificate and the Higher School Certificate.

These were primarily grammar school exams. Some education authorities established their own leaving examinations for youngsters not taking GCEs.

1964: Comprehensivisation: Harold Wilson's newly elected Labour government abolished the secondary modern/grammar school division and instituted comprehensive schooling, emphasising the importance of equal access to educational resources, combining pupils of all ability levels in one school that served a specific catchment area. However, not all grammar schools closed during this time; some remain in operation today.

1965: The Certificate of Secondary Education (CSE) was introduced for secondary modern pupils to cater for those not sitting O-levels.

1973: School-leaving age was raised to 16.

---

[5] One sector of the British educational system left entirely unaffected by the 1944 act was that of the independent, fee-paying 'public' schools, the most noteworthy being Eton, Rugby and Charterhouse. These institutions continue to run with minimal state regulation and, in their exclusive nature, have spawned political debates regarding equality of access not only to educational resources, but also to higher positions within British Society.

1976: Another Wilson administration compelled all local authorities to introduce comprehensives but the Tories repealed this legislation in 1979.

The 1988 Educational Act. After Margaret Thatcher came to power in 1979, she dismantled comprehensive schooling and reduced the power of local educational authorities. Thatcher felt that comprehensive schooling did not provide the same degree of varied, specialised education that the previous grammar and modern schools had. She also claimed that comprehensive schooling did not encourage family values and that graduates were not armed with the skills necessary to create a nationally competitive economy.

Thus, in 1988, the Conservative party introduced an act that was to 'revolutionise' the education system in Britain. It was also an attempt at marketization: parents were encouraged to choose schools that were best suited to their children, and the education system was thus exposed to the market forces of supply and demand.

capitalist
approach.
schools
run like
businesses

Some other key reforms of (and responses to) the 1988 Educational Act included:

Reform	Response
A national curriculum complete with universal state teaching guidelines and standardised testing. The National Curriculum, stipulating subjects to be studied until the age of 16, was also introduced. The General Certificate of Secondary Education (GCSE) replaced O-levels and CSEs.	This reform was met with great resistance by groups of teachers who felt that the rules were confining - teachers actually went on strike in the summer of 1993 in response to the state requirement of standardised testing.
A 'local management of schools' system, which was intended to balance the power that had been transferred to state authorities, with the introduction of a national curriculum. However, grant-maintained schools could 'opt out' of local authority in favour of state funding as well as the right to select up to 50 per cent of their students. *often had elective admissions process*	This spawned much criticism, as many people felt that the competitive selection process would create further inequalities among students; they much preferred the 'equal access' principles behind comprehensive schools. Further, the schools which were keen to attract students who would do well on their GCSE exams, thus boosting rankings, made costly marketing efforts. Budgets were often redistributed, and, in several instances, money was transferred from less profitable areas such as Special Educational Needs to marketing departments. Researchers have emphasised that not all parents were well informed when it came to school selection process; school choice largely depended on parents' social class backgrounds and their access to cultural resources.

1994: An A* grade was added to GCSEs to differentiate between top and lower A grades.

1995: The government introduced National Curriculum Tests, often called SATs, for all children aged 7, 11 and 14 (tests for seven year olds were first tried in 1991).

younger testing more academic the more ?

1996: General National Vocational Qualifications (GNVQs) were offered as a more work-based alternative for non-academic students.

1997: Education Policy under New Labour. Like the Conservatives, New Labour wanted to get rid of mixed-ability classrooms; they instead encouraged streaming or setting students. Streaming is when students are split into several hierarchical groups based on ability, and setting is when students with similar abilities are put together for certain lessons. Both methods are founded on the idea that children should progress at rates must suited to their capabilities.

Upon entering office in 1997, Prime Minister Tony Blair made educational reform one of his top priorities, claiming that Britain's educational system did not live up to international standards.   New Labour has since introduced a variety of reforms, including the following:

- The introduction of Literacy and Numeracy strategies in primary schools. It aimed to raise literacy standards to those of the UK's main competitors
- The encouragement of competition and diversity amongst school
- The introduction of specialist schools (such as in technology, arts, maths etc.). Also, the creation of City Academies in deprived areas
- The channelling of capital to underprivileged areas to attract more teachers with higher salaries; these initiatives form what are known as Education Action Zones.

2000: Advanced Subsidiary (AS-level) exams were brought in for 17 year olds. These were qualifications in their own right but also served as a halfway stage in the A-level course, unlike the Advanced Supplementary exams they replaced.

Plans were also revealed to replace the lower tiers of GNVQ with vocational GCSEs, with the stated aim of putting academic and vocational education on a par.

2002: Several hundred A-level papers were re-graded amid fears that the reforms had been rushed through.

2004: Mike Tomlinson, the former inspector of schools in England, proposed replacing GCSEs, A-levels and the "soup" of vocational qualifications with a four-part diploma for 14 to 19 year olds. It called for "core skills", such as numeracy and literacy, to be compulsory before pupils could qualify. If it had gone through, the plans would have altered the English education system more radically than any others since 1944. However, Tomlinson said the changes would be "evolutionary, not revolutionary", taking around 10 years to implement.

2005 Education Act covered many educational issues without major controversy, such as: the inspection of schools, the provision of day care and childminding, nursery education and careers services and staff training.

2006 Education and Inspections Act: This was a more controversial piece of legislation, which was eventually only passed with support from the Conservative opposition for the then Labour government. It caused the largest rebellion sustained by a Labour government at the third reading. This Act paved the way for more school autonomy and freedom from local authority control.

2007: The Qualifications and Curriculum Authority (QCA) began consulting on a new secondary curriculum, which was eventually introduced in 2008 as part of a wider updating of Key Stage 3 and 4 teaching.

2008 Education and Skills Act.

2009 Apprenticeships, Skills, Children and Learning Act.

2010 Children, Schools and Families Act.

2010: Academies Act becomes law under the Coalition Government (2010-2015), with the then Education Secretary (Michael Gove) announcing the first wave of conversions to Academy Status from existing schools. By 1st September 2010, 142 schools were set to convert to Academy status. Academies were (and still are) controversial educational policy. They were advocated by the Coalition Government because they allowed schools to be more autonomous, with teachers having more control over the running of the school rather than the Department for Education or the local authority (who under the previous Labour government were the two governmental bodies who had the power to set teachers' pay and formulate the National Curriculum, which all state schools had to follow).

2010: The Importance of Teaching: The Schools White Paper 2010 was published, outlining the Coalition Government's case for reform to the education system. This reform is now underway at time of writing (June 2015). This programme of reform includes restructuring of A-level syllabuses and the scheme of assessment, including A-level Sociology. The Schools White Paper 2010 can be read here:

https://www.gov.uk/government/publications/the-importance-of-teaching-the-schools-white-paper-2010

Jan 2011: 400 Academies open, with more schools converting to Academy status over the course of the year.

The Education Act 2011: This is a vital piece of recent legislation which seeks to end all forms of educational inequality based on the ascribed statuses of gender, socio-economic class, ethnicity and disability or Special Educational Needs. You can read the report which was instrumental to the Education Act 2011, the Equalities Impact Assessment, here. It contains some very useful data on education attainment by pupil gender, socio-economic class, ethnicity and disability:

https://www.gov.uk/government/publications/the-education-act-2011-equalities-impact-assessment

2013: The Academy Conversions (Transfer of School Surpluses) Regulations 2013 enacted. These Regulations state the timescales under which budget surpluses need to be transferred from local authorities to schools converting to Academies. This is because Academies are independent of local authority control, and have the power to manage their own finances.

June 2014: The Education Secretary approved 38 new free schools to be created, which have created 22,000 new school places across England, in a move aimed at improving school standards. Free schools are brand new schools set up by teachers, parents and charities in response to demand from the local community.

March 2015: Prime Minister David Cameron announced 49 more new free schools. Further information on the Coalition Government's vision for free schools available here:

https://www.gov.uk/government/news/prime-minister-announces-landmark-wave-of-free-schools

Summary of the 2010-2015 Coalition Government's educational strategy regarding free schools and Academies available here:

https://www.gov.uk/government/publications/2010-to-2015-government-policy-academies-and-free-schools

May 2015: End of the 2010-2015 Coalition Government; start of the Conservative Government 2015-2020.

A detailed and informative chronological account of education in England can be read online, with a focus on how the state school system was established, and how successive governments since then have altered educational policies, and for what ideological purposes. This overview of the major educational policies, legislation and trends will provide you with much more insight, should you wish to research these in further detail:

http://www.educationengland.org.uk/history/index.html

Activity 9 -

Using the Education England website to conduct your own additional research, summarise the basic implications of the following:

The Forster Act of 1870

The Educational Act (Butler Act) of 1944

Comprehensivisation, and the Education Reform Act of 1988.

Admissions Policies

Children can be assigned to a school in a number of difference ways and this has generated a significant amount of debate in terms of how appropriate some of the criteria set, is. Here are some factors that have been considered:

1 - Religion

As we discussed above, prior to 1870, poorer children could only attend schools that were run by churches. Historically speaking, faith selection has been central to schooling. Although faith schools tend to produce better exam results, many criticise these institutions for segregating children and, thus, surrounding communities.

Despite secularisation in Britain, many people still support faith schools. Statistics indicate that they have produced higher results; also, many participants note the supportive community ethos produced by these institutions. Some would argue that the values instilled at faith schools help to preserve family values. On the other hand, many find these institutions imposing and constraining, arguing that children should be exposed to a variety of religions so that they may choose for themselves. Also, many are critical of the segregating impact of faith schools: they sometimes create social tensions with surrounding communities.

Activity 10 - How does religion influence the allocation of children to secondary schools?
What are the positive and negative perspectives on this?

2 - Ability

As stated earlier the first state secondary schools were introduced in 1944 on the premise that children would be admitted based on ability. However, this practice has changed: the remaining grammar schools, as well as some specialist schools, still select students based on ability. Some are supportive of entrance exams, claiming that they ensure that education is personalised and tailored to students' needs, but others feel that aptitude tests are biased and are culturally entrenched in the norms and values of the middle class. *creates class divide*

3 - Catchment area

A catchment area is a geographical area that surrounds a comprehensive school and determines its intake. The use of catchment areas was introduced in the 1960s when comprehensive schools changed their admissions policies. Many support this approach as it ensures equality of access regardless of social background. Others argue that not all of the schools are of the same quality and that families tend to overcrowd the more desirable catchment areas, driving up house prices and thus driving out people of poorer backgrounds.

4 - Parental Choice

This is another important factor in the admissions process. During Thatcher's leadership when public services were increasingly marketised, parents were encouraged to 'shop' for suitable schools for their children: the idea being that market-based 'competition' between schools would improve school quality. Unfortunately, some parents were more informed than others, so this practice actually ended up creating social biases.

5 - Banding

This is still a common practice today: children are siphoned into different ability levels (high, middle and low) after they have been admitted to comprehensive schools. In this way, schools maintain diversity by accepting students from all backgrounds and ability levels. Some parents, who may feel that their children have been inappropriately banded, are against this practice.

Non-government involvement

Private schools

Many of the famous fee-paying 'public' schools (e.g. Eton, Harrow, Rugby, Charterhouse, etc.) are considered by the majority of British society to be the most exclusive and elite schools in the nation. Many of these institutions were opened in the thirteenth century as prestigious alternatives to faith schools; they were thus 'public' in the sense that they were open to all members of the fee-paying public.

Today, many people feel that these institutions provide the best education: they are free of political agendas (ostensibly), have smaller class sizes, etc. Others argue that the pricey schools are too exclusive and exacerbate social differences in the UK.

They say that recent voucher schemes, which were introduced to give children of less-privileged backgrounds the opportunity to attend private schools, are not generous enough to provide education for members of the poorest sectors of society, and that these vouchers only subsidise the wealthy.

Home Schooling

Outside of formal education is the option for parents to school their children at home. Also known as Home Education, this approach to education may be taken up as an option for a number of reasons, including, dissatisfaction with the current system or the system available, a personal belief system that is not accommodated by the formal education system and so on.

Under Section 7 of the 1996 Education Act, parents are responsible for ensuring that their children receive an education suitable to their age, ability and aptitude, as well as any special needs the child may have. In order to home school a child, the following factors apply:

- Permission of an LEA is required in order to home educate a child (unless the child attends a special needs school)
- There is no need for any particular qualifications
- There are no predetermined hours or times that have to be adhered to in order to tutor your child at home
- There is no need to conform to the National Curriculum
- A child with special needs can be home schooled
- Home educated children are not required to undertake examinations or SATs
- The Education Welfare Service (EWS) will ensure that the duty to provide an education to the child is adhered to

Business and Industry

Governments have also encouraged involvement in education by the private sector. The Education Reform Act of 1988 introduced City Technology Colleges (CTCs), which specialise in maths, science and technology and are partially subsidised by private businesses. The idea was that these institutions would drive capital into deprived areas and provide more educational and subsequent career, opportunities. However, some are critical of these initiatives for subjecting educational curriculum to the private agendas of corporate managing directors.

Activity 11 - How do you think the economic function of education has influenced social policy?
In your opinion, is home schooling as effective as formal education?

Vocational Education and Training

There has been much political debate regarding the practical applications of skills and knowledge that citizens acquire through education, and many argue that solid vocational training programmes are key cultural necessities which can directly match the needs of the UK workforce. In the 1980s, the UK saw a surge in such training opportunities with the New Vocationalism Movement, which introduced the Youth Training Scheme, as well as the NVQ and GNVQ qualifications. Also, New Labour emphasised the importance of Key Skills (e.g. numeracy, communication, IT, problem solving, and team work skills) in the post-16 curriculum.

Again, there is much debate about vocationalism. Many feel that these training programmes are not as valued and esteemed as academic pathways and are subject to social bias. While some see vocational training programmes as essential to the running of British society, others feel that academic educations are necessary in that they produce 'well rounded' citizens.

Activity 12 - Consider some of the debates surrounding the importance of vocational education versus academic education. Which do you think is important, and why?

Education and the economy

In order for the economy to continue running, it must be constantly fuelled with individuals who have different capabilities and skill levels. Functionalists, Feminist and Marxists have all said that education serves to filter the population into different career paths that combine to stabilise the economy. The extent to which this is done and the level of equality in terms of access to different career paths and opportunities is where these perspectives differ in their analysis.

Sociological Explanations for Processes within schools

Symbolic Interactionists, as discussed previously, are interested in small-scale interactions that occur in educational settings. Studies of how teachers perceive, relate to and 'label' their student have revealed much about the socialising influence of education whereas Functionalists such as Talcott Parsons felt that the educational system provided children with a window of opportunity to 'escape' the status that was ascribed to them by their families. Labelling theorists, such as Symbolic Interactionists, essentially argue the opposite - the way that students are categorised and 'labelled' by their teachers can have lasting social implications.

Labelling and Self Fulfilling Prophecy

When teachers make initial judgements regarding their student (often in a discriminatory manner), students can take on this ascribed status (for example, 'a troublemaker'), firstly because they are treated or responded to according to the label that has been attached to them, and secondly students come to see themselves as they have been labelled.

Eventually, regardless of whether the initial label was true, students can become real 'troublemakers' through a self-fulfilling prophecy. This is the power of labelling: once someone has a label (especially a negative one) then they act this out because it is only what they were expected to do by others around them.

Student subcultures

A subculture can be described as a culture within the mainstream, and dominant culture in terms of the norms and values of a given society or institutional environment. In terms of education then, students may either conform to or rebel against the norms of educational institutions to varying degrees (Pupil Subculture). Those who fully oppose the values and norms of a school often form collective, 'rebellious' anti-social school subcultures. David Hargreaves (1973) would argue that these subcultures are a result of negative labelling. Peter Woods (1981) expands this by identifying eight types of school subcultures known as pupil adaptations: these range from groups that fully subscribe to institutional norms to groups that openly rebel, with many 'shades of grey' in between.

The Curriculum

We have already mentioned the formal (official) and informal (hidden) curricula that are imparted to students. Many sociologists argue that the official curriculum is shaped by the cultural values of the middle classes and thus creates difficulties for underprivileged or lower class students, often leading to under achievement. The hidden curriculum is not specifically or readily identified within a school system and therefore can be described as the unintentional and informal teaching of values, attitudes, modes of behaviour and perspectives. The hidden curriculum begins from an early age in a child's education. A child will learn about acceptable modes of behaviour, opinions, how to interact with their peers, acceptance of authority figures and so on via an informal mode of instruction that is internalised by the student recipient. In terms of the formal curriculum the hidden curriculum can often 'package' certain subjects as more or less appropriate for students of certain gender and social backgrounds. For example, Interactionists might look at how activities or examples used in certain subjects might appeal to one gender over another. Therefore, this is a subtle and non-formal way of determining gender roles.

The way in which school staff are distributed across levels of authority according to gender and ethnicity may also shape students' conception of what their social roles are to be as adults e.g., more female primary school teachers = women as caregivers; fewer ethnic minorities and females in higher positions of authority = women and ethnic minorities as less authoritative.

While some sociologists point to home environments, and others to wider social constraints, as factors leading to educational underachievement, others think that problems actually arise when there is a cultural 'mismatch' between home and school environments. This is better known as the educational difference hypothesis.

Labov (1973), for example, argues that underachievement is the result of linguistic differences; when children of non-middle class/white backgrounds are allowed to communicate in the words and phrases that they are familiar with, they can express advanced ideas. Whereas those who do not use or are not familiar with more linguistically complex modes of communication, such marginalised students often struggle to achieve.

Lastly, when parents of certain social and ethnic backgrounds lack the knowledge and confidence to seek certain educational opportunities, children will experience disadvantages.

Gender and Achievement

Despite all of the literature highlighting female disadvantages in adult work environments and the greater burden of childcare and housework women take on in the home, one thing is certain: for the past 20 years, girls have consistently outperformed boys in most school subjects. It used to be that girls fared better than boys in their younger school years but that boys pulled ahead during their 16+ years, but this has all changed.

Gone are the days of male-dominated curricula and male favouritism: it is a widely known fact that young women are on the whole more diligent with their studies, achieving higher marks. The increasing number of failing male students has become a huge concern for social researchers, economists and law enforcers alike. This decline in academic performance is linked to nationwide increases in crime, unemployment and drug use. There are currently fewer unskilled, manual jobs for men with weak educational backgrounds. On the contrary, however, there are more service industry jobs available, most of which are taken by women though many of these are still low-paid.

Why the shift?

A lot of the 'gender swap' trend (in terms of educational achievement) can be attributed to the women's movement. For example, the Sex Discrimination Act of 1975, which made gender discrimination in employment illegal, was a major turning point for women.

Young women have, in recent decades, become increasingly surrounded by working female professionals: this has raised levels of self-esteem as well as career and life expectations. Further, the majority of educators are now much more aware of the confining gender socialisation practices of their predecessors; many teachers attempt to steer clear of gender stereotyping in the classroom (though this is not to say that gender stereotyping does not still go on in the modern classroom).

Social researchers have also noted that differences in communication styles have an impact on women and men's respective abilities to succeed in academic environments. Girls are quite verbal in their exchanges, often sharing thoughts and feelings with friends through focused conversation.

Boys, on the other hand, socialise more actively by engaging in group or sporting activities, conversing less, and playing more. Some would argue that education has become 'feminised', with more emphasis on discussion and creativity instead of high-stakes exams. The 'girl' way of communicating is more naturally suited to the classroom environment, and in this way girls are advantaged.

Researchers have also identified a recent phenomenon in schools in which bands of (most commonly) boys decide that education is 'uncool' and useless to their lives, thus partaking in rebellious, anti-learning behaviour.

According to sociologist Martin Mac an Ghaill, these young (usually working class) men are attempting to develop a sense of masculinity during confusing economic times; the manual waged labour jobs of their fathers (formerly centre points of working-class masculinity) are disappearing, and their life paths are thus unclear.

Criticisms

Some researchers think that all of the attention that is currently directed towards 'saving the boys' is misdirected. They feel that this new focus detracts from the major inequalities that still exist in the educational system, for though girls may perform well in school and pursue higher educational degrees, they still lose out in the job market because they have not mastered the competitive science and technology subjects; jobs that require this background are still male-dominated. Moreover, there is still a gender pay gap (where women are paid less than men for equal work) and women take on the majority of unpaid (but necessary) childcare and domestic labour. This must be to the detriment of their careers: in general, then, women are still disadvantaged in the job market.

These gendered subject choices could be the result of many factors, including early socialisation in the home, teachers' differential expectations for girls and boys, and the structure of the job market and economy which clearly still discriminates against women and has yet to accommodate the reality of care-giving as an adult role performed by both genders within working life.

Other researchers hold that class and ethnicity are much more important issues that we need to work out; for example, 70 per cent of children from top professional class background receive 5+ pass grades as compared to 14 per cent of working class students. Underachievement issues, therefore, might have more to do with class than with gender. As with many complex social trends, though, multiple factors can interlink.

Activity 13 - How do you think patterns of educational achievement vary by gender, class and ethnicity?

You may like to research this topic in further detail by looking at some statistical evidence – make sure you know some key facts and figures about this topic. You can start your research into this topic here:

https://www.gov.uk/government/uploads/system/uploads/attachment_data/file/280689/SFR05_2014_Text_FINAL.pdf

http://www.genderandeducation.com/

http://www.guardian.co.uk/news/datablog/2009/dec/15/gcse-statistics-free-school-meals-race-local-authorities-poverty

http://www.statistics.gov.uk/hub/children-education-skills/school-and-college-education/pupils-and-students

What are the links between education, the economy and social inequality?

For many years, sociologists who work on researching education have noticed a strong link between academic achievement at school and social stratification in later life and in wider society.

Sociologists have noticed the following trend: pupils from a working class background (of either gender) usually do much worse at school compared to those from the middle classes or higher. Sociologists reject an explanation for this based on heredity: in other words, they would reject an explanation that claims that the working classes are not as intelligent as the middle classes or upper classes by nature.

NB: However, note that the government does not measure 'social class': they use an 'eligibility of free school meals' indicator (which indicates low income).

"Eligibility for free school meals is strongly associated with low achievement, but significantly more so for White British pupils than for other ethnic groups. Other indicators of disadvantage, such as...the proportion of parents with low educations qualifications...are also statistically associated with low achievement."
Joseph Rowntree Foundations, 2007a

Sociologists feel that the expectations, values, beliefs and culture of schools and of the working class make succeeding at school much harder for pupils from a working class background compared to those from the middle class.

For example, a famous and landmark piece of sociological research conducted by Paul Willis in 1977 investigated the issue of cultural reproduction. This is the term sociologists give to the process whereby the values, norms, ideas and beliefs of one generation are passed on to the next. Education plays a key role in cultural reproduction, and this is often viewed in a negative way.

Willis's key research topic was to try to find out why it was that children from the working classes – despite universal access to free education in the UK – still typically left school and worked in 'working class' jobs such as manufacturing. Why was it that free access to education for all social classes had not resulted in a more flexible level of social mobility, as some had predicted? In other words, how was it that the cultural values, norms and beliefs of the working class (some of which did not value educational achievement) were passed on from one generation to the next through their schooling?

Willis's qualitative research focussed on a group of 12 mainly white working class boys in a Birmingham as they made the transition from school to work. He discovered that the boys did not see themselves as 'fitting in' to the school system, and enjoyed challenging the authority of the school, rather than accepting its rules. They also did this in order to maintain their status amongst themselves as being 'cool' or tough, and keeping this image proved to be more important to the boys than achieving at school or receiving qualifications.

On leaving school, then, the boys typically had not done as well as their middle-class counterparts, and so they could not aspire to jobs beyond those traditionally associated with the working class. In this way, cultural reproduction had effectively taken place where class inequality was passed on from one generation to the next, despite both working class and middle class children receiving a free education.

Some other sociologists argue that this form of cultural reproduction is a vital part of enabling society to function effectively. There are roles in society that have to be filled in order for society to be ordered; therefore some workers have to be skilled whilst others are unskilled. Therefore, in the best interests of society and to ensure that those of the working class stay in the working class on leaving school and not aspire to any other kind of career or educational attainment, the education system is structured in a way that is in keeping with the capitalist system and economy.

4.1.2: Methods in context

A Level: 4.1.2

As stated in the introduction to this course, it is essential that you apply sociological research methods to the different topics that you study. In this case, we will briefly discuss how some research approaches can be applied to the Sociology of Education.

Surveys

Surveys are key forms of research that generally measure quantitative (large-scale, statistical) data on a given subject. Sociologists use surveys to attempt to assess data objectively. One popular type of survey is known as a questionnaire. Questionnaires allow for more precise comparisons among larger groups of people but often can be too highly standardised, thus producing information that does not reflect the true concerns and opinions of the people being studied. Even open-ended questions can pose problems, as people may answer what they profess to believe rather than what they actually believe. Also, surveys can exclude non-literate and non-English speaking individuals.

Examples:

'Women Graduates Paid Less'[6] Caroline Benfield (2007)
Approximately 25,000 students were asked to complete questionnaires three years after graduating.

'The Other Side of the Gender Gap'[7] Molly Warrington and Michel Younger (2000)
This was a survey of 20 eastern English secondary schools looking at the gender gap that made girls feel alienated from traditional male subjects even though they consistently outperformed boys at age 16+.

Activity 14 - What do you think are some of the advantage and disadvantages of using surveys as a research method?

---

[6] Higher Education Statistics Agency
[7] Gender and Education, Vol.12, No.4

Interviews

Interviews are usually conducted by sociologists in intimate environments for the purposes of gathering either quantitative facts or qualitative (small scale, biographical, detailed and/or opinionated) information. Interviews can be hugely informative and eye-opening ways to understand social processes from first hand accounts; however, they have limitations. Often, interviewers can steer conversations in certain directions in order to suit their own research objectives, thus failing to discover the true concerns of those interviewed. Interviews can be either structured or unstructured. Structured interviews are usually based on a prescribed set of questions, with very little or no deviation from the script. Unstructured interviews may have a general theme of questions from which the interviewer and interviewee can elaborate if it is felt that it is necessary to do so.

Examples:

'Family Linguistic Culture and Social Reproduction: Verbal skill from parent to child in the preschool and school'[8] Kurt and Farkas (2001)

This study examined the effects of social class background on children's oral language development.

'Racism in Children's Lives: A Study of mainly-white primary schools'[9] Barry and Hatcher (1992)

This was a study of the effects of social class background on children's oral language development. Interviews were conducted with students aged 10 and 11 over a period of 2 years.

Activity 15 - What do you think are some of the advantages and disadvantages of using interviews as a research method?

---

[8] Population Association of America conference paper
[9] Routledge

Ethnographic methods

Sociologists (and anthropologists) employ the research approach of ethnography in order to gain in-depth understandings of their topics. Ethnography is a qualitative approach, which involves first-hand study of, and often direct engagement with, the people that researchers wish to learn about. Ethnographic researchers predominantly use the method of participant observation, becoming assimilated into the specific groups that they wish to study by living and/or working alongside group members.

Ethnographic researchers will often take part in daily tasks and contribute to the overall well-being of a group, organisation, or community. Ethnographic researchers often conduct interviews (usually informal) to gather information, and can sometimes perform non-participant observation research during which they are observing social behaviour objectively as outsiders. Overall, ethnographic fieldwork not only generates rich, detailed information about individual and group behaviour but also allows for an understanding of broader social processes.

Example:

'Class, Codes and Control' Basil Bernstein (1971)
A study of the relationship between social class and the use of language within the context of the family and the school and how this can affect educational achievement.

Secondary data

Sociologists of education often rely on secondary data that has initially been collected by others. This includes official statistics published by the government as well as school reports, textbooks and other personal documents.

Activity 16 - Imagine that you wanted to do research into how parental values can influence students' achievement levels in school. How would you go about designing a research programme to investigate this? What research methods would you choose, and why?

I think ethnographic methods would be the best method for this as to really see the relationship between interviews would be the best method

Some Key Concepts related to the Sociology of Education	See also...
Economy	
Class structure	
Differentiation	
Social Class	
Gender	
Ethnicity	
Teacher/Pupil Relations	Labelling Self-fulfilling prophecy
Cultural Reproduction	
Identity	
Subcultures	
Hidden Curriculum	
Formal Curriculum	
Educational Policy	
Selection	
Marketisation	
Privatisation	
Equality of opportunity	Access to education
Globalisation	
Qualitative Research	
Quantitative Research	
Surveys	
Secondary Data	
Official Statistics	
Participant Observation	Covert and Overt
Ethnography	
Questionnaires	Structured and unstructured

Conclusion

Like many areas of sociological research, education is a politically important topic because of its direct links to social policy and government strategy. If you have enjoyed this introduction to the Sociology of Education, then you may like to continue your work on education policy and strategy (and how this links to sociological research) by visiting the website for the Department for Education:

http://www.education.gov.uk/

4.1.3: Theory and Methods

Key Areas:

- Quantitative and qualitative methods of research; their strengths and limitations; research design

- Sources of data, including questionnaires, interviews, participant and non-participant observation, experiments, documents, and official statistics; the strengths and limitations of these sources

- The distinction between primary and secondary data, and between quantitative and qualitative data

- The relationship between Positivism, Interpretivism and sociological methods; the nature of 'social facts'

- The theoretical, practical and ethical considerations influencing choice of topic, choice of method(s) and the conduct of research

- Consensus, conflict, structural and social action theories

- The concepts of modernity and post-modernity in relation to sociological theory

- The nature of science and the extent to which Sociology can be regarded as scientific

- The relationship between theory and methods

- Debates about subjectivity, objectivity and value freedom

- The relationship between Sociology and social policy

Introduction

We can speculate about the answers to sociological questions by reading up on relevant sociological literature. Eventually, however, if we truly want to tackle a specific problem or question for ourselves, we must employ formal research methods.

The Research Process

We already touched upon some basic terminology related to sociological research in the previous sections. Now, it's time to dive right into the specific steps and approaches that sociologists follow in order to design and carry out a research project.

1. Defining research problem and aims

This can be the most difficult part of the entire process. Often we are interested in a broad social issue and have to plough through lots of literature and case studies before we can begin to narrow our research aims. Within the topic that we wish to pursue, we must find a research problem to solve. It is usually best to devise a particular question that can be answered with a research project.

For example, let's say that you are interested in learning about youth crime in England. You must then think of other practical considerations. Is there a specific city or region that you would like to focus on? A specific form of crime: say, knife crime? Or perhaps a specific ethnic minority, gender or age category? Let's say you decide to conduct comparative research on knife crime amongst young, working class white and African Caribbean groups in Manchester. More practical issues to consider:

- Do you have the time and resources required for the project? Can you relocate to Manchester for an extended period of time?
- Do you have access to the subject matter? Will you be able to gather information from people in, likely, dangerous parts of the city? Most importantly: will you be able to conduct research safely?
- Is funding available?
    - If you cannot answer 'yes' to all of the above questions, then you probably will have to start the process all over, selecting a topic that is more manageable.

However, for an amateur or novice sociologist, it is easiest to look at your immediate surroundings and circumstances when devising a research topic. For example, you could think about your school, home, workplace, local area or community. Perhaps you could investigate how age, ability, class, gender or ethnicity (or another social concept) have an impact on performance or participation in work or school.

Consider some areas of investigation and make a note of your ideas. An example question or topic for study could be one of the following:

- How does age affect the amount of time spent online in the home?
- How does gender affect academic performance at school?
- How does social class affect promotion and performance at work?

However, bear in mind that these types of question are still too general; make sure that you ask yourself a question that is specific to your own personal circumstances. For example, your question could be about your own school or workplace, and so on.

2. Reviewing evidence

Now it's time to read up on all of the literature that you can find to support the creation of your research project as well as your prediction, or hypothesis (and later, in presenting your final results, your argument or thesis). You will probably consider some broad theories that were created by past sociologists related to crime and deviant behaviour. You would want to look up some statistics on youth crime. You then might want to read up on any laws that were created that relate to the prevention of knife crime. Next, you will want to look at any case studies or ethnographies that exist regarding your topic. These are usually more difficult to come across.

3. Making a problem precise (hypothesis)

Having researched your topic thoroughly, you will not want to narrow your intentions by creating a hypothesis (a prediction or educated guess based on your reading), which indicates what you may discover.

4. Design

Now you must undergo the task of designing your project. We have already discussed different types of research methods that you can use (e.g. survey, ethnography) in order to carry out research about your topic. It is best that you try to incorporate both qualitative and quantitative forms of research. Researchers tend to use multiple methods in order to gather more reliable data: this is known as triangulation. For example, a researcher may use qualitative data from interviews and quantitative data using reports or official statistics, to build up a more comprehensive picture of a social situation.

5. Research and data collection

You will then carry out your research, step-by-step, based on your design. You will collect many forms of data throughout your research, including the following primary data and secondary data:

- Primary data: is collected personally in the form of questionnaires and fieldwork interviews and observational studies
- Secondary data: originates from a source other than personal research and can include newspaper articles, books, mass media and the research of other social scientists. Sociologists should take caution in the way that they present information gathered from non-academic publications, which could be biased and under-researched. e.g. when conducting research on the Internet, make sure that you are looking at legitimate academic articles from academic journals

Quantitative and qualitative data:

- Quantitative data: quantifies the relationship between two or more things and is represented statistically or numerically, based on surveys and statistical polls (for example, the results of a survey that was sent to a representative sample about the employment conditions of pregnant teenagers)

- Qualitative data: specifies the quality of the relationship between two or more things and involves interpretation based on either fieldwork or surveys (for example, a detailed analysis of the information gathered from an observational study)

Activity 17 - Look at the table that follows and think about the different kinds of data. Fill in some examples of forms of data that fit into each different category. When you have done that, continue reading below.

	Qualitative data	Quantitative data
Primary data		
Secondary data		

Throughout the research process, you will probably run into problems with gathering the data you are after. Often, the statistics that researchers need have not been recorded or are confidential and incredibly difficult to access. As such, you will likely have to re-evaluate your approach and modify your research design several times.

6. Interpretation and evaluation

After collecting all of your data and information, you will compile your facts and begin to analyse your results. It is important not to pigeonhole your facts into a neat summary that reflects your original hypothesis. You must analyse your results objectively, using 'sociological imagination' and steering clear of any bias that you may have, based on your personal experiences.

7. Report Findings

Lastly you must structure your conclusions into a coherent, user-friendly format that includes both an analysis of your qualitative findings and/or quantitative data, as well as charts and graphs that present your survey statistics.

8. Reality

You must keep in mind that while the above steps appear to provide a neat structure, the actual research process can be unpredictable and chaotic, requiring re-thinking and re-structuring almost every step of the way. For example, it can be the case that the original research brief that a sociologist starts with will not be what they end up researching, as the reality of the context takes them in new directions or gives them new ideas or understanding. Also, society is made up of social beings, individuals, who are notoriously unpredictable!

The research process

To recap, the stages in the research process of academic Sociology are as follows:

- Choose a subject for research – define the nature of the problem for investigation
- Read the existing sociological research on the topic
- Decide what you think is the relationship between the variables being tested
- Decide on the research plan – what are the most suitable methods of data collection?
- Carry out the research according to this plan
- Record the results and analyse the findings
- Report the research, discuss the findings in terms of your preliminary thoughts – do they match up or not?
- Discuss your findings with the wider research community

Activity 18 – Consider how sociologists plan and design a research project. Can you design a research project on a topic related to either Health or Education, of your choosing?

Ensure that you include an example of triangulation in your research design.

Research Methods

It is important that you can understand (and apply on a small scale) the following methods:

1. Fieldwork (Ethnography)

Sociologists employ the research approach of ethnography in order to gain in-depth understandings of their topics. Ethnography is a qualitative approach, which involves first-hand study of, and often direct engagement with, the people that researchers wish to learn about. Ethnographic researchers predominantly use the method of participant observation, becoming assimilated into the specific groups that they wish to study by living and/or working alongside group members. Ethnographic researchers will often take part in daily tasks and contribute to the overall well-being of a group, organisation, or community.

Ethnographic researchers often conduct interviews (usually informal) to gather information and can sometimes perform non-participant observation research, during which they are observing social behaviour objectively as outsiders. Overall, ethnographic fieldwork not only generates rich, detailed information about individual and group behaviours but also allows for an understanding of broader social processes.

Sociologists use these research methods but more often within specific communities in their home regions contrasted against anthropologists who may study cultures further afield. For example, a sociologist studying knife crime among working class men in Manchester would first relocate to Manchester, and perhaps start contributing to the local economy in some way. The sociologist would need to find a SAFE way to become integrated in the local communities in which knife crime occurs as a way to collect data in context and yet not to risk their own lives or compromise ethical standards. Like any research method, ethnography has its limitations and problems. Ethnographers may face ethical problems, especially when working in areas where they may feel obliged to help and support individuals in ways that they cannot. Also, ethnographic research can sometimes provide a very limited scope, producing results that may be hard to apply cross-culturally.

Participant Observation (PO)

Whereas questionnaires typically collect quantitative data (though not always), there are different approaches. These are qualitative methods, and they collect data which is descriptive rather than numerical. One example of this method is participant observation (PO).

PO is grounded in observing subjects of study in action. For example, a sociologist undertaking PO may join an interest group, club, school or other form of social structure. They do this 'covertly', that is, they do not necessarily announce that they are sociologists who intend to study people in real life.

Rather, they assume the cover of joining that group as a member of the public, and they then use this cover as a way to watch how people in real-life situations actually do think and behave. Sociologists do this so they can understand and describe their subjects. The understanding comes from the fact that they too have joined the group, club or other social structure, so they too can see how it works 'from the inside.' However, as time goes on, it may be obvious that the sociologist is in fact an 'outsider' and so the sociologist will have an interesting role: a participant in the group but as an obvious 'outsider' by virtue of the fact that their age, class, ethnicity, gender or social background de-bar them from being considered full and normative members.

An alternative approach is for the researcher to operate on the basis of overt PO, in that he/she takes part in what is being observed but those being observed are aware of that fact.

Activity 19 - What do you think are the advantages and disadvantages of PO as a research method?

Make a list of around 5 points on either side, and then continue reading below.

Advantages

Subjects are studied in their natural environments, in real life and in 'real time'. This means that sociologists can gather much detailed and real-life data.

Sociologists are more able to understand subjects on their own terms. For example, it can be tempting to assume that as a sociologist, one 'knows' more than the subjects themselves about what they think or feel. In this instance, it is much harder for a sociologist to do this because they allow the subjects to demonstrate what is actually important to them through their day-to-day and natural, real-life activities.

Sociologists, as fellow participants, can share and discuss events and experiences with the subjects, and so can gain much more detailed and direct information, and in particular, how the subject has interpreted his or her own experiences.

PO reduces the risk of subjects altering their behaviour because they know they are being observed as part of a study. Remember, key to this method is that the sociologist is, broadly speaking, 'undercover', and so the subjects should not be fully aware that they are actually under observation.

PO can therefore be an excellent way for sociologists to gain access to groups that they would normally be denied admission. For example, a gang. Provided the sociologist had a good cover, and could convincingly play the required role, then he or she could carry out observation of gang members and collect much valuable data, in a way that no one else could.

Disadvantages

PO is time consuming and laborious. It must be done properly if it is to be worth anything; imagine what difficulties could arise if the cover of the sociologist was broken or revealed in a difficult situation, for example.

Since PO relies on good cover, then many sociologists would be denied access to some groups by virtue of being unable to disguise themselves effectively. For example, it would be highly difficult for a woman sociologist to enter the Freemasons to undertake PO (they are a male-only group), and in this case, a woman sociologist is excluded from this kind of data collection and observation by virtue of her gender. It would be ob·

right from the start that she was not a serious 'participant', and so any admissio.

the group would always be as an outsider witness.

It can be hard for a sociologist to ask questions when they are undercover. It may become suspicious or break their cover if they act too much 'like a sociologist'; they may thus be restricted to observation but unable to find out much about why people are behaving as they do (because they cannot ask too many direct questions) or else discover much about people's feelings and opinions.

Although PO can be an excellent method of gaining access to some hard-to-access groups, there are still those where entry would be very hard indeed. For example: a gymnastics club. A sociologist would have to also be proficient at gymnastics in order to convincingly join this kind of club, and also be of the right age and possibly gender in order to 'fit in' well enough. It is unlikely that there are enough available sociologists who also have such a wide range of other skills, talents, attributes and qualities and so on to make study of a large number of different groups by this method possible! Thus, the sociologists themselves restrict and determine their areas of research and study. If there are no gymnast sociologists, then there can be no data collected from the gymnast club (if PO is the only method employed).

Non-participant observation (NPO) is another form of observational sociological analysis, and is similar to PO. In this instance, the sociologist still observes an individual, group or social structure in action, but this time, there is a crucial difference. The sociologist is not 'undercover' as an active member of that group. Rather, he or she works with the knowledge and awareness of the subjects. That is, the sociologist is not in disguise or undercover, but is openly conducting observational research as a sociologist.

The advantages of NPO are similar to that of PO, but there is a crucial disadvantage which they do not have in common.

The Hawthorne Effect

In the 1920s, some sociological studies were carried out in Chicago of the workers at the Western Electric Company. The researchers observed and measured how different working conditions (such as length of hours worked, levels of lighting and pay) all affected the productivity of the workers. The sociologists found that productivity did indeed vary when these types of factors were changed. However, that was not the major insight of their work. Far more important, the sociologists discovered that regardless of what they were measuring, the subjects (workers at the Western Electric Company) all worked harder when they were being watched.

In other words, the researchers had found that the very act of observation, measurement and analysis (regardless of the experimental aims of the researchers) changes human behaviour. This gave rise to the now widespread term 'the Hawthorne effect' to describe any instance of behaviour change when under outside observation.

Indeed, the Hawthorne effect can be seen in action in human interactions all around us, if one cares to look. For example, school children who know they are being watched by their teachers are more inclined to be quiet and less disruptive; adults in a street may prefer not to drop litter when a policeman or other adults are passing by and so on. In fact, we have all altered and modified our behaviour (especially if we were intending to do something that we know breaks social norms or the rules a little) as soon as we suspected that we were being watched when we previously thought we were not. It is a powerful effect indeed, and because of its undoubted influence on human behaviour, it is impossible to discount in NPO. The subjects, whatever is being researched and whoever they are, know they are being watched and so some alteration or change of behaviour is likely as a result. Thus, it is harder perhaps to draw conclusive results from data gathered as a result of NPO since any results must include the question of whether the behaviour observed was 'natural', normal or in-line with what would have happened if the sociologist had not been present.

Activity 20 - In the light of your reading about the Hawthorne Effect, what do you think is the key ethical principle to follow in sociological research?

Interview

Typically, the interview is conducted in real time, and is a series of questions posed by the sociologist to the subject or subjects of their research. The case study of Jane Smith that you read earlier is of the kind that could have been written by a sociologist based on a brief interview with the subject Jane Smith. Interviews can be used to gain both quantitative and qualitative data. Interviews can also vary by format: some can be formal; the subject can be aware they are being interviewed by a sociologist for example (and in this case, the Hawthorne effect may come into play). However, interviews can also be more informal, open-ended and unstructured, or could take place within the context of PO (the sociologist would simply be 'having a conversation' with a subject, though he or she would not know that this was really an 'interview').

2. Social Survey

In order to apply ethnographic research findings to larger cross-sections of a population, it is often necessary for sociologists to employ the quantitative approach of the social survey, in which questions are sent or administered directly to a selected group of people (often consisting of thousands) known as a population. In conducting surveys, sociologists use questionnaires and sampling methods. Questionnaires can be conducted in two formats: standardised (with a fixed selection of answers) or open-ended. Questionnaires allow for more precise comparisons among larger groups of people but often can be too highly standardised, thus producing information that does not reflect the true concerns and opinions of the people being studied. Even open-ended questions can pose problems, as people may answer what they profess to believe rather than what they actually believe. Sampling is often used when the group being studied is too large for the sociologist to question each individual. Thus, a representative sample (a group of people that represents the typical characteristics of a population based on factors such as ethnicity, age, and gender) or random sample of a given population will be administered questionnaires. Other methods include quota sampling (choosing people from a range of different quotas or groups which fairly represent the population) and stratified sampling (dividing the population into levels or strata which are representative and then choosing at random from among these). Due to the numerical insight needed to carry out accurate sampling, it can be a complex process which requires specific statistical knowledge.

Sampling in action

For example: a sociologist may be interested in investigating how women's attitudes to work in the UK have changed over the last ten years. The first stage would be to get some data to establish what current attitudes are, and then to look back over the previous ten years to understand what changes (if any) have taken place.

The first stage then clearly involves asking women about their own opinions or feelings about work. But to ask all women in the UK these questions is clearly impossible and undesirable: in which case, the sociologist could first take a representative sample (choosing a manageable number of women who represent the demographic of the UK in terms of age, class or ethnicity, for example) or a random sample (choosing women at random from the electoral roll or birth records, for example) in order to gain a sample for study.

Most sociologists will use a combination of fieldwork and survey research to gain the best overall understanding of social processes in a given population.

Activity 21 – Reflect on social surveys. What are the advantages and disadvantages of a social survey?

3. Comparative Research and Other Methods

Comparative research can be very useful in that it provides sociologists with well-rounded, relative perspectives regarding their concentrated ethnographic and survey research. Comparative research can be conducted cross-culturally e.g. measuring teen crime rates in western societies against those in non-western societies and also historically, measuring the change in statistical values over time.

Other research methods include experiments, life histories or longitudinal studies and content analysis.

Experiments

You will recall that sociology is a social science. This means that it partly makes use of the scientific method. The scientific method tests theories through data collected from observation and measurement. An experiment is the major way in which scientists do this: a scientist will propose a question, then will test whether the question is 'true' or 'false' through changing an independent variable (a cause) to observe the dependent variable (the effect) while keeping all other factors the same (the extraneous variables, or other factors which may otherwise disrupt the outcomes). Experiments are controlled, and they can take place in the laboratory or in the field (outdoors or in nature or real life). Although experiments are the major methodology in the natural sciences and in psychology, they are far less common in sociology.

However, some sociologists, depending on their ideological position, favour experimentation more than others. Those that do favour scientific experimentation do so because (as in the physical sciences) the results are seen as objective, re-testable and thus a solid basis for drawing up an argument or conclusion about social trends, patterns or behaviours. However, those sociologists that do not favour experimentation claim that sociology is far more about why people do what they do, not just what they do. Thus, an experiment may yield a great deal of data about, for example, the shopping patterns and consumer habits found in a regular high street.

But this may only get the sociologist so far: examining why people shop, what motivates them to shop, when and how they do, and so on, is something that only a more qualitative or meaning-based approach (rather than pure experimentation) can possibly begin to understand. It is this, as some sociologists say, that is far more valid than endless data which has no reference to the values and meanings behind why people behave as they do.

Finally, as we have already noted, the Hawthorne effect poses another practical problem for experimentation in sociology. As soon as subjects are aware they are being examined, observed or 'checked 'up on' they are more inclined to change their behaviour as a result. This makes clear data much harder for the sociologist to find. Moreover, the sociologists themselves may have their own strong expectations regarding the results of the experiment. In fact, the sociologist may already have a strong belief in the validity of his or her hypothesis. Thus, he or she may take any kind of evidence, or look for evidence, that confirms this expectation regardless of how good the evidence really is.

A sociologist who wants to use scientific experimentation must therefore be aware of the Hawthorne effect, and should also guard against looking too hard for confirmation of a hypothesis that may not actually have much evidence to back it up.

Activity 22 – Summarise some of the problems that may arise due to bias and objectivity in carrying out sociological research.

Longitudinal studies

A longitudinal study is one that is conducted over time. For example, a sociologist might interview Jane Smith (our earlier case study) at age 16, then at age 21, then at age 25, 30, 35 and 40 and so on. Such a study, though obviously time-consuming and an inherently slow process, is valuable for the depth of data it can provide. The subject is watched for development over time, and analysis and long-term trends can be researched and analysed in this regard. For example, a sociologist may wish to research whether children whose parents divorced when young (as Jane's did) experience any adverse effects of this later in life. Perhaps it affects their schooling, their work, their own adult relationships? In which case, a good way to find out if this is so is to test this by observing a subject over time.

Content analysis

Content analysis is a broad term for a type of research methodology used in the social sciences, though it can cover lots of different approaches. It is a method of studying communication and communication strategies. The 'content' of content analysis refers to any kind of communication content. This could take the form of a letter, a book, a newspaper article, a radio programme, a conversation or even a painting (which is a form of visual rather than aural communication).

A sociologist using content analysis as a method would then examine what was really being communicated, what meanings were intended, in that particular 'content'. The sociologist aims to do this in a scientific way, using linguistic analysis and measurable data, in order to try and be as exact as possible and to allow any findings to be repeatable (by another sociologist using the same method). In this regard, content analysis is similar to experimentation in that it uses a key plank of the scientific method: repeatable and testable hypothesis backed up with data gained from experimentation.

Research Strategies

What should be clear now from the various methods of obtaining sociological data as outlined above is that there is no one way in which sociologists work. In fact, Sociology is broad and diverse, and different sociologists use different methods according to their own backgrounds, beliefs and ideologies and as appropriate to the context and content of their own special areas of study.

What is also important to realise is that the method or methods chosen by the sociologist are very important indeed, because they actually dictate the type of data it is possible to find. With this in mind, continue to the tasks below.

What factors should be considered when evaluating a piece of sociological research? 'The method of data collection and the form of presentation may influence the information given and the conclusions reached.'

It is very important that you are fully aware of the implications of the statement made above for the purposes of this course. The truth of this is best demonstrated through a real life example, as follows: the social scientist Durkheim conducted some research into suicide in 1897. He gathered many statistics on suicide and then drew some conclusions on the reasons for suicides based on this evidence. What is interesting about Durkheim's study is what then happened much later, in 1952: sociologists re-evaluated the data from the 1897 study on suicide but this time, they drew very different conclusions. They argued that there was an error within the data Durkheim had based his research on; they questioned how a death had come to be defined as a suicide.

In many cases, the deaths were sudden or unexpected, but how could it be assumed that they were all also suicides? In fact, it was possible that some of the deaths were accidental rather than deliberate; what was really important, the sociologists therefore concluded, was to research how and why a death in suspicious or indeterminate circumstances came to be defined as a suicide by the medical establishment or police. This research would say a lot about the sorts of assumptions or beliefs that were being applied in instances of suspicious deaths, and would thus be useful for sociological research into social and cultural attitudes surrounding death by suicide.

The interesting point about this real-life example is how important the methodology of data collection is for sociological research. What at first glance may seem like a cold, hard, factual statistic (on suicide) turns out to hide a great deal of ambiguity and subjectivity. What is suicide? How can we be sure a death is a genuine suicide or accidental? Who defines and determines this? All these questions come into play, and remind us that for all data, what is vital is to ensure that it is gathered with as much clarity and accuracy as possible, but that it always has its limitations of which the sociologist must be aware.

What is the relationship between theory and methods; positivist and anti-positivist approaches?

We are now clear on the fact that the sociological research method affects the type and quality of data obtained by the sociologist. For example, some sociologists favour experimentation as a methodology more than others, and this is because of their own personal ideological position. It is time to examine these in more detail now.

A summary of the positivist perspective

A sociologist who describes themselves as a positivist is one who thinks that the only kind of valid data (in any field of human study) is the scientific. That is, only data gained from close and rigorous application of the scientific method is worth any attention.

In which case, a positivist sociologist strongly favours scientific experimentation as a research method. A positivist sociologist would take the approach that statistics about society (for example, crime rates, the divorce rate, the suicide rate and so on) all indicate and describe wider social and societal trends. However, a positivist sociologist does not welcome all data or statistics regardless. What is important is that the data has been collected objectively and in accordance with the scientific method; in this respect, positivists are very highly concerned with good research methods and overcoming any problems associated with achieving these. A positivist sociologist would therefore not hesitate to disregard data that was irrelevant or unreliable.

A summary of the symbolic interactionist perspective (or 'anti-positivist')

In contrast, an interactionist sociologist thinks that statistics and data of the type favoured by the positivist are not objective or 'value-neutral', as the positivist thinks. Rather, data and statistics are just as prone to the Hawthorne effect, researcher bias and other problems that the positivist is trying to avoid by being careful about the research methodology used.

This means that an interactionist sociologist questions whether statistics and data are valid for the sociologist to use in research, since for this sociologist there is no such thing as 'objectivity', or value-neutral data.

Therefore, in practice, a symbolic interactionist sociologist would question and investigate the ideological basis behind data; even research data that has been conducted on so-called 'objective' grounds according to the scientific method because the assumptions and beliefs of the researchers still intrude to shape and influence the results.

What are the theoretical, practical and ethical considerations influencing the choice of topic, choice of methods and conduct of research?

To explain this further: a positivist sociologist may have all the data and statistics for the UK crime rates over the past ten years, and would use these to draw conclusions about social trends with regards to crime. However, an interactionist would question whether it was valid to draw these conclusions based on this kind of statistical data.

An interactionist would ask: but who has defined this event or act as a crime? How has that definition been reached? What kinds of criminal behaviour or criminal acts have possibly been discounted from police reports? Why would this be so? What kinds of acts have been included as crimes, and if so why? Thus, an interactionist would argue that data and statistics are not value-neutral or objective. Rather, they throw up just as many questions about the assumptions people, society and social structures make about crime and about patterns of human behaviour.

Social Facts

This is another important sociological concept, and one that was coined by Durkheim. Durkheim's view of sociological research was that it should be focussed on 'social facts'. By this, he meant the parts of social life that mould our actions as individuals. For Durkheim, each society had its own reality and its own characteristic ways of acting which were external to the individual and typically more powerful. For example, economic reality or religious institutions are all social facts according to Durkheim, since they all have the power to deeply affect who we are as individuals.

However, social facts are very hard to study because typically individuals think of themselves as acting freely, when in fact their actions and self-identity have been deeply conditioned by those same social facts since birth.

For Durkheim, the entrenched reality of social facts meant that sociologists were required to approach the study of society with a scientific mind-set and method. Since social facts can be hard to see, it is necessary to approach society with an open mind and without pre-conceived ideas in order to find out the true nature of social reality.

Sources of data

One way to ensure that statistics, if they are used, are reliable, is to go to a trusted source. One problem with internet-based data is that unless you are very sure about the source or the origin of that data, it can be hard to trust. One way around this is to go to sources of official data and statistics as examples of reliable secondary data.

Official statistics concerning UK society are gathered by the government from research such as the population census. Every ten years, the UK population is counted and asked questions about themselves for the purposes of drawing conclusions about social trends. For example, it is very useful for planning purposes for the UK government to know how many people there are in the different age categories.

At the moment, it is known that as a society, the UK (in common with many other western nations) is ageing. In terms of planning, this means that governments need to consider putting resources into care or residential homes, into pensions and into medical research on ageing health issues in order to accommodate this social trend.

(This is also a good indication of how important sociology is as an area of study; a sociologist could conduct important research on ageing in the UK to aid governmental decisions on how best to prepare and plan for this demographic change, for example.)

In fact, so important are statistics for social planning that in the UK there is an 'Office of National Statistics' which deals with collecting the kinds of relevant data all governments need in order to plan and prepare effectively.

Activity 23 - Here is the website of the Office of National Statistics: http://www.statistics.gov.uk/default.asp

Browse the website of the Office of National Statistics (ONS) and look at some of the data you personally find interesting which you can find there.

What kinds of data and statistics does the ONS collect and publish? Why do you think this is useful or important? How is the data categorised? Why do you think official statistics might need to be used with caution? Finally, think about how sociologists can make use of secondary data such as those found in the ONS.

Other statistics

Besides the official statistics collected by the ONS for the UK government, individual social institutions and structures collect and record their own data. For example, every single school in the UK keeps data and records of their pupils and staff. It does this not only because pupil record keeping is a legal requirement (for example, schools must know about pupils' health requirements, their attendance records and their academic performance each year) but also because without these data and records, it would be much harder for the school staff to teach and work effectively. Good information is vital to the functioning of modern institutions and organisations.

However, this kind of data is still fairly formal (you would find similar data on the patients of a hospital, for example) and in many cases is private (such as health records), though it is not official in the same way that data collected by the ONS is both official and in the public domain. Besides this type of formal data, there are all sorts of different statistics collected by a number of organisations, businesses, charities, foundations, trusts and other bodies which may prove useful to the sociologist.

Published studies

The sociologist also has the option of turning to academic research or published studies for further information. The work of current professional sociologists is often helpful for sociological research, since it can provide the groundwork for a new area of investigation. Moreover, published studies may well have a great deal of useful existing research data that a sociologist could use in a new investigation or as the basis for conducting new research.

Activity 24 - Here is a website where it is possible to access sociological data from published studies:
http://www.socresonline.org.uk/home.html
Browse through this website and look at some of the archive material that interests you, so you can get a feel for the kinds of work that professional or academic sociologists are currently engaged in.
Ensure that you can name and describe at least three sources and three types of secondary data.
What is the distinction between reliability and validity?

We now need to pay close attention to two terms that have already been used to describe data, though are easily misunderstood. Although it may seem as though the terms reliability and validity are similar, in fact in sociological research it is very important indeed to understand their different definitions and different applications when we come to evaluate the worth of data.

Reliability

A key question for sociologists is this: if a sociologist repeated any piece of research, following the same methodology, would he or she obtain the same results? It is expected that if research is reliable then the answer to this question would be: yes. In other words, reliable research and the data that results is that which conforms to the scientific method and the principle of repeatability. In general, quantitative data is more reliable than qualitative, if we follow this definition of reliability.

Validity

The next question sociologists ask themselves when evaluating research is this: how far does this data give us a true or valid picture of the subject of research? In order to answer this question, the sociologist must do some analysis of the methodology used to obtain the data. For example: how well does the method used match the research subject? Is it appropriate for the topic? Was the research carried out ethically and correctly? This is how a sociologist evaluates whether or not data is valid.

It is not always the case that data is both valid and reliable. Sometimes it is one but not the other, sometimes both. We shall now investigate this further.

Valid but not reliable

Often, observational and qualitative data is valid but not reliable. It is not reliable because PO or NPO is hard to replicate. For example, if a sociologist were to join a group and make observations (using PO) and then write up the data and draw conclusions, this would be a valid method and one that most likely would prove insightful of the group that the sociologist had joined.

However, it is very unlikely that it would be reliable data: if another sociologist then attempted to do the same a few years later, it is very likely that he or she would make different observations. The group members would probably have changed; different events or circumstances would have changed how the group operates; the group could have expanded or contracted. In other words, time would have made its inevitable impact on the group and so it would not be possible for the sociologist to repeat the original research; this form of data is therefore valid but not reliable.

Reliable but not valid

In contrast, a sociologist could draw up a questionnaire or survey. This could then be sent out to a sample, the results returned, quantified and turned into charts or graphs and conclusions drawn from the results. It is fairly easy to imagine that another sociologist could repeat this research later; he or she could take the same questionnaire or survey and provided that it was sent to the same kind of sample then the results returned would be the same or similar; especially so if the survey was to gather quantitative data. This would mean that the data was reliable because if the research were repeated it would yield the same or very similar results. However, the questions or survey basis itself may well not be valid.

For example, a sociologist could be researching the effects of crime, and could gather quantitative data to determine the colour of shoes that victims of crime were wearing at the time of the offence. The sociologist would then have a great deal of data to represent in the form of pie charts or graphs showing how many victims wore black shoes, how many blue, how many white and so on.

This data would be reliable; it is likely that if the research were repeated then similar results would be obtained, but it is not at all valid when it comes to the topic of research (the effects of crime). This is because it is a trivial line of research; the colour of the victims' shoes is most unlikely to be very significant when it comes to evaluating the effect that the crime had on the victim. Clearly, it is not the colour of the victims' shoes that really matters when it comes to how they handle and deal with what happened to them.

Moreover, there can be a problem with qualitative data gathered from questionnaires. It is not always the case that subjects tell the truth to sociologists when they ask them questions for survey purposes. Similar to the Hawthorne effect, the fact that you are being asked questions by someone 'official' is very likely to change your own answers in response. This is especially the case when sociologists research topics which are sensitive or taboo: for example, it is very likely that people would lie about their sex life or attitudes to sex to a sociologist unless they were first assured about their privacy and anonymity. In which case, the research methods and manner of conducting the survey would be vital to ensuring that the data was valid as well as reliable.

Activity 25 – Explain the practical issues that researchers must consider when choosing a research method so they can ensure their data are as reliable and as valid as possible.

Ethical Considerations

As mentioned above, sociologists will always encounter ethical dilemmas when conducting research among human subjects. The following are key ethical considerations that all sociologists must consider when conducting research:

- No one should be harmed as a result of the research. Though this may seem obvious: researchers should never harm participants, whether it be physically, emotionally e.g. insensitive questions, or socially e.g. harming social reputation
- Researchers need be honest about what they are doing by seeking informed consent and letting participants know who is conducting the research, why it is being done and how the results will be used
- Researchers should respect participants' rights to confidentiality and privacy by concealing participants' identities when they write up their research
- Researchers will not break laws or cause others to break laws

The role of theory

You should now be coming to an understanding of the role played by a sociologist's theoretical position and the relationship between that and the methodology selected by a sociologists for their research. A sociologist in the positivist school, for example, will tend to favour some data collection methods over others; likewise a sociologist in the interpretivist tradition. Although both sociologists may be researching the same topic, they may very well collect entirely different data sets as a result. This shows us the close relationship between theory, methods and data. However, there are additional theoretical approaches in sociological research. So far, you have already covered consensus, conflict and structural theories: you may like to pause briefly to consider what methodological approaches a sociologists working in one of these theoretical traditions would be likely to select, and why. There is one more theoretical position to cover.

Social Action Theory

This term refers to a theoretical position which was originally founded by Max Weber. Social action theories are those sociological theories (such as interpretivism) which see social interaction or relationships between people as individuals as being fundamental, rather than wider scale social structures or systems (in contrast to Durkheim).

Activity 26 – Now read the following article on theoretical positions in sociology and how these relate to the research methods used by sociologists. Make sure you can explain how and why a sociologist's theoretical background informs their data collection methods:

http://www.historylearningsite.co.uk/sociology/theories-in-sociology/social-action-theory/

Modernity

The discipline of sociology arose in response to the massive changes that went on in the late eighteenth and early nineteenth century, as society transitioned from pre-modernity to modernity. This transition was caused by the effects of the 'twin revolutions': the democratic revolutions and the Industrial Revolution, which caused a breakdown in the traditional value systems that had defined pre-modern societies. Several of the classical sociological theorists, such as Durkheim, Marx or Weber described the structural, intellectual and political changes that occurred during this shift from pre-modernity to modernity.

Durkheim

Durkheim claimed that pre-modern society achieved **social order** through **mechanical solidarity** (or a shared set of beliefs, such as religious or cultural beliefs) whereas modern society, he predicted, would be (more loosely) bound together by **organic solidarity**. Organic solidarity involves economic ties (such as those between employer and employee) and occupational associations (such as those between colleagues in workplaces).

Weber

Weber felt that in modern society, there came an 'iron cage of rationality', in which all people's actions were goal-oriented and based on rational thought, and that this mode of thinking was the only socially sanctioned one.

Marx

Marx was highly critical of the capitalistic societies that emerged with modernity. He felt that capitalism divided society, creating inequality and exploitation.

Postmodernity

Postmodernity (the period that, several sociologists would claim, we operate in today) is characterised by plurality and relativity. Gone are the days in which science could lead humans to objective truths; postmodernity challenges these views of the Enlightenment, claiming that science is just one of multiple ways that people can choose to seek truth. There are no such universal truths: truth is relative.

Postmodernism also negated the **metanarratives** (that is, grand narratives) that were put forth by classical sociologists. Society does not simply move in one, progressive direction, with everyone falling into matching step. Again, society is characterised by **plurality**: we can pick and choose from elements of different belief and value systems to formulate our own identities.

Late modernity

Some researchers would argue that we have not yet entered a period of post-modernity; they feel that scientific technologies still have the potential to lead to human progress. Instead, we are in a period of **late modernity**, in which society and social relations are being continuously transformed by **globalisation**.

In late modernity, social relationships are no longer confined to specific localities; people communicate, work, marry, shop and are educated internationally. Also, we live in a society that is characterised by **reflexivity**: people actively think about themselves in relation to society, they are thus **reflexively** living their lives and creating their identities.

The second age of modernity

Others feel that we have entered a 'second age of modernity', within which postmodernist ideas are dated and irrelevant. Sociologists thus need to adopt the **cosmopolitan outlook**, which addresses the current interdependencies that exist between people across national borders. The ideological viewpoint of **cosmopolitanism** (for example, the sociologist Ulrich Beck proposed this) is one where the national outlook is critiqued as being too narrow in an age of globalisation. So what are the conditions of the cosmopolitan condition that Beck claims we currently live in?

Beck claims that in a globalised world, the nation state is not strong enough to protect its citizens from dangers and threats that are global in scope and which cross national boundaries (for example, climate change or a global financial crisis). This means that in order for each nation state to withstand these threats, international mobilisation and agreement at the transnational level is necessary.

A post-societal stage?

The sociologist John Urry argues that globalisation undermines the notion of a distinct, definitive society. We now operate in a series of complex, global networks; as such, sociologists have entered a 'post-societal stage' in which they can examine the global flow of people, information, images and objects. For this reason, sociologists must employ **methodological cosmopolitanism**. This is whereby sociologists take the global perspective and the international dimension as fundamental to their analysis of national societies and cultures.

The science debate

In our discussions of sociological theories such as positivism and interpretivisim, and the consideration of the relationship between Sociology and other subjects such as Biology, Psychology or Anthropology, we have touched upon an ongoing debate among sociologists. That is, to what degree can sociology be considered a science, if at all?

1 - "Yes, sociology is a science"

a. Description of natural sciences in general

Examples of natural sciences: biology and chemistry

Characterised by empirical, objective inquiry

Objectivity = free of bias and prejudice

Empiricism = using observable facts to test theories

Scientists aim to discover natural laws, which explain patterns in the natural world

They conduct research through experiments and statistical methods

In order for their laws to become accepted, scientific knowledge, they must test theirhypotheses using **replication**

b. Sociology as a science

Like psychology, anthropology and economics, sociology is often categorised today as a **social science**. However, the pioneering sociological thinkers pursued the discipline as a natural science. Like these early positivists, some still argue that, as in the natural sciences, sociologists can pursue research objectively and empirically. These sociologists tend to support one of the following two approaches: Positivism or Popper.

i. Positivism

Sociology was developed at the turn of the nineteenth century, a time that was strongly influenced by the ideals of the Enlightenment, e.g. science dominated religion; reason was seen as the cure to societal ills (Marx developed the concept of reason).

The earliest sociologists, such as Marx, Comte and Durkheim, were positivists.

Comte: Sociologists should use the methods of natural sciences. The discipline of sociology was the apex of scientific study: the 'queen of sciences'.

Durkheim: We must study social facts objectively, as 'things': just as objects are studied in the natural sciences.

Positivists used **inductive** methods: they examined data, created a theory and defended the theory.

ii. Popper

Karl Popper expanded on his positivist predecessors in 1959, arguing that sociology could only be a valid science if based on **falsification**.

Falsification = the idea that researchers should aim to refute hypotheses.

Sociologists thus needed to use testable hypotheses. The longer that these hypotheses are not falsified, the truer they are.

Sociologists should use deductive methods (as opposed to the positivist **inductive** methods), starting with a theory and testing it against evidence.

2 - "No, sociology is not a science"

a. Interpretivism – Sociology is not a natural science

Sociology cannot be studied as a natural science.

People are not objects; they are social beings that engage in meaningful interaction.

Interpretivism is based on Weber's concept of *verstehen*, or empathetic understanding.

Sociologists must study social behaviour empathetically, from the perspective of the person they are researching.

Interpretivist approaches are inherently subjective; because researchers interpret social behaviour in different ways, sociology is not a natural science.

b. Thomas Kuhn – Can we even pursue objective truths to begin with?

Argues that science transitions through 'paradigm shifts', moving from one stage to the next. These stages are: pre-science, normal science and revolutionary science.

Born out of 'pre-science', or an experimental period of science with no central paradigm, 'normal science' is a period in which scientists use a shared set of techniques and theoretical values.

Normal science, therefore, reflects the above description of the 'natural sciences', based on empirical, objective modes of inquiry. (Thus, if sociology is, indeed, a natural science, it would fall under the category of normal science).

When normal science reaches a 'crisis point', in which its underlying explanations are scrutinised, it will shift to 'revolutionary science'.

So to summarise: normal science operates within a specific paradigm, which will eventually shift; the pursuit of objective truths through universally recognised techniques and theoretical values is combined to a specific paradigm, which is subject to change.

Thus, it may not be possible to pursue objective truths through the natural sciences, much less the social sciences, to begin with.

<u>c. Realism – We should approach science differently to begin with - we should get rid of positivism altogether.</u>

Unlike positivists, who systematically research observable things, realists think that both the natural sciences and the social sciences should investigate unobservable, underlying phenomena.

Natural scientists currently examine underlying processes using closed systems (controlled laboratory experiences) and open systems (systems in which variables cannot be controlled and precise predictions cannot be made, e.g. studies of the weather and evolution).

Realists focus on open systems. Natural scientists need to pursue underlying structures of open systems, such as the process of natural selection.

Social scientists, too, can study social life by going 'beneath the surface' to expose social processes.

The value freedom debate

There is a major debate among sociologists regarding whether sociology can or should be value-free. Going into this section there are two concepts that you must know:

- **Value freedom**: when research is entirely objective and not biased in any way by a researcher's values
- **Value relevance**: when the selection of research topics, and the construction of concepts, are based on the values and interests of the researcher

1. "Sociology can be objective"

<u>Positivism</u>

- Sociology can, and should, be value free
- Sociologists should study observable phenomena, using the same modes of inquiry that scientists use
- Sociologists should use quantitative research methods that can be tested for their validity and reliability
- Sociologists can keep facts separate from values

<u>Weber</u>

- Sociological research has the potential to be carried out objectively, but only after a value-relative concept, which can generate meaningful research, is selected
- Sociologists can choose their topics, and formulate concepts, based on their views of the world
- Once research topics are conceptualised, sociologists can carry out objective research to test them
- If a topic fails to generate meaningful research, a new one should be selected

<u>Positivists and Weber: value neutrality in the research process.</u>

Both positivists and Weber argue that research should be carried out objectively, with value neutrality. However, researcher's values can influence the research process at multiple stages, for example, in choosing questions for surveys or interviews and in interpreting findings. Many would argue that sociological research is thus an inherently subjective process.

2. "Sociology is inherently subjective"

<u>Interpretivists</u>

- Sociology cannot be objective and value-free; all sociological research is inherently subjective. However, sociologists can acknowledge how their personal perspectives may have influenced their research, thus making it valid

- Sociology is not a natural science; the subject matter of sociology is fundamentally different from that of the natural sciences and, as such, must be approached differently

- Social behaviour is not controlled by external, overriding structures; people behave based on their interpretations of different situations

- People's day-to-day social actions shape society

- People make sense of the world through the interpretation of meaning

- Only qualitative research methods will give sociologists insight into people's behavioural motives and meaningful interpretations

- The personal and political beliefs of the researcher will inevitably influence their interpretations of social behaviour

- As such, in order to keep their research valid, sociologists should acknowledge how their personal perspectives may have influenced their interpretations and posed certain limitations. (In other words, sociologists should be reflexive in their interpretations)

<u>Values in theory: political alignments</u>

Some theories are political in nature and thus cannot be value-free e.g. Marxism, feminism; both of these methods are inextricably linked to political action, in that they argue for society to be changed in line with class or gender equality.

Social constructionism and subjectivity

Sociologists cannot pursue research objectively: the frameworks that they operate in are socially constructed to begin with.

Knowledge is socially constructed through discourse. Widely understood concepts and categories are relative to certain moments in history and certain cultural influences.
A good example of this is the (previously discussed) perspective that 'mental illness' is a social construct.

Sociologists should figure out how and why the social categorisations that they study were socially constructed to begin with. They should do this through a process known as deconstruction.

Key point

It is vital to remember that methodological approaches are definitive. They are definitive because they define and conceptualise not only the scope of research that a sociologist undertakes but also the kind and type of data that they will gather as a result. Whenever you evaluate sociological research, it is very important to uncover the methodological approach and the ideological underpinnings of that approach in order to be sure that the research is as valid and as reliable as possible. To conclude this unit, you will now undertake a practical exercise on the relationship between sociological research and social policy.

Activity 27 – Read the following blog entry on the history of the Educational Maintenance Allowance (EMA), as an example of a government social policy which was informed by social sciences research:

http://blogs.lse.ac.uk/politicsandpolicy/scrapping-ema-and-fairness/

What do you think the relationship between social policy and social sciences research should be? How closely should sociologists work with government to form social policy? Use this case study and your own research to justify your answer.

Discussion

There are a few key criticisms of the use of sociological research to inform social policy:

- Many argue that this type of research is too positivistic in nature; it is usually based on quantitative data rather than sociological interpretation
- Also, because these projects rely on government funding, sociologists often experience time constraints or, even worse, have to compromise their research objectives
- Lastly, theories of postmodernity and the 'second age of modernity', as discussed above, challenge the existence of social class identities and national boundaries, respectively. Social policy is often based upon such categorisations; as such, some sociologists are critical of the way in which social policy-focused research is conducted

Conclusion

It is important that all the work you have done so far on research methods, data collection and analysis informs the rest of your sociological study. Remember that the question of how a sociologist collects their data and what methods they use is closely tied to the kinds of data they gather as a result, and so to the conclusions they will draw from their research. Having a clear and accountable research strategy is therefore of the utmost importance, as is being able to justify this with reference to a theoretical position.

Whenever you come across new sociological ideas, try to ask yourself the following question:

How could sociologists 'operationalise' this concept?

Remember, to operationalise means to define a concept or variable so that it can be measured or expressed quantitatively, rather than qualitatively.

4.2.1: Culture and Identity – Optional

A2 (Optional 1) - 4.2.1

Key Ideas:

- What is culture?
- Types of culture - Different conceptions of culture, including subculture, mass culture, high and low culture, popular culture, global culture
- Theories of culture
- The socialisation process and the role of the agencies of socialisation
- What is identity?
- Theories of identity
- Sources and different conceptions of the self, personal and social identity and difference
- The social construction of identity

The relationship of identity to age, disability, ethnicity, gender, nationality, sexuality and social class in contemporary society

Identity in relation to production, consumption and globalisation

What is culture?

Culture is a very important concept indeed in sociology. In terms of a definition, most sociologists would say that culture is the shared beliefs, values, norms, skills, roles, customs, rituals, language, symbols, history and knowledge that altogether make the life of a society. It is socially transmitted and therefore transmitted through socialisation. Therefore, culture can be many different things: it can be the music, visual art, soap operas, newspapers, theatre, film, public events and occasions, internet blogs and websites, rituals, ceremonies or religious observances which collectively make for the shared life of any group of people. All human societies create culture, and this is accomplished by one of the distinctive aspects of being human, which is language (a system of advanced and symbolic communication). When speaking of culture in this context we are talking about the mainstream or dominant culture of a society.

Cultural norms: a case study

Now imagine that you are sitting in a quiet university library, revising for a difficult exam. Without realising it, you are upholding a widely-held value in contemporary society: that of the importance of working hard at school. Opposite you, a fellow student stands up on her chair and begins to sing; to your left, an acquaintance enters the room wearing only his boxers: he takes a seat and begins to read silently.

Activity 26 – Consider the above scenario. From a sociological perspective, what do you think has just happened? Try and use sociological terms such as culture and social norms in writing your answer.

Analysis

Your fellow students, in behaving as they did, were challenging social norms. Social norms are 'rules' (both formal and informal) by which members of a given social setting (usually unconsciously) abide. The singing girl was breaking the cardinal library rule, or norm, of silence and would likely be asked to quieten down or to leave. Your nearly naked friend, though abiding by the library-specific norm of seated, silent study, was challenging a widely-internalised social norm of wearing clothing in public places. Most breaches of norms involve swift punishment in one form of another, though most usually, the punishment given is that of social exclusion and rejection, such as the singing girl would receive.

Sub-cultures

Simply put, a sub-culture or sub-cultures can be described as a culture operating within the mainstream culture (see figure below), sometimes as a variation of the mainstream, other times in opposition or contrary to the mainstream culture.

Obviously, not all people will conform to the values and norms that are widely recognised in their social settings. When a group of people band together based on a shared set of values that are different from (or opposite of) mainstream culture, they form a subculture. Examples include hippie communes, animal rights groups, criminal gangs, and political activists.

Figure 7: Subcultures are cultures within the mainstream culture

A recent sub-cultural phenomenon regarding working class macho lads has been discussed in depth by the sociologist Mac an Ghaill (1994). He claims that many young working class men wish to follow in the footsteps of their fathers by earning respectable livings in manual labour jobs; however, they cannot do so due to job shortages and, as such, are experiencing a 'crisis in masculinity'. They feel that the 'traditional' role of men was diminishing, leaving many young men facing an identity crisis. As such, many young working class boys cannot visualise themselves as becoming breadwinners and protectors like their fathers; they see education as useless in helping them to secure careers, and thus act in delinquent ways. These boys have formed a youth subculture which is characterised by anti-educational values and behaviours adhering to and following a set of values that is contrary to the mainstream culture.

There can be many reasons why small groups of people feel this way, but those who do have these feelings in common of being 'outside' or different to the mainstream often group together to create an alternative of subculture which is in some way different to mainstream culture. This is a new way of creating a different identity. Sometimes, this subculture can be associated with being 'cool' or with subversion, and can be accepted into the mainstream or become better known for this reason.

However, subcultures which are very distinctive can also remain broadly unaccepted because in order to join, you have to have very specific or specialised interests or skills (such as skateboarding or computer hacking, for example). Subcultures can either be non-threatening or benign, such as those centred on specific interests or hobbies (such as skateboarding) or a particular subculture that grows up among a small and select group (such as those working in isolated or remote communities, like scientists who are stationed at the Arctic) or they can have a more negative, exclusive or threatening edge.

For example some social scientists suggest that, the secret society known as the Freemasons only accept male members and have their own distinctive culture which some others could find threatening, because individual members tend to give special advantages and privileges to fellow members over non-members when in mainstream culture. This could be interpreted as a form of discrimination.

Moreover, criminal groups, both small and large (such as street gangs or organised crime such as the Mafia), have their own particular cultures and customs. Clearly, these types of subculture are especially threatening and negative because they are outside the mainstream and are what sociologists would refer to as deviant.[10] The sociological study of subcultures can prove very fascinating because they give us another way to think about culture. Subcultures, because they are different to mainstream culture, inevitably make us ask the questions:

- What is good or bad about mainstream culture?
- Should we accept mainstream culture as it is, or should it be changed?
- Why is mainstream culture the way it is?
- What do subcultures tell us about the norms, values, beliefs or ideology of mainstream culture?

Definitions of Culture

What constitutes culture is dependent upon a number of social factors, including, time, political and social climate, social attitudes and so on. As such, there are difference definitions that can be applied to the concept of culture. The mains ones are:

- Mass culture
- Folk or Traditional Culture
- High Culture
- Low Culture
- Popular culture
- Global Culture

No other animal besides the human can communicate in language as we do, and it is through our communication or language that we can transfer meanings from one to another individual in a way that (to current scientific knowledge) no other animal can. Therefore, as a human group or society we can create symbols or meaning (such as ritual, art, shared history and stories) which we can then communicate to each other or participate in together. This is culture, and it can cover familiar and everyday activities.

---

[10] Deviance is addressed in the A Level, Crime and Deviance Unit 4.3.1

Mass Culture

Mass culture is often associated with types of consumption as well as the effects of the media in perpetuating and directing mass culture. Members of the Frankfurt School of Sociologists, namely Adorno and Horkheimer, were concerned with the effects of mass culture (particularly the culture industry of mass media) on society. They felt that the culture industries of mass media entertainment were perpetuating capitalist values and as a result replacing traditional working class folk culture. Sometimes Mass Culture is referred to, interchangeably with Low Culture, due to the negative connotations and its association, which is used to describe certain cultural tastes, associated with those of the working class (e.g., soap operas).

Folk or Traditional Culture

Not only do cultures vary according to place (e.g. if you compared British culture to Jamaican culture) but they have also changed over time. Since industrialisation [the revolution in industry, technology and society that changed most people's way or life from rural to urban] there have been massive changes in society that have also had an impact on culture.

Folk or traditional culture is a rural culture and is associated with pre-industrial society where tales, songs, dances, medical remedies, were passed on by word of mouth. However, mass culture has eradicated this, and according to some schools of thought, making the recipient of mass culture passive and manipulated.

In the UK, there are still groups of people who practise or who are interested in traditional folk culture. In other countries, more survives of traditional or folk culture because these countries are less industrialised, or the process of industrialisation happened later, so there is more that survives. In the UK, we could consider folk or traditional culture a form of subculture, since it has now been overtaken by mainstream or western, globalised culture.

High Culture

High culture has class related connotations that would suggest that this type of culture falls within the domain of the upper classes. High Culture is considered to be more discerning and elite, being associated with things like Shakespearian literature, gourmet eating, the opera, ballet, classical music, 'good taste'. These aspects of culture are often regarded as being good and of benefit to society to the extent that government bodies may in fact subsidise the 'arts' with different forms of funding. This is quite interesting in the sense that Low culture (to be discussed next) due to its very nature tends to generate more money than high culture, which as stated previously is often subsidised by government funding. High culture is seen to be enjoyed by the few.

Low Culture

Often regarded in a negative light and associated with Mass culture (discussed earlier), Low Culture is seen to produce cultural products such as pop songs, soap operas, fast food, mass advertising and mass consumption. Some schools of thought, particularly Marxists, believe that there is no such thing as High and Low Culture. Rather, Marxist writers such as Pierre Bourdieu argues that the notion of a 'High Culture' is a manipulative elitist ideology created by the ruling classes, imposing what is considered to be 'culture' on the masses (everyone else). As such it is exclusive. Bourdieu argues that High Culture is presented in a positive light, as it is a culture that is promoted positively by the ruling classes that have easy access to it. Conversely, Low culture is regarded negatively. Cultural capital is a term that was coined by Bourdieu, who argued that when looking at the education system, which is one of the ways in which culture is transmitted to members of society, students from middle class backgrounds not only had an economic advantage over working class students, but also a cultural advantage due to the way they have been socialised. Middle class children, prior to attending school, through the process of primary socialisation, would learn to speak and behave in certain ways and have been raised to have more refined cultural tastes. Because of this they would fare better in educational settings. Consider the advantages that a student would have on a Shakespeare or Literature course who had attended Shakespeare plays with his or her family since he or she was a young child.

Popular Culture

This type of culture is based on the notion that society's members actively engage in the process of formulating and developing Popular Culture, to the extent that they can shape and change how the culture is presented, followed, transmitted and developed. Often some things that are regarded as part of popular culture can fall into the category of sub-culture – making the 'exclusivity' of the culture even more popular.

Global Culture

There has been a social, economic and cultural trend that has become known as globalisation. This is the trend towards cultural uniformity [sameness]. This is because societies, businesses and industries are increasingly globalised, meaning that we live in world where many industries or products that we rely on are located or produced abroad. In the same way, products or industries that are located in the UK find customers or clients abroad. This means that countries are connected at the international level by links of trade and money.

Rapid development and improvements in communication technologies mean that we can easily and quickly communicate with people all over the world (and even create internet-based subcultures with them!) provided we can access the internet or have a phone, television or other form of digital communications technology. As a result, culture has become more shared or more globalised. Adverts, TV programmes, music and art which originate in one country are now commonly also popular in other countries far distant, and as a result some sociologists feel that the values, norms, beliefs and ideologies of western globalised culture are now increasingly shared by more and more countries.

Activity 27 - Can you think about difference cultural influences from other countries that are evident in your everyday life and activities?

Globalised culture means that alternatives, such as folk cultures and subcultures, become even less dominant, which in turn decreases cultural diversity.

Even the mechanics of the transportation of goods has influenced the development of a global culture. Goods can be transported across the world. For some sociologists like Klein (2001) this is a concerning cultural trend leading to cultural homogeneity, and subsequently resulting in the loss of the cultural diversity that helps keep cultures strong and vibrant. Cultural diversity challenges us and makes sure that we keep questioning and re-evaluating the norms, values, beliefs and ideologies of our own culture.

In particular, American commercialism seems to dominate global culture.[11] Disney is a great example: consider the global spread of Disney theme parks, songs, films, books and merchandise. Many would argue that Disney is an example of American cultural imperialism.

Some schools of thought see cultural globalisation as a positive thing in that it enables societies to share identities and cultural practices, thereby creating a plurality of cultures and even the reinventing of cultures as they combine and mix creating new forms of themselves. It is the access, freedom and choice to do so that is a positive thing.

Note, however, not all people will passively consume the ideas and objects of mass or popular culture. This is where Antonio Gramsci's concept of hegemony (and counter-hegemony) comes in. Remember, every culture will also have subcultures that have been formed to resist the dominant cultural, or hegemonic, values of our society.

Activity 28 – Think about subcultures and hegemony now. Do you consider yourself a member of a sub-culture, and if so, what is it?
Can you describe the sub-culture, and in what ways do you consider it to be outside or different from mainstream society?

---

[11] For an in-depth discussion of the pervasive, far-reaching influences of American consumer culture read *The McDonaldization of Society: Version 5* by sociologist George Ritzer.

This graph could be used by sociologists to represent membership of the dominant culture contrasted against membership of subcultures of different kinds.

The role of society in culture

Sociologists are dedicated to unravelling how the structure of social relationships influences cultural traits such as social norms, values and mores. There are several theories which try to describe how societies influence culture, and it is important that you have an awareness of some of the major academic trends.

Socialisation:[12] a case study (fictional)

The parents of twin boys, Thomas and Mark, get divorced when the boys were infants. Before the twins could walk, they were split up: Thomas went with his American father to be raised in Baltimore, and Mark stayed with his mum and 7-year old sister in Bristol. Neither parent remarried. Mark was closely looked after by his mother and had a fairly good relationship with her, but he never had any significant male role models at home who could teach him sport and take him camping: typical activities that his male peers would do with their fathers. Instead, Mark spent much time with his older sister and her friends, who tended to watch films and play imaginary games around the house. Thomas, on the other hand, was not closely looked after by his dad but they played football ('soccer') together on the weekends and took occasional camping trips with the American Boy Scouts organisation.

---

[12] Note: Agencies of Socialisation will be discussed later.

Mark would grow up to have very close female friends, both in his age bracket and possibly older. Granted that his mother and sister behaved in what could be considered as socially 'feminine' ways. Mark would be well-versed in topics and issues that are of concern to many females. Thomas, on the other hand, might have formed bonds with several male football friends from a young age, spending more time playing games with mates and less time talking to females in intensified settings. He, therefore, ended up with fewer female friends, finding it more difficult to engage with women, and would happily interact with large groups of men.

Activity 29 - Consider this fictional case study. How do you think a sociologist would interpret these data?

Primary Socialisation – Analysis

A sociologist could argue that Thomas and Mark underwent completely different primary socialisation processes within their separate households, which shaped the way that they interacted with women as adults.

Socialisation is the process through which we learn from others how to behave within our cultures. Just like Thomas and Mark we, underwent the process of primary socialisation in the early years of life when we learnt basic ways of interacting with others through daily encounters with friends and family. By observing the behaviour of those who looked after us, we would have formulated our own perspective on the social roles, that, supposedly, men and women play in society. For example, you may have learnt from your mother or another female family member that women are to love and care for others; this may shape the way that you interact with others (if you are a woman) or the way you perceive women and expect them to behave (if you are not).

Like Thomas and Mark, you are also a social being who has undergone primary socialisation into your current social role.

Activity 30 – How do you think the process of primary socialisation in your childhood home shapes the way that you interact with male/female friends today, or how differently you expect men and women to behave?

Secondary Socialisation – Analysis

It is important to realise that we are not solely products of our childhood home lives. The socialisation process continues outside of our families through secondary socialisation; we are influenced by anyone and everything that we see and interact with on a daily basis: from friends, to teachers, to criminals, to religious institutions, to the media. Thomas, for example, underwent a much different secondary socialisation process than Mark by living in America. He would have learnt to speak and communicate differently and would have experienced a completely different educational system to Mark, thereby being fully emerged into American culture.

Researchers of other subjects (namely of biology or genetics) might challenge the sociological perspective: that the way that we are shaped by these primary and secondary socialisation processes. Though our 'twin study' was fictional, studies of the rare cases in which twins are 'separated at birth' are used to fuel the ongoing nature-nurture debate, as sociologists unravel the extent to which our behaviours are shaped by social and cultural factors rather than biologically-inherited factors.

1. Functionalist (Durkheim)

According to some sociological schools of thought, the Functionalists in particular, there are five components that can be identified with culture in any given society. They are:

- Norms – social standards and/or rules that regulate behaviour within a given society
- Values – collective ideas and beliefs that set out what is considered acceptable (good/bad; right/wrong) thoughts and behaviour within a given society
- Symbols – "anything that carries a particular meaning recognized by people who share a culture". (Macionis 2005)
- Language – a way of communicating using signs, symbols, vocalisation, written word that is significant to a given society and is what is said to be the element that separates humans from animals
- Material Culture – any tangible thing that a given society produces

Functionalist sociologists, such as Durkheim, look at society in terms of a system. A society is a complex system: one with many parts, but one which essentially works together. Therefore, in terms of culture, a Functionalist perspective would regard it as the 'glue that holds society together', and as such is a way of uniting people in a cohesive way that benefits society as a whole.

This approach can often lead functionalist sociologists to overplay the things in society, which create cohesion, and to overlook the things in society which create tension or discord. In fact, functionalism has fallen out of favour a little since sociologists are often concerned to look at those very social factors – such as class, religion, gender or ethnicity – which so often do create tensions and divisions between people leading to conflict rather than social stability.

Durkheim claimed that society could be structured differently depending on forms of government and leadership (if any) and degrees of social cohesion due to religious practice. Pre-modern, egalitarian societies, he claimed, were characterised by mechanical solidarity in which people shared equally in daily tasks and were bound together by religious practice. In modern, industrial societies, people hold a variety of different beliefs and practice many different types of work. It is, therefore, difficult to uphold any sense of collective conscience or culture.

2. Marxist

This perspective would fall into the category of the Conflict Theory. Marx claimed that the basic infrastructure of society e.g. services such as transportation and power generation and supply that uphold economic activity, determines the shape of the complex superstructure which comprises institutions such as law, education, religion and politics. As culture is a part of this superstructure, economic infrastructure directly impacts the values, norms and mores of a given society.

For Marx, because the ruling class dominate and dictate, this is the key to understanding both society and culture as a whole. Economic activity is unequally divided into the working classes (who do the manual work and are poorly paid) and the owner or elite classes (who own the means of production and thus benefit from the labour of the workers).

3. Feminist

Feminist discussions of the role of culture in society focus on power; particularly as distributed differentially among men and women. Feminists would argue that we live in a society that through mainstream culture perpetuates the norms and values of a patriarchal society in which men have more power and status than do women; women thus experience many disadvantages which are specific to being a woman in an unequal and misogynist society.

In terms of popular culture, feminist thinkers such as McRobbie (1978) and Ferguson (1983), in conducting research into the content of magazines, found that they tended to promote what was considered, within mainstream society, as traditional female roles.

Activity 31 – Considering the research of McRobbie (1978) and Ferguson (1983). Do you think that magazines in the present time still represent female roles in the same light?

For a feminist, gender is thus the key to understanding society and culture. Inequalities of gender role (such as the unfair division of work between men and women, the nature of the work that both do in and outside the family and the pay and social status they receive as a result) are fundamental to how society is ordered and thus to cultural expression.

4. Post-modernist

In the post-modernist perspective, there are no 'grand narratives', and no sense of history progressing towards a goal. Rather, for the post-modern sociologist, the world is instead very diverse, and very disconnected. Through modern media technology, we can access images, ideas, content from all around the world, but these do not necessarily have anything to do with our own particular location (either in time or in place). In effect, we no longer have the kind of relationship with the past which people in pre-modern societies did, because we can pick and choose from the flow of media images we are all exposed to.

One result of post-modernism is that categories such as social class, gender or ethnicity become less important in favour of the media. For the post-modern sociological analysis, it is the relationship of the individual to the media that matters; how they consume the media, what they think about the media, how the media shapes their reactions, that matters, rather than their social class or even other traditional concepts of social division, such as gender, ethnicity or sexual orientation.

Agencies of Socialisation:

Sociologists are also keen to understand how it is we are socialised into society in terms of learning what are considered to be the acceptable norms and values of a society, cultural expectations, social and self-identities. Most sociologists would agree that there are four major agents of socialisation (primary and secondary).

1. Family

We have already discussed the most significant agency of socialisation which shapes the way that we internalise our cultural values: that of the family. If you have taken the IGCSE course, you know that there are many different types of families in the UK, from extended to single parent to single person. Yet perhaps the type of family that often comes to our minds (as often depicted on TV programmes) is that of the nuclear family, which consists of married parents and their two children (2.4 children being the average UK family size).

For the first few years of our lives, almost everything that we learn about the world is through interactions with family, particularly through primary relationships, which are characterised by personal, face-to-face interaction. Often these relationships involve the process of emulation and behavioural copying or role modelling. This includes the process of learning behaviours that are deemed 'appropriate' for our gender; we do this by looking closely at the social roles that members of our families play. For example, mothers in nuclear families may tend to hold care-giving positions. Feminists argue that the traditional nuclear family is inherently patriarchal and thus is not symmetrical: men and women do not share tasks equally, and thus their children are inevitably socialised into unequal gender roles as a result.

Activity 32 - How is the family an important agency of socialisation?
Give an example from your own life to illustrate how your own family socialised you in a certain way.

2. Education

Beyond the family, we learn much about how to behave and interact with one another through education. Our society, like all industrial societies, has a formal education system, which transmits values and norms to young people. Students learn both a formal curriculum, comprising academic subjects, lectures etc., as well as a hidden curriculum, or all of the other rules, regulations and peer interactions from which students learn behaviours and social roles.

Theories regarding education and secondary socialisation:

- Talcott Parsons (Functionalist) - Talcott Parsons thought that education served an important socialising role that families did not. At school, children have a universal opportunity to earn achieved statuses through a meritocratic system based on the principle that through hard work they will succeed as well as be allocated their role within society. This is in contrast to the home, where children take on 'default' ascribed statuses from young ages based on how their family members interact with them. In school, children learn that success and advancement is based on ability from the formal curriculum, but the hidden curriculum also serves an important socialising function
- Bowles and Gintis (Marxist) - Bowles and Gintis had a more critical view on education as a socialising agent. They felt that education served to perpetuate class distinctions, and that the students who succeeded were actually the ones who conformed to the rules and regulations of the hidden curriculum and behaved in the ways that their middle class teachers expected them to. Also, they held the typical Marxist view that working class students learn to accept the organisation of society as 'fair'. Education thus allows the ruling class to prevent working class rebellion

3. Religion[13]

In Durkheim's discussion of mechanical solidarity, religion is an important socialising agent in pre-modern societies in that, like the family, it helps to reinforce what is considered right or wrong, acceptable or unacceptable behaviour and values. In modern, industrial societies, religion is still important to many people; however, some sociologists would argue that the process of secularisation has taken place and religion is thus a less significant agency of socialisation, as other agencies, such as the Mass Media, have become more and more dominant in this area.

4. Mass Media

The mass media (T.V, newspapers, films, internet etc.) have an ever-pervasive presence in our day-to-day lives. Since the time of the Frankfurt School in the 1930s, discussion of the role of mass media in the socialisation process has been quite negative. Their view is that the mass media is the main way in which a capitalist ideology is transmitted. And most recently there has been much concern regarding violence in the media, and children 'copying' behaviour that they would not be exposed to if it were not for violent video games, films and TV programmes, thereby demonstrating, according to some schools of thought, the pervasive nature of the media.

Also, many feminists are concerned about the way that women are portrayed in the media, claiming that they are symbolically annihilated, or under-represented. This could lead young female viewers to take the social message that they are less important than men. Feminists also argue that young women's perceptions of beauty and body image are skewed by the media, leading to eating disorders, and that this is perpetuated by popular culture via the media. Lastly, the media have been criticised for portraying minority ethnic groups in negative ways, which in turn contributes to stereotyping and prejudice or discrimination. Because the mass media is associated with popular culture and the promotion and reinforcing of some aspects of popular and mass culture, this is an important area to consider in any discussion of culture and identity.

---

[13] The topic of religion is covered in more detail in the Religion unit.

Agencies of social control

With socialisation and its transmission of the norms and values of a given society, there has to be a means of reinforcing and maintaining those norms and values, and this is done through agencies of social control. Social control is about enforcing and/or encouraging conformity and discouraging behaviour that violates accepted norms and values. The process of socialisation teaches acceptable ways of behaving and cultural values and agencies of social control sanction rule breakers and non-conformists. In order for norms and values to be not only reinforced but also conformed to, there has to be in place, certain agencies of social control. These agencies provide different ways in which social roles, behaviours and cultural values are maintained. These are divided into two broad categories.

Formal

Formal agencies of social control such as the police and the criminal justice system, schools, the armed forces etc. within our society, ensure that people conform to institutionalised behavioural norms by enforcing laws. There has, however, over the years, been much debate about the fairness of the police and criminal justice system, particularly regarding the differential treatment of certain social groups, with cultural and social bias and prejudices being cited as one of the reasons for negative differentiated treatment. In addition, it has been argued that the police side with particular political parties rather than investing in the interests of the people.

Informal

Informal agencies of social control are not set up specifically to enforce rules but still transmit the norms and values of society and ways of behaving through sanctions. We receive positive sanctions through acceptance, praise, inclusion etc. when we behave in socially acceptable ways and negative sanctions being shunned, excluded, reprimanded, punished etc. when our peers or family disapprove of our behaviour. The mass media can be used as an informal means whereby it transmits sanctions indirectly by showing us how people are punished for breaking laws or challenging norms.

Activity 33 - Review the notes on Functionalism, Marxism, Feminism and Post-Modernism. It is important that you are aware of these as critical approaches

and can understand how a sociologist working in one of these academic traditions would interpret sociological data differently.

What is Identity?

Identity can be regarded as an individual's sense of self – how a person sees him or herself, not just personally but in relation to others. Conceptions of the self begin to formulate within us from birth, through the process of primary socialisation and through the remainder of our lives through secondary socialisation. Charles Cooley coined the term 'looking glass self' to describe how people re-evaluate themselves based on how they think others see them. Actors and singers, for example, experience a heightened version of this constant self re-evaluation because their careers often depend upon the reviews and responses of their peers and of the public.

As society's members, we have multiple identities and they can fall into two categories, Personal Identities and Social Identities.

The Personal identity is based on the notion of agency, making a conscious decision about how we see ourselves and how we want others to see us, both of which are based on personal choice. Social identities can be imposed e.g. society says you are either male or female and as such should act in a certain way, this also relates to how we present ourselves to the social world.

Identities in context

It is important to be aware that identities will vary according to the time and circumstance. For example with your family you may be mum, dad, brother, sister but at work you are a manager, whereas at college you may be a student or teacher and so on.

Activity 34 – What is meant by the term 'looking glass self'? Give an example from your life to illustrate your definition.

The self: a case study

Let's focus on a specific (rather heightened) example. Many of you have probably seen the reality TV show X Factor or similar. Those of you who have watched are familiar with the first few episodes in which pop star hopefuls flock to audition venues to show off their (presumably) innate singing talents. Every year, there are always a few contestants on the first episode that are completely and utterly tone deaf. Out of those tone deaf candidates, there are always a select few that genuinely think that they possess musical talents, until the judges tell them otherwise. These people perhaps spent their entire lives seeing themselves in terms of their identity in one way but, only after being rejected publicly, were pushed to reassess their capabilities as human beings and as such, the part of their identity that presented them as a singer or musically gifted.

The issue of meaning

Of these 'rejected' X Factor candidates, there are always a few that absolutely refuse (at least on camera) to acknowledge the negative responses of the judges. These contestants are questioning the meaning of others' actions as they continue to re-evaluate themselves. Like these contestants, we are all able to interpret the actions of others in different ways. We will attach different meanings to things that are said to us such as "They didn't like me because I was too good for them." Depending on the circumstances, we may accept another's criticism literally or interpret it differently.

Erving Goffman, who approaches this from an Interactionist perspective, puts another spin on concepts of self and self-representation. He goes by the saying that 'all the world is a stage' and that we shape our identities by our interaction with each other and managing the impressions that we give to others in particular ways. As such, we are always 'acting'.

Activity 35 – Think about the way that you communicate with members of your immediate family versus your teachers and professional colleagues.
Do you communicate as openly and honestly with your colleagues as you do your family and friends? Think about this and write your answer now.

Analysis

It is highly likely that you do not communicate in the same way to family and friends as you do to work colleagues, and the reason why is entirely due to the different social role you play in respect to these different groups of people. Indeed, we construct our social identities by comparing ourselves to individuals and groups and labelling ourselves in certain ways.

For example, let's pretend that you are applying for a loan. Think of what you would write on the application on the line next to 'profession': 'Student'? 'Bartender'? 'Banker'? 'Mother'? You probably would never dream of writing something like 'impoverished library dweller' or 'underpaid beer drinker' or 'taxi driver to my children' — because, whilst these descriptions may be characteristic of your day-to-day experiences, they are not acceptable ways to label yourself on a formal application. We categorise and present ourselves using terminologies that are digestible and acceptable to the greater public.

In addition, as we age, the pressure to define ourselves in terms of tangible career and family-orientated things tends to increase; we may 'rethink' our social identities at several points in our lives as we renegotiate our relationships to those that we interact with (e.g. 'student' – 'tutor' – 'teacher' – 'headmaster' or 'sister' – 'aunt' – 'mother' – 'grandmother'). The social roles that we play and the norms and values that go along with these roles e.g., becoming a mother, also shape our social identities.

Social stigma

In some cases, social roles are unproblematic: at one point in our lives, all of us are children and later many of us are parents. These kinds of common social roles are not usually associated with stigma.

However, that is not always the case: many of us are faced with the problem of social stigma, meaning that we may, based on our physical appearances or social affiliations, be labelled by others in a way that could preclude us from becoming fully integrated in society.

Erving Goffman cites the following three factors that could cause people to be stigmatised:

1. Physical defects e.g. missing limb
2. Membership of religious or ethnic minority group
3. Personal weaknesses such as criminal records

He also notes three ways that people tend to deal with social stigma:

1. Attempts to hide the stigma e.g. plastic surgery
2. Recognising the stigma and accepting treatment (this applies to the 'personal weakness' category)
3. Protesting against the stigma e.g., gay rights

Activity 36 – Have you (or someone you know) ever experienced social stigma? What were the effects?

Importance of the Self; individual and collective: identity, social and cultural life

Some sociologists argue that people who deviate from social norms and partake in deviant or criminal activity do not do so because they are innately rebellious or 'bad' people, but rather, because they are labelled as such to begin with this known as the Labelling Theory. People from certain sectors of society are more prone to being labelled as 'deviant' (as breaking social rules: formal or informal) than others.

For example, a group of working class boys might be punished by local authorities for trampling through a neighbour's garden (most likely, they had, prior to this, been labelled as 'delinquent' at school or within the neighbourhood) whereas a middle class girl might not receive any label or strict punishment for stealing berries from her neighbour's garden to make a pie. According to the sociologist Howard Becker, once an individual is labelled as deviant by a figure of authority, he or she will be treated differently by others and could eventually internalise the label, seeing him or herself as deviant and therefore acting as such as a result, this is known as the Self Fulfilling Prophecy.

The role of agencies in defining identity and status

We have already discussed several agencies of socialisation; these (and others listed below) also influence our sense of identity in significant ways.

Families

Our gender identities tend to be shaped, in part, based on how we respond to the social role that our parents and siblings take on in the household as well as our own positioning, relative ages, levels of responsibility and roles within those households. These are all factors that influence our ideas about status.

Peer Groups

Through processes of secondary socialisation among peer groups, identities are shaped in complex ways. Our relationships with peers tend to be more 'balanced' than those with our caregivers, and thus we learn about ourselves through more mutual sharing of ideas and support.

Education

Education can definitely have a strong influence on one's identity: particularly regarding affiliations with different social classes e.g. Public vs. state funded schools. Also, in schools with 'streaming' or 'setting' processes, those who are placed in lower streams or sets may have more negative perspectives of their capabilities. It is also during this stage of socialisation that associations and connections made with peer groups have an instrumental role to play in the formation and development of identities.

Religion

Affiliation with a certain religion can also shape one's identity, as individuals, due to their affiliation with a particular religious group may present their identity in the way in which they dress, and as such are symbolically sending a message to the wider society that they are associated with a particular religious group For example, different religions may convey different ideas regarding women's roles and status in society.

Mass Media

As discussed, the media can influence how we see ourselves and our statuses in relation to other members of society and even what we 'should' aspire to be like.

Workplace

Certain professions in our society are associated with certain levels of status and with different social classes. If a child is born into a family with a strong tradition of holding a certain occupation (such as within medicine or law, for example), then it is likely that this expectation will have a significant impact on their self-identity and will be a key part of their socialisation process.

Therefore, what we do professionally or choose to do can be part of what forms our identity. Think about when you meet someone for the first time: once you have passed the conventional formalities of getting each other's name, during the course of a conversation with them you may ask them what they do for a living. What their profession is, and depending on their response, can give you some indication of their identity. It is often a way in which we make assumptions about what a person is going to be like, and certain professions command more respect and status than others, due to certain social conventions.

Sociological categories and identity

In order to try and demonstrate the impact socialisation and social structures (such as education, family and class) have on behaviour and identity, read the following case study and then consider the questions that follow.

Case Study: Jane Smith

After completing the first term of her A-level qualifications at her secondary school in Manchester, Jane decided that school was not for her, so when she was 16, she left school and went to live with her mother, who had divorced her father when Jane was aged 5, and relocated to Germany. There, Jane's mother had got married a second time to a German hotel owner and together they lived in Munich. So Jane left her father's home (who worked in a factory and came from Manchester) and went to Munich. When she arrived, she moved around, spent a few months travelling and sightseeing. She then got a job as a receptionist in a hotel owned by her mother and stepfather. She was a quick learner and good at languages, and soon became fluent in German in a couple of years. She also had excellent customer service skills, and became a key member of staff.

At age 21, Jane returned to the UK and found a job as an assistant manager at an upscale hotel in Kensington, London. She easily beat the competition for this job because of her good German language skills which were to her advantage, and previous job experience. She was promoted to top management level at age 25, and soon afterwards married a Londoner whom she had met while organising some business events for his bank at the hotel conference rooms. They had a child together, and Jane continued to manage the hotel until age 30.

By this time, Jane had 13 years' experience in the hotel industry, and her only child was in primary school full time, so Jane felt ready for a change. She started looking at some distance learning websites and found subjects that interested her. She chose A-level Sociology, because she had always loved customer service and working with many different people as part of her job. She therefore felt that studying Sociology was a good 'fit' for her, and enrolled on this course.

Activity 37 –

Now think carefully about the case study of Jane Smith. What does Jane's life story tell you about the following:

- **Her social class?**
- **Her home or family background?**
- **Her educational background?**

Analysis: Jane Smith

Jane Smith's story raises several issues and questions that are of sociological relevance, and tell us a great deal about how social categories impact on identity.

First, let's consider Jane's family and household situation. Jane's parents were one couple of many whose marriage eventually broke up. As such, Jane's personal story contributes to a growing trend of divorces in the UK, and Jane's childhood family structure falls under the social category of single parent households. As a child, her parents' divorce would have no doubt had a profound impact on her, and this would have been one of the key incidents that shaped her adult personality.

Next, on the subject of education: Jane dropped out of school at the age of 16. She never received a university education, and so this places Jane in a second category of youths that have not completed secondary school and who did not go on to tertiary level. It is more likely that children whose parents do not have a university education will drop out of school before they themselves reach university level. As such, Jane's story is part of a wider social trend, and her class background and upbringing will also have contributed to her identity and to how she saw herself regarding her education – perhaps it was never a part of her identity that she would get a degree, even though she was intelligent and had the ability to do so.

Lastly, let's consider the controversial subject of social stratification. We know that Jane's father was a Manchester-based factory worker. We also know that her husband is a London-based banker with a university education. Though we cannot be sure (for example, we don't know where her husband is originally from, or what his parents do for a living), we can assume that Jane's life path represents one of social mobility [progression from one class to a higher one].

Jane's father is of working class origins, as demonstrated by his job, whereas Jane's own job is in senior management. Moreover, her marriage is to a man who is likely from a higher class than her father and so she now most likely works and socialises at a level higher than that of her father, and more in line with that of her step-father. We can also speculate that Jane's mother, in divorcing Jane's father and remarrying a German hotelier, followed a similar life trajectory of social mobility, moving from one lower class to a higher one. The reasons why Jane followed this life path could all be uncovered by further sociological study, and the fact that she has made these decisions in her life will have also shaped her sense of who she is in society and her personal self-identity (as a woman from the working-class who has achieved a higher class status than her birth family).

Identity and Class

Class is always a complex subject to discuss. Traditionally speaking, we are all aware of the class divisions that exist within our society: working class, middle class and upper class. Studies have shown that class is still a major source of identity, particularly for working class people but some think that increasingly, due to the rise of individualism, class lines have somewhat dissipated. Some people think that class is no longer a strong source of identity and that people (particularly of middle class backgrounds) are engaging in varied forms of work, seeing themselves according to their individual contributions to society rather than as products of their class backgrounds. Moreover, some think that identity is largely shaped by leisure and consumption. Another important thing to note for your exams: concepts of identity aside, children born into working class families tend to have more depleted life chances than those of middle and upper class backgrounds. Life chances are defined in your books as 'the opportunities a person has to achieve good health, social prestige and economic prosperity'.

Identity and Gender

Sociologists (particularly feminists) have identified important differences between sex and gender. Sex is something biological that we are born with; gender is developed through the process of socialisation. We assume, for the most part, that men are socialised into having masculine behaviours, and females, feminine. But this is not always the case. For example, lesbians and gay men may experience gender in varied ways. Overall, however, feminists would argue that our society is shaped by patriarchy and that women are socialised into more submissive roles (and thus assume stereotypical gender identities) from young ages.

Submissive feminine roles include stereotypes that women are softer, weaker, more caring, less assertive, less aggressive, less ambitious, less career- or success-focussed and more altruistic and concerned for others than men are. Feminists would highlight that such gender stereotypes serve to benefit men, primarily since women are socialised into being the care-givers and nurturers of men from their infancy and throughout their adulthood, but at the expense of developing their own talents, interests and abilities for themselves. Other sociologists note a 'crisis in masculinity' in which shifts in the working class labour market have affected young men's aspirations to become family breadwinners, resulting in a confusion of gender identity.

Sexuality can also be an important source of identity; as mentioned above, in recent decades, lesbians and gay men have expressed their sexual identities openly and publicly. This has changed society enormously: gay sexuality used to be a huge social taboo (even as recently as twenty or thirty years ago); now, in most parts of UK society, it is not.

What is patriarchy?

This refers to a society where the male sex is in general given power, authority, prestige, rank, status, education, wealth, choices and life chances superior to, and over against those of the female. In effect, it makes wives inferior to and dependent on their husbands, daughters subject to their fathers until they are married and the ability of women to be single an impossibility (women uncontrolled and undefined by either husband or father). Patriarchal societies both have been and still are exceedingly common, and it is fairly typical to find societies stratified by gender and characterised by inequality on these grounds.

Identity and ethnicity and nationalism

Firstly, it is important to distinguish between the concepts of ethnicity and race. Ethnicity is a term that is widely used by academics. 'Race', on the other hand, is a term that has been discredited by academics, because 'race' is usually a term used by people who see human beings as divided into categories based on biological characteristics. Ethnicity, on the other hand, refers to language, religions and cultural traditions that are shared by a group of people.

Therefore, although race, like sex, certainly has a biological component, sociologists would argue that the definition and understanding of race is also socially constructed, just in the same way that gender is socially constructed as a category. For this reason, sociologists prefer the term ethnicity since this makes it clear that the differences between people are largely social constructs.

For example, clearly there are physical differences between individual humans, such as in skin colour, but biologists have discovered that that can be just as much genetic variation among members of the same racial group as there can be between members of different racial groups. Also, although humans vary by skin colour, they also vary by height, weight, hair or eye colour. However, skin colour has usually been the variation given more social significance than any of the other physical variants. Therefore, race does have a biological component, but is clearly also socially constructed. When sociologists talk about race, they are aware of this social construction, and sociologists who investigate race are primarily concerned to find out how a racial identity is constructed both by society and the individual.

When sociologists use the term ethnicity, they are referring to the socially constructed identities and meanings that surround race. An individual's ethnicity is the cultural, social and symbolic meanings associated with belonging to one or another race, and refers to the cultural heritage, history, language and shared contemporary culture between those of a particular racial background. How an individual self-identifies their own ethnicity (that is, which ethnic group or groups they see themselves as belonging to) is of importance in finding out how they construct their entire social identity, since race and ethnicity, like sex and gender, have a very important part to play in an individual's social identity and socially constructed role. As we have already discussed, ethnic minorities are often stigmatised; ethnicity is also a source of social inequality in the UK. The mass media have enhanced such problems by creating moral panics and by scapegoating ethnic minorities. Unfortunately, we do turn to external sources such as the media whilst formulating our personal identities in relation to others. On the other hand, membership of an ethnic minority group can give individuals a feeling of community and collective identity. This can be taken a step further: agencies of socialisation, such as the media, can contribute to a sense of nationalism or shared national culture.

Activity 38 - Like any member of society, you are also a social agent. You have your own identity and sense of self.

Consider the important social categories of gender, class, ethnicity and sexuality that we have covered so far:

- **To what extent do you feel that you have been shaped by these social categories?**
- **To what extent do you feel that ideas about these social categories have determined your own adult identity?**

Try to identify gender, class and ethnic stereotypes in particular, and be aware that though we are all individuals, we also all social agents and therefore inevitably influenced by the society and time into which we are born.

Identity, Age and Disability

Age: As stated previously, when we look at identity we do need to look at it in context. As such, be aware that identities change according to circumstance and time so it is inevitable that as an individual ages, so too will elements of their identity change. Research shows that middle-aged people tend to experience the most economic advantages whereas younger and elderly people experience more inequalities. After they retire, older people tend to experience negative cultural stereotyping and limited income.

Disability: In terms of identity, often people can be identified and therefore responded to, according to a disability, and as such the person, aside from the disability, is often overlooked and their disability becomes their identity. Therefore, the experience of being disabled is a social construct. If you think of disability in terms of labelling theory, once people are labelled as 'disabled' or inferior, they might internalise these stigmas and see themselves as 'inferior' members of society, and society may treat them as such.

Activity 39 -
Consider the social (and biological) categories of age and disability.
What attitudes and cultural stereotypes do you think there are towards people of your age and dis/ability?
To what extent do you think social assumptions and stereotypes of people of your age and dis/ability have shaped your own current self-identity?

Leisure, consumption and identity

It is said by some schools of thought that we live in a consumer society and that our daily activities are often governed by the process of buying goods and services. Those with greater economic power are able to be active participants in a consumer society and therefore purchase goods and services as a means of reflecting and portraying their identity.

Economic power is the power an individual, group or organisation has when they have greater wealth than others. In our society, money brings with it power: the rich have the power to consume much more widely and freely; the rich can use their money to buy influence and advantage to make sure that they achieve their own aims; the rich usually have greater freedom, time and leisure since they are free from the worries and stresses that come from being poor. For all these reasons, the rich have a form of power which is economic.

Social class can have a big impact on the choices people make, how they live their lives, how they experience the world and the chances and opportunities they have, how they can participate or not in a consumer society. For example: the way in which the working classes, the middle class and the upper class spend their leisure time and their money; have jobs and occupations; set behavioural norms and standards; interact with social institutions or authorities (such as the police or government); celebrate and mark important key events (such as births, deaths or marriages); experience education or achieve educational goals and participate in political power, all these can vary enormously.

Activity 40 – Consider the claim made by some sociologists (especially Post-Modernists) that individuals are free to shape their identity through their personal leisure and consumption choices, and that this freedom is now more powerful than the old defining limits of class, gender or ethnicity.

Do you agree with this claim? Do you think people do deliberately express their identities through their leisure and consumption choices?

4.2.2: Families and Households

A2 (Optional) – 4.2.2

By the end of this unit you should have an understanding of the following:

- The relationship of the family to the social structure and social change, with particular reference to the economy and to state policies
- Changing patterns of marriage, cohabitation, separation, divorce, child-bearing and the life-course, and the diversity of contemporary family and household structures
- Gender roles, domestic labour and power relationships and the nature and extent of changes within the family
- Relationships and the family and households in terms of marriage, cohabitation, separation, divorce and child bearing
- The nature of childhood, and changes in the status of children in the family and society
- Personal life and the diversity of the contemporary family and household structures
- Demographic trends in the UK since 1900; reasons for changes in birth rates, life expectancy, ageing population, family size, migration and globalisation

Introduction

The family has a crucial role to play in the process of primary socialisation. In today's society families are incredibly diverse, and as such nuclear families are no longer the norm, which is why it is important to define the concept of family. Broadly speaking, Family can be described as a unit of people, usually living in the same household, who are bound together by marriage and/or kinship ties.[14] Families typically involve one or two parent/guardian figures that care for younger family members. Families, however, can be scattered across more than one household (especially in the case of blended families). Note, the title of this unit, 'Family and Households'; therefore we should also define the concept of household. A household can be described as one or more persons living together that may or may not be related.

There are, in contemporary society, many forms of family structures:

- Nuclear families are the types of families that were once identified as the 'typical' family. Often presented as the ideal family in television commercials. Nuclear families, also known as the cereal packet family, consists of married parents and one or more children. This family is a self-contained unit whereby family members are expected to support each other, socially, psychologically and economically according to socially acceptable, prescribed roles

- Extended families are comprise three generations living together, consisting of grandparents, their children and their grandchildren. Today, extended families are increasingly giving way to nuclear families because of the geographical mobility of the latter

- Beanpole families are nuclear families with one or two children that maintain close relationships with their grandparents. They are therefore 'horizontal' in that they maintain relationships through more than two generations

- Reconstituted or blended families are those where one or both of the parents have had a previous marriage or relationship and so bring children from that old relationship into the new one. This introduces various combinations of step-father, step-mother etc.

---

[14] A relationship with others that stem from a blood connection, marriage or adoption.

- Single parent families, also known as the Lone Parent Family, are those with one adult parent and children residing in one household
- Empty Nest Families are families where the children have moved out of the home, and the parents reside together
- Gay/lesbian families are those with same-sex parents and children
- Symmetrical Families are families where the roles of the husband and wife or cohabiting partners are alike or equal

As well as structures, it is also possible to place family structures into different types of categories:

Categories with asset related or financial implications:

- Patrilineal Family: property and title inheritance passes down through the father's side
- Matrilineal Family: property and title inheritance passes through the mother's side

Categories based on leadership or dominance:

- Patriarchal Family – a male dominated family where the male/father is the head of the house
- Matriarchal Family – a female dominated family where the female/mother is the head of the house

Categories based on the type of adult relationship:

- Monogamous Family: a husband only has one wife. This is the most typical form of marriage in the west
- Polygamous Family: the husband has more than one wife at the same time
- Polyandrous Family: consists of a wife with more than one husband

Categories based on location:

- Patrilocal Family: a married or cohabiting couple lives with or near the male partner's family
- Matrilocal Family: a married or cohabiting couple lives with or the female partner's family
- Neo-Local Family: When a couple sets up a home separate from either side of their families

Activity 41 - Describe the differences between nuclear, extended and beanpole families.

Consider your own family situation. Which family category best defines your own current family situation, or the one in which you were brought up?

Diversity

As society has changed over time, there has inevitably been a decline of the nuclear family, and this has subsequently contributed to more diverse family structures being found in society. Sociologists, Robert and Rhona Rappaport (1982) were the first to identify this decline. The subsequent increase in family diversity is seen as a positive change in society, in that, people have more freedom of choice in how they arrange their personal lives and feel that they no longer have to conform to the nuclear family stereotype. Feminists are equally supportive of family diversity as most feminists hold that the nuclear family instils patriarchal values (with the man being the primary breadwinner and the woman being the lower paid or unwaged primary carer).

Cultural and Structural Differences in the Family

In this section, we will touch upon some more cultural and structural differences focusing on class, ethnicity and gender.

Class

The rates of marriage, child bearing and child rearing patterns, the makeup of the household and the stability of the family unit can be significantly influenced by social class. Therefore, class can be a source of family diversity. In terms of care-giving practices for example, whilst middle class families may have nannies or au pairs to look after their children, working class families may turn to family or friends. When looking at the family in terms of marriage and social class, figures from the ONS reveal that in 2001, 64.8% of around 4 million people in Social Class 1[15] were married. By 2012 that had risen to 66.3% of 5.1 million. However, in social class 7[16] the figures fell from 52% of 4.3million in 2001, to 44.5% of 5 million in 2012. This would invariably have an impact of the family unit.

Activity 42 - In your own words, write a short paragraph explaining how social class can affect the family unit.

---

[15] Such as professionals e.g. doctors
[16] Which includes dustmen and cleaners

Ethnic Diversity in family patterns

Ethnicity also has a strong influence on family patterns. Some Asian families living in the UK, for example, come about due to the cultural expectation that a marriage would be arranged.[17] Also statistics show that Asian families tend to be larger than white families, and about 25 per cent of Asian households in the UK are considered to be extended families.

A significant portion of African Caribbean families in the UK is single-parent. An Equality and Human Rights Commission report in 2011 found that as many as 65% of African-Caribbean children are raised by one parent – nearly always the mother. This could be for many reasons, which are related to employment, cultural traditions and heritage, but this fact is a key subject for social study.

Single-parent or Lone-parent families

Single parent families are becoming increasingly common in the UK. According to the ONS there has been an increase in Single/Lone-parent families with there being nearly 1.9 million lone parents with dependent children in 2004 rising to 2.0 million in 2014. Single/Lone parents represented 25% of all families with dependent children in 2014.[18]

Of these 2014 figures women made up 91% of single/lone parents with dependent children and men making up 9%. These striking statistics should also remind us of social categories. Sociologists investigate what it is about the social category of gender that makes women far more likely to take on the role of single parent than men.

---

[17] This practice is much more common than you think; in fact, the idea of 'romantic love' is a modern day construct, as discussed in-depth by Anthony Giddens in his Sociology textbook *Sociology: 5th Edition* (2006). See Giddens pp. 204-206.
[18] ONS Statistical Bulletin: Families and Households 2014 - http://www.ons.gov.uk/ons/rel/family-demography/families-and-households/2014/families-and-households-in-the-uk--2014.html#tab-Lone-parents

Reasons for increase in single-parent families:

- Divorce and changes in the law - 40% of UK marriages end in divorce; The Divorce Law Reform Act of 1969 has made the process of divorce more attainable. Also, the increase in economic opportunities for women and feminism have given more economic empowerment to women, and thus have enabled women to support families independently, without the need of a man's wage. However, social stereotypes about women as carers and nurturers have also ensured that women are far more likely to become single parents than men (who are more likely to cut ties with their children and move on to new relationships)[19]

- Social acceptance or changes in social attitudes - What was once a bit of a social taboo has become normalised. This has a lot to do with secularisation: religion has less of an influence on the way that we are socialised and our attitude to marriage, and going back to the nineteenth century when divorce was a massive taboo we can see the impact a less religious society has had on social trends

- The welfare state - Women do not have to rely on men and marriage to support themselves and their family (see later discussion on New Right perspectives) whereas only around two centuries ago, due to misogyny, sexism and a patriarchal culture, it would have been essential that a woman had a male husband or relative to support her since she would not have been able to vote, earn a wage or otherwise live independently

- Working practices of women - Due to changes in social attitudes, the law and therefore the working environment, women are now more able to take up working opportunities that enables them to exercise a level of independence whereby they can support their family independent of a partner

Activity 43 – Why has the number of single-parent families grown so much since the 1970s?

Why are most of these families headed by women?

---

[19] Refer to previous section on Lone/Single Parents

Why over 90% women?

- Legal reasons - Women are far more likely to gain custody post-divorce, though this must be seen in its social context; people (including those in the legal profession who help arrange affairs after a divorce) due to prevailing social attitudes, are more likely to perceive women as care-givers when compared to men because this is a core part of female gender role

- Men and work - Men are less likely to give up their (better paid) jobs, and it is still the case that women earn less than their male counterparts for doing work of equivalent worth and they are still relegated or stereotyped to the lower-paid and marginalised jobs in society. These are the so-called '5 Cs': cleaning, catering, clerical work, caring and cashiering, and they are all still heavily dominated by women

- 'Preservation' of masculinity - Due to social expectations and social attitudes, men are more reluctant to give up work when compared to women because care-giving is still not generally seen in society as a core part of male gender role and identity

- Socialisation - Women typically learn the social role of 'nurturer' and 'caregiver' from a young age and thus would find it harder and would receive more tangible social sanctions by refusing to take on this role as mothers. Think now about how you feel about mothers who abandon their children compared to fathers, or times when the media has reported that a woman has committed an offence against a child. The social and moral outcry can be quite significant

Activity 44 - If you feel more shocked that a mother would leave her children compared to a father, then reflect now on the gender and cultural stereotypes that create the social idea that women should do the majority of the care-giving of the young.

How has women's role and status in society changed?

Women's lives are now radically different to how they have been in any other time in the past. If we think back to how women lived in the nineteenth century in the UK (and it was also similar in other western countries), then we will find many distinct differences. For example:

- Women (alongside criminals and the insane) had no vote at all. Voting for women over a certain age was only achieved in 1918, and it took a longer time for all adult women to achieve full voting rights equal to men. Full female suffrage was granted in 1928

- Married women could not own property. When a woman married, then all her property went into the legal ownership of her husband, and he could do with it as he wished. In 1870, Parliament passed the Married Women's Property Act, and married women were then allowed to own property but this was still limited. Married women could then only own property up to £200; anything over that still went into the ownership of their husbands on marriage

- A woman did not have legal guardianship over her own children; her husband was considered the sole legal parent. Regardless of how a husband behaved, the children were considered his, and a woman had no legal right to them if the marriage broke up

- A husband could divorce his wife on the grounds of adultery, but a wife did not have the same legal rights to divorce on these grounds. It was only in 1923 that a wife could sue a husband for divorce on equal grounds

- It was legal for a husband to beat his wife until 1923. This meant that there was no legal case for prosecution for cases of domestic violence

- In 1736, Sir Matthew Hale said that a husband 'cannot be guilty of rape committed by himself upon his lawful wife, for by their mutual matrimonial consent and contract the wife hath given up herself in this kind unto her husband which she cannot retract.' In other words, it was legal for a husband to rape his wife. Marital rape was viewed as an impossibility since it was thought that one proper role of a wife was to have sex with her husband whenever he wanted it, regardless of her own feelings or preferences on the issue. In effect, a husband owned the body and person of his wife. This part of British law remained in place until as late as 1994, when the law was changed to include 'marital rape' (rape within marriage) as well as 'male rape' (rape by one man of another)

- Maternal mortality was very high due to a lack of good medical knowledge, widespread ignorance and a fear of sex and the realities of pregnancy and birth. This meant that many women indeed died in childbirth, which for most was dangerous and risky. Good medical care and attention (such as it existed) would have only been available to those with the money to afford it

- A woman would have had little control over her own fertility. Information on reproduction and sex was limited and not always very accurate; women had little access to contraception or abortion and it was an expected gender role that women would be mothers and housewives and would therefore be pregnant often regardless of whether this matched their own wishes

- Women were expected to derive their status and social role from their husbands. There was no social role, status or prestige attached to being an unmarried woman and few choices available. If a woman was from the middle classes and she had an education, she could become a governess (a private teacher of children), but this was often a lonely occupation that was not well-paid and had small social recognition. A woman (married or unmarried) could not advance in a career in the way that a man could

- Both poor men and women had few options available; work was often dirty and dangerous (such as working in mines or factories with poor safety standards) but women had an even worse deal since they were typically paid much less than men, even if they did work of an equal type

- Poorer women from the working classes had the majority of the responsibilities for housework and childcare. Housework was hard and demanding with none of the modern labour-saving devices (such as vacuums or washing machines) available now

The reasons for the changing role of women

Many factors have contributed to the changing roles of women (and thus to the family and society) since the nineteenth century. Some of them are outlined below:

- Medical - The developments made in medicine, such as in abortion (which has become much safer) and in contraception (such as the invention of the contraceptive pill) have allowed women a greater degree of freedom and control over their own fertility. For a woman, being able to control if and when she becomes pregnant, is an important part of having increased power and control over her own life

- Intellectual - Feminism as an intellectual and social movement has campaigned for significant changes to the law, so rape within marriage is no longer legal, neither is discrimination on the grounds of sex, domestic violence or not paying men and women equally for equal work

- Social - As a result of feminism and women's changing social roles, women are more likely to desire a career outside the home, intellectual achievement or the types of success that were previously associated only with male gender roles. Women are less focussed on marriage and family as their main goals in life, as they were in the early to mid-part of the twentieth century

- Sexual - A greater freedom in sexuality and sexual expression has made information on sex and sexuality more widely available, so women are no longer misinformed about their own sexual identities, about sex or about biological processes specific to women such as pregnancy, birth or menstruation

- Political - In the UK, women achieved the vote in 1918 (though not on an equal status to men) and since then, women's participation in the wider life of society (such as in politics or government) has taken women out of the home and made staying at home less central to female gender role. Look up the role of women in making munitions for the war in the trenches, for example, and the impact on their expectations[20]

- Employment - In the Second World War, women took on many of the jobs that had previously been done by men (because men were away fighting in the army). As a result, women experienced the world of work and found they

---

[20] See http://www.bbc.co.uk/news/uk-scotland-south-scotland-28565239 for a fascinating insight into this side of warfare and its consequent social impact.

enjoyed it (see footnote below also, although whether 'enjoyment' is the right word is a moot point!), which gave a whole generation of women the desire to have a career or work outside of the home, family, marriage and children

What has been the impact of equal opportunities policies on women's lives?

This is an ideal subject area for sociological research, and indeed, many sociologists who do research into gender have looked into this very question to assess the impact that feminism and women's increased role, status and rights has had on the lives of individual women.

Activity 45 - Using the UK web archive of women's lives (link below), which is maintained with the help of the Women's Library, research how individual women's lives have changed as a result of equal opportunities policies.

Your research should primarily focus on the world of work, since equal opportunities legislation (such as equal pay and the sex discrimination act) have mainly focussed on women in employment.
http://www.webarchive.org.uk/ukwa/collection/98537/page/1/source/collection

More family variations

Singletons

A singleton is a person who lives alone. According to the Eurostat 2011 Census, 13% of the usually resident population of England and Wales were living alone.

Reasons for this variation:

- Later marriages
- 20s/30s women are more independent
- Less social stigma about living alone in 20s/30s for women in particular
- Middle aged divorced men tend to live alone
- Increasing number of widows live alone
- Changing social norms: a heterosexual marriage is no longer seen as the only acceptable adult family structure
- Same sex
- The Civil Partnership Act of 2004 allows gay couples legal recognition of their relationships, and to enter into a 'civil partnership' (though not a marriage)

As of March 2014, the Coalition government gave gay couples the right to marry, meaning that homosexual people could enter into a marriage (though the option to have a civil partnership remains for gay people or else to convert a pre-existing civil partnership into a marriage), in equality with heterosexual people.

Reasons for this variation:

- Secularisation (some religions condemn homosexuality, though religious taboos now hold less sway in many Western countries)
- Increased social acceptance of homosexuality
- New reproductive technologies and surrogacy practices allow homosexual couples to have children (also adoption)

Childbirth, family size and mortality rates

Family sizes in Western societies have become smaller in recent decades; a woman will, on average, give birth to 1.6 children in her lifetime (vs. 2.7 in the 1960s and 6 in 1870). There are many reasons for this. Firstly, due to a decline in the infant mortality rate, more children are living to be adults and thus there is less of a 'need' for continued reproduction. Birth control and other forms of contraception have also decreased birth rates. Also, as we will discuss below, we now live in a child-centred society, meaning that children have become big expenses. Also due, in part, to the feminist movement, women are prioritising their careers first and giving birth later than they used to, though this trend also reflects the fact that the way the world work is structured (by men, for men) has not caught up with women's equal status and increased public role.

Even though family sizes are becoming smaller, the population is growing because people are living longer; the average life expectancy for a man is 75 and for a woman is 80. Today we have better healthcare and improved knowledge of diet and exercise. Also, we have improved hygiene and things like sewage disposal systems, cleaner water and refrigerated food. Jobs are also less dangerous and labour intensive. Elderly people receive pensions from the welfare state and generally are medically supported.

Remember, it is important to be aware of the impact that demographic factors have on society (therefore looking at a population based on factors such as age, race, sex, economic status, level of education, income level and employment, etc.)

Analysis

Overall, it is important to understand the family life cycle and how that relates to diversity. Every individual will have their own, unique life cycle based on factors such as class, ethnicity and gender. The case study that follows is an illustrative example of how factors such as class, ethnicity and gender can present itself in an individual's life cycle.

- Robert is born as an only child (age 0 – 15) living with his mother who is a stay-at-home mum, and his dad works as a hospital porter. (Nuclear Family)

- Robert's father dies leaving Robert and his mother. (Single/Lone-parent household)

- Robert goes away to university and lives alone (18-22). (Single/Lone-person household)

- Robert goes on to do further study and shares a flat with friends whilst he gets his master's degree (22-24). (Communal household)

- Robert lives alone again whilst he does his doctorate and subsequently teaches (24-29). (Single/Lone-person household)

- Robert moves in with his male partner (29-34). (Same sex household)

- Robert and his partner enter a civil partnership and adopt two children from different ethnic backgrounds from each other and from Robert and his partner, thus creating a gay parent family. (34-54). (Gay family unit)

- The children leave home, leaving Robert and his partner alone again (54-75)

- Robert's partner dies, leaving him on his own (75-90). (Single/Lone-person household)

Activity 46 – Reflecting on your own personal life. Can you write your own family life cycle, in the style of the case study above?
When you reach your current situation, can you then draw up a projection for how you see your own personal situation in the future?

Theoretical Perspectives on the Family

It is also important to be aware of how different sociological perspectives view the family as a social concept.

Functionalist

The functionalist school thought argues that families serve as key socialising agents, instilling cultural values in children from young ages so that they may, ultimately, contribute to society and perpetuate the socialisation process by having families of their own.

American functionalist sociologist Talcott Parsons specifically states that the family serves to:

Socialise children through the process of primary socialisation. This is where personalities are moulded and society's norms and values are taught and reinforced by the family. For Parsons the family would be a safe environment where personalities are formed in a secure and nurturing way. Stabilise adult personalities. This aspect of the family unit focuses on the needs of the adults within the family unit. It is through the family that marital relationship emotional security can be found for the adults. The family unit would act as a cushion for the stresses and strains of life. The sexual division of labour in terms of male/female roles, with the female being 'expressive' (care giver and nurturer) and the male being 'instrumental' (the breadwinner) are all contributory factors to the stabilisation of adult personalities. Functionalist sociologist George Peter Murdock stated that the family serves four vital universal functions. They are:

- Reproductive – procreation, having and caring for children
- Sexual – regulation of sexual activity so as to encourage fidelity and contribute to the maintenance of social order
- Educational – socialisation, learning the norms and values of society
- Economic – division of labour within the family unit – breadwinner and nurturer, caring and providing for the family

Activity 47 -

What criticisms do you think can be made of Parsons and Murdock's view of the family?

Some criticisms that can be made of the functionalist view on the family:

Murdock's theory discounts same sex marriage.

Feminists criticise the idea of different and unequal gender roles in family (where men work and earn money but women don't, though their unpaid labour is vital to ensure this).

Too positive or optimistic: it does not account for unstable families and domestic violence, which is primarily a form of gender violence (Most domestic violence is perpetrated by men on women).

Too much emphasis on key functions of nuclear families, not enough focus on the positive outcomes of single parent families. (Many sociologists are actively investigating the extent to which single parent families and traditional nuclear families differ in terms of the outcomes and life chances for the children brought up in this way.)

New Right

New Right views are generally more conservative than are functionalist views; they were also perhaps most influential during Margaret Thatcher's leadership in the 1980s. New Right theorists very much in favour or and support the traditional nuclear family in which the father is bread winner and the mother is care-giver, and therefore are seen to be against single parent family units. They feel that the nuclear family is a better, more balanced formula for primary socialisation. In addition, they think that single-parent families are a burden on society in that they cost too much in welfare benefits. As part of their analysis of the family, they do make assumptions about single/lone parent families being more commonly associated with the underclass, idle, unmarried etc.

Some criticisms of New Right:

They fail to acknowledge that there are some nuclear families that do not socialise children properly despite their appearing to represent the 'ideal' family type; therefore nuclear families are not 'best' by virtue of being nuclear families.

Feminists regarding this perspective as sexist and, as such, based on a patriarchal ideology: women need to and should be able to work to support families and as a means of self-expression and use of their talents. These options are open to men so it is sexist if they are denied to women by virtue of gender alone.

Reynolds et al (2003) argue that there is no evidence to confirm that non-traditional roles, i.e. the 'mother' going out to work as opposed to staying at home, negatively impacts the family unit.

Children will suffer if welfare benefits are cut from single parents.

Feminist

The Feminists school of thought argues that women are constrained by the social implications of patriarchy and must therefore fight for equal rights, independence from men and for a revolution in the social structure. Feminism has its own subdivisions and categories: therefore, you need to be aware of the following:

- Liberal Feminists
- Radical Feminists
- Marxist Feminists
- Black Feminist

Liberal feminism

Liberal feminism is associated with the so-called 'first wave' of feminism, which saw women granted increased social and political equality with men from the end of the nineteenth century onwards and, as such, they regarded changes occurring within the family as being positive, with roles becoming progressively more equal. Therefore, besides equal rights to divorce, the most significant achievement was the granting of universal women's suffrage (the right to vote) in 1928.

Later in the twentieth century, important gains in public life and the workplace were won in the 1960s and 1970s, as part of the 'second wave' of feminism. Key legislation was the Equal Pay Act 1970, which made it unlawful to pay women less than men for work of equal value. Before this, it was common employment practice to pay women less than men for work of equal value because women's social role was thought to be primarily that of housewife and carer, and were not considered to be the main breadwinners. It was also common practice for women to leave their jobs on marriage, in order to devote themselves full time to their husbands and families.

The Sex Discrimination Act 1975 went further than the 1970 Equal Pay Act and outlawed further forms of gender discrimination, and both these changes were actively supported by liberal feminists.

Jenny Somerville (2000) argues that with better access to divorce, access to better job opportunities, control of their own fertility, and fewer social pressures to marry, women's roles within society had improved considerably.

Liberal feminists still campaign on important feminist issues such as the prosecution of perpetrators of sexual violence and domestic violence, as well as closing the gender pay gap. However, liberal feminists typically do not see women's oppression as part of a systematic or structural sexism. Instead, they focus on individual examples of women's discrimination or oppression and on changing these, but do not have a desire to radically overturn social norms and conventions. This is in contrast to other forms of feminism.

Radical feminism

Radical feminists see society as patriarchal as characterised by the domination of women by men, in a social contract, which men benefit from at the expense of women. As such, men are fundamentally the cause of the inequality women experience within society. Moreover, patriarchy is not confined to the modern western world but has been common in many cultures both now and in the past. This makes it a near-universal structure of systematic oppression and, from this perspective, is a system that has to be eradicated, particularly the family which is at the centre of the oppression women experience.

Many radical feminists focus on issues such as sexuality, body image, the family and male sexual and domestic violence against women as key ways in which men systematically oppress and subjugate women. Radical feminists engaged in sociological research may well research these topics, for this reason.

Marxist/Socialist feminism

As its name suggests, this form of feminism is closely allied to the class and labour movements of the nineteenth and twentieth centuries. Marxist feminism developed out of Marx's conflict theory. This perspective looks at gender inequality in terms of economics, that is the inequality generated because of a capitalist society. The unpaid labour of the working class housewife who maintains the home and cares for the family and is thus entirely dependent on her husband's wage is fundamentally necessary in order to maintain this system of injustice. Without her unpaid labour, the low paid and dangerous labour of her husband would become impossible and there would thus be no production surplus to maintain the rich owner elite. Some may argue, for example, that because there is no economic value placed on the work women do, within as well as outside of the family unit, they are fundamentally at a disadvantage as a result of a capitalist society.

Both Marxist and Socialist feminism are critical of liberal feminism, and see women's oppression as part of a systematic or structural social-set up. Therefore, society needs a radical overhaul in order to end women's oppression and the powerful vested interests that are allied against women achieving equality.

A key strand of both Marxist and Socialist feminism is to see capitalism as an economic and social structure that creates and perpetuates women's oppression and discrimination, as well as that of working class men. In order for wealth and power to be concentrated in the hands of the male elite (the owners of the means of production), then the low paid and often dangerous labour of the working class man is required.

Black feminism

Black feminists and feminists from the global south have argued that the forms of feminism outlined above are problematic because they are ethnocentric. That is, they focus on white society and on white women and do not take into account ethnicity as well as gender. (In this regard, Black feminism can be compared to Socialist and Marxist feminism, which sees gender-class as a compound issue; Black Feminism sees the problem as one of gender-ethnicity.)

A key Black Feminist is bell hooks (lower case deliberate) whose book Ain't I A Woman (1981) focuses on documenting the American black woman's experience of both racism and sexism. She felt the need to write the book (as a black American woman herself) because she saw black women as being 'symbolically annihilated' by twentieth century American culture. For example, she stated that when the topic of racism is discussed in American culture, then usually people focus on the experience of black men. And when the topic of sexism is discussed, then usually the focus is on the experience of white women.

In this book, bell hooks analyses the sexism that black women have experienced from black men in the black civil rights movement who wished to achieve equality with white men but still wanted to dominate women at home and in the public sphere, and the racism that black women experienced from the white women in the feminist movement who wanted equality with white men but did not want to give up the white privilege that was theirs in a racist society, and ally with black women.

Thus, neither black men nor white women were in full solidarity with black women, and black women therefore found themselves caught in a double bind of racist-sexist oppression and in this way doubly marginalised in society.

For this reason, bell hooks and other black feminists have argued that it was important that the black female experience was properly documented. Whereas white radical feminists might point to the family as the key social structure which maintains white women's oppression, black feminists have argued that the black family is often a source of strength for black women who have experienced racism in society. In this way, categories that apply to white women cannot necessarily be 'carried over' to black women unthinkingly, and therefore it is necessary for a black feminist movement to record black women's experiences and to highlight that any theory of gender discrimination must also include racism, and any theory of racial oppression must also account for sexism.

Finally, many black feminists often include class as well as gender and race in their analysis of society, and argue that it is impossible to understand social oppression without understanding how these three factors intersect. Understanding oppressions as intersecting in this way is known as intersectionality.

Criticisms of feminism in general:

Many different types of feminism: different schools of feminism are seen to argue with one another and possibly weaken the overall message.

Feminist views do not always apply to 'real world' aspirations of women who wish to have children with their husbands and become housewives (though as most feminists would argue, these women are certainly a product of gender-role socialisation that has made women more likely than men to view unpaid care-giving as their self-identity.)

New Right would argue that working women either neglect their children and husbands, or take on too much work by trying to balance their careers with care giving. Thus, it would be easier to focus solely on care giving duties and so the key feminist objections to patriarchal society would disappear.

Social Policies in the UK and the Family

It is important to note how government policies have influenced patterns in family structures over the years. Social policies introduced by the government have directly influenced marriage, divorce, childhood, welfare and domestic violence.

Marriage – Marriages must be monogamous and to someone of opposite sex, though since March 2014 in the UK, gay people have full equality with heterosexual people with regards to their right to marry.

Divorce – the Divorce Law Reform Act of 1969 (came into effect in 1971) identified the grounds for divorce as being: adultery, desertion, unreasonable behaviour and 'no fault' in that neither partner had to prove fault on the part of the other; one just had to demonstrate that the marriage was no longer suitable or working. Couples could also apply for divorce if they had been separated for two years or five, if only one of them wanted the divorce.

The Family Law Act 1996 (FLA 96) promoted mediation and conflict resolution between the parties concerned, though this was considered by some to be underutilised and ineffective.

It is important to bear in mind that in the early twentieth century, a woman still could not obtain divorce from a husband on the same grounds as a man could from his wife.

Children – Policies require children to attend school from age 5 and prevent them from working part-time prior to the age of 13. A person has to be 18 years old before they are allowed to buy cigarettes. A person can enter a pub at age 16 but are not allowed to be served or buy alcohol; if the 16 year old goes into a pub/bar with an 18 or over individual, they can buy and consume alcohol with a meal. In terms of sexual activity the law stipulates that a 16 year old can give consent.
You can do some research into other areas of social policy and law that ensure the welfare of children.

Welfare – child benefits, single parent benefits, unemployment or housing benefits and pensions have all played a role in how people choose to arrange their personal lives, because they have created economic support structures which many have found invaluable.

Domestic Violence – The laws that protect family members against violence and give police and courts power to intervene. How the police treat domestic violence has changed remarkably since the mid-twentieth century, when it was not taken seriously as a crime. This change is the product of changing attitudes towards women but has also shaped the structure of the family since it has increased people's options (especially women's) if their partners become violent.[21]

Activity 48 –
Research how social policies in the UK have impacted the family.
You may like to focus on this particular legislation:

- **1945 Families Allowances Act**
- **1980 Housing Act**
- **New Labour's 'Welfare To Work' programme (1997 onwards)**

and you may wish to use this website:
www.legislation.gov.uk to research them.

---

[21] This is discussed in more detail below

Recap of the social scientific perspectives on policies and the family

Functionalist - welfare is a positive mechanism that supports families as key agents of primary socialisation.

New Right – critical of welfare benefits; single-parent welfare benefits should be eliminated and the nuclear family should be bolstered as an economically sound option. They are also critical of 'easy' divorce laws.

Feminist – support benefits for single parents, especially for women who are in such positions against their wishes: Also support divorce laws because they give women more independence e.g. free from patriarchal control. Feminists are also in favour of laws against domestic violence (as is any right-minded individual!).

Marxist – Some think that policies such as free education are just put into place to placate the masses or discourage the working classes from rebellion; upper class members of society still enjoy the top private medical and educational resources.

Marriage, Divorce and Cohabitation

Over 40% of UK, marriages end in divorce; this is a massive shift from the mere 4,000 divorces that occurred in 1931. Divorce rates have increased steadily since 1970. Reasons for this:

Legal

- The Divorce Law Reform Act of 1969 (as discussed previously)
- The Matrimonial and Family Proceedings Act of 1984 (allowed couples to get a divorce after one year of marriage)
- The Family Law Act of 1996. This was actually introduced to slow divorce rates, requiring 18 months of marriage prior to divorce, as well as counselling

Feminism

- Women have become more independent; around 70% of divorce petitions are now from women. This potentially shows us that women are not content with the still patriarchal and sexist assumptions of modern marriage and gender relationships

Welfare State

- Benefits for divorced women mean that women now have more options. In the first half of the twentieth century, it would have been far more likely that a woman had no choice to remain married because she had no economic independence. Women's choices in public life and career were severely limited solely because of their gender

Changes in Social attitude toward divorce

- Less social stigma to divorce than there ever has been.

Secularisation

- Less religious taboo about divorce than there has been.

In contemporary society, people usually marry 'for love' instead of, as was the case in the past, for economic or social stigma reasons (being a single unmarried woman was a difficult social role to negotiate; women needed men for economic support since they were denied careers of their own). However, people expect their relationships to be 'perfect' and constantly 'romantic', so many find the reality of marriage to be disappointing.

Increased life expectancy

Longer marriage periods = more time for a divorce. The longer you are married to someone, perhaps the more time you have to become dissatisfied with him or her as a partner!

Note: In addition to divorce rates, we must take into account marriages of convenience or loveless marriages (in which partners never did or now no longer love one another, so there is no actual relationship though they are legally married) as well as separation. Neither of these social trends is covered by divorce statistics, though they both point to dissatisfaction with marriage as a social construct. It is important therefore to bear in mind that divorce statistics do not tell the complete social story in this regard.

Activity 49 –

Do you have any personal experience of divorce? It is fairly likely that even if you are not divorced yourself, a friend or family member has experienced the break-up of a relationship.

How do people describe their own experiences of divorce; what reasons do they give and how do they view the process?

Do you think the increased divorce rate implies that marriage as an institution is now less socially important, or do you think this conclusion cannot be drawn?

Cohabitation

With such an increase in divorce rates, along with the rise of secularisation and recent shifts in social attitudes, it makes sense that people are marrying less. Cohabitation is becoming an increasingly popular alternative to marriage.

Feminism has had a strong impact on adult relationships. As careers become increasingly important to women versus care giving and having children, women are choosing to marry later or not at all, opting for cohabitation instead.

Secularisation is also an important trend in this regard: it would have been a huge social stigma which would have occasioned massive social shame to be cohabiting in the nineteenth century; now it is commonplace.

Activity 50 –

Do you or someone you know have any personal experience of cohabitation?

Why do you think that more and more people are choosing cohabitation, and do you think this social trend equates to a rejection of marriage as an institution?

Childhood

Most sociologists would label childhood as a 'social construct'. This means that the differential treatment of children from adults e.g. required schooling, different doctors, different activities, different foods, etc., has not always existed and exists less (or does not exist at all) in other cultures.

For example, prior to the industrial revolution, from 1760 onwards, most children assisted adults in daily land-focused work; it wasn't until children started working in factories that they became protected by labour laws. Going even further back, then 'Childhood' as a separate phase of life than adulthood did not exist in the middle ages; it wasn't until the first public, or fee-paying schools opened in the thirteenth century (yet only for privileged boys) that children started to be treated differently. (Refer back to the Education unit and the history of education.)

Compulsory schooling was not introduced until 1870, when the minimum leaving age was 10. Now, many children in the UK attend school from ages 5-17 and then go onto university. Also, it is illegal for children to work part time prior to age 13.

We live in what some sociologists call a 'child-centred society', in which children are protected and treated very differently to adults. Some would argue, however, that childhood is not always 'blissful' and that many children suffer from child abuse and bullying at school. Also, Neil Postman (1994) argues that, due to internet and media access, children are growing up a lot faster today and that it is no longer possible for parents to withhold information from them. This has increased parents' worries and fears about their children's safety, and so has made it more likely that they will try and maintain childhood as a safe and special time.

Activity 51 – Briefly summarise the reasons as to why childhood is a social construct.

Domestic Labour and Gender Roles

Whilst we have already touched upon the topic of domestic labour in our discussions of feminine social roles in the household, it has been reported that, though men are taking more of an active role at home and family units are more symmetrical, women still perform the majority of housework and childcare duties.

Feminists argue that this inequality is a result of patriarchy, or male domination in society; they feel that women are doing the so-called 'double shift' of full time jobs and full time housework and that some women even partake in a 'third shift' (that of emotional work, or of providing love and emotional support to children and family members). If this is the case, then the fact that around 70% of all marriages are ended by women who seek divorce becomes less surprising; women are dissatisfied with the unequal burden of caring and nurture that society and socialised gender roles assume that they have to perform.

Conjugal roles

Conjugal roles are the roles and duties that people take on during marriage. Throughout the majority of the nineteenth and twentieth centuries, married couples took up segregated conjugal roles, meaning that men were typically working breadwinners, and women stayed at home as caregivers. This balance has shifted significantly, especially since the 1970s. Now, we are seeing an increase in joint conjugal roles, in which men and women share the housework and childcare roles equally.

However, though this relationship is becoming more common, studies still show that, even though around 75% of married or cohabiting women have paid jobs, women still are doing the majority of home-related work, and in fact, only 1 in 10 of all heterosexual relationships are actually 'equal' in the sense that housework, domestic tasks and childcare are split fairly between the man and woman. It is notable that as women have entered the workforce in ever greater numbers since the 1960s and 1970s, men have not taken on a correspondingly greater share of housework land childcare. This is a significant social trend and one that sociologists concerned with gender issues frequently return to.

Functionalist and New Right views on domestic division of labour

While feminists would argue for women's independence, stating that women should be able to pursue careers and should not have to be bogged down with housework, Functionalist and New Right theorists would argue that segregated conjugal roles represent a more 'natural' division of labour and is necessary in order for the family unit to function effectively.

They would say that men are more suited for full time employment and women for childcare and housework. Women should not take on two, full time roles (career and home) i.e. it is much easier for each partner to take on one full time job, and that the 'natural' way to divide this is for the man to be the primary wage-earner and the woman the primary care-giver.

Power relationships and domestic violence

Studies have shown that men have, historically, exercised more control over joint finances and have usually dominated decision-making processes within marriages. However, a study by Hardill *et al* (1997) does indicate more equality in decision-making processes among middle class couples.

Some would say that men tend to dominate decision making processes because they tend to earn higher incomes, and are socialised into being dominant rather than co-operative or consensual. This is due to the social construct of masculinity which holds that men are better suited than women when it comes to being more authoritative, commanding, stronger and more capable of good decision making. Feminists would likewise argue that it is the patriarchal nature of society that socialises women into being more passive and to have less confidence in their own decisions and abilities, and so they are more likely to defer to male judgement.

The Dysfunctional aspects of the Family - Domestic Violence

There is no legal or statutorily agreed definition of domestic violence and because of this measuring the extent of domestic violence in the UK is a difficult exercise. However, various sources can be utilised in order to gain some idea of the extent of domestic violence. It is accepted within social scientific circles that, due to the very private nature of domestic violence, there is a tendency for individuals who are victims not to report incidences to the police. According to data collected by the CPS (Crown Prosecution Service) in 2012/13, 88,110 domestic violence cases were referred to the CPS. This was less than the previous year but higher than 2007/08 at just over 70,000.[22]

Other UK-wide studies have shown that domestic violence will have an impact on one in four women, and one in six men in their lifetimes. However, most women do not report cases of domestic violence out of fear, and when they do, it is after an average of 35 offences. Men, on the other hand, might be reluctant to report cases of domestic violence at all due to embarrassment over the social stigma of being physically assaulted by a woman. It is important to be mindful and aware of domestic violence within gay and lesbian relationships, too.

Activity 52 – Review your research and your work on the family.

Make sure that you can explain the different sociological perspectives on family diversity as well as outline the key demographic and social changes that have taken place in the family in recent history.

To consolidate your work, you may wish to research further the most recent UK social policy as it affects the policy.

You can start your research at the Department for Education looking at social policy on Families and Children.

http://www.education.gov.uk/childrenandyoungpeople/families/

You may also want to find out more about demographic changes in the UK since 1900, such as birth and death rates or marriage and divorce rates. This governmental research paper is an excellent overview:

http://www.parliament.uk/documents/commons/lib/research/rp99/rp99-111.pdf

---

[22] Violence against Women and Girls Crime Report 2012-2013 - CPS

4.2.3: Health (Optional)

A2 Option 1 - 4.2.3

Key Areas:

- What is Health?
- The social construction of health, illness, disability and the body
- The biological/biomedical model of health and illness
- Models of health and illness
- The unequal social distribution of health and illness in the United Kingdom by social class, age, gender, ethnicity and region, and internationally
- Inequalities in the provision of, and access to, health care in contemporary society
- The nature and social distribution of mental illness
- The role of medicine and the health professions, and the globalisation and health
- Sociological explanations of health and illness

What is Health?

According to the World Health Organisation (WHO), health is:

"...a state of complete physical, mental and social well-being and not merely the absence of disease or infirmity."[23]

A biomedical definition sees health as the absence of illness, whether physical or psychological. From a sociological perspective health is more than just the absence of illness and feeling unwell: health is to a certain extent, also a socially constructed[24] thing, meaning that as a concept it can change according to time and place, and as such can be affected by socio-economic factors. Sociologists look at health in relative terms: to be 'healthy' or 'ill' has different meanings in different social settings. For example, to be diagnosed as HIV positive in San Francisco in the 1980s was a tragic death sentence. Today, with all of the modern medical advancements that have been made, people can live with HIV for decades, experiencing virtually no signs of illness. The same could be said of many illnesses and conditions which perhaps a century ago were a sure death-sentence and today are manageable, preventable or curable. Such changes remind us yet again that health and illness are social (as well as biological) categories: defined by society and subject to social change which varies over time. Further, sociologists examine how individual ideas of 'good health' may vary depending on age, class, ethnicity, and/or gender, and how health and illness are unevenly distributed across society, by age, class, ethnicity and/or gender.

Activity 52 - Think about your own health now. Have you ever been seriously ill? If so, have you had any experience of the National Health Service (NHS)? How did you manage your illness, and has it had any long-term effects on your current lifestyle?
Reflect on this and on the social factors at work: to what extent do you think your class, ethnicity, gender or age have had an impact on how you have experienced ill-health?

---

[23] Preamble to the Constitution of the World Health Organization as adopted by the International Health Conference, New York, 19-22 June, 1946; signed on 22 July 1946 by the representatives of 61 States (Official Records of the World Health Organization, no. 2, p. 100) and entered into force on 7 April 1948.
[24] A product of society and subject to social definitions.

Models of Health

The Medical Model

The medical model of health focuses on biological and physical causes of illness, viewing the body rather mechanically, as something that can be fixed with prescribed treatments. When the body can no longer be fixed, doctors endeavour to extend life for as long as possible, making people feel more comfortable with medications.

The Social Model

The social model looks beyond physical and biological factors, placing health and illness in broader social contexts; for example, sociologists look at how poverty, unemployment and other living conditions influence health and also at how patterns of ill-health and disease are distributed across society by factors such as class, age, gender and/or ethnicity. Often, sociologists who follow this model are critical of doctors for over prescribing medication from powerful drug companies and failing to recommend alternative therapies. Others are less critical of doctors, seeing the benefits of modern western medicine and acknowledging that doctors are genuinely concerned with their patients' well-being.

Activity 53 – Summarise the differences between the medical and social models of health.

Disability

Often, disability is looked at in association with health as the social assumption is that a person who is classified as disabled is unhealthy. Whilst sometimes this may be the case, in that, for example, a physical impairment could be as a result of a physiological condition, it is a social assumption that can be disputed. Due to this rather contentious issue, some sociologists have only turned to the subject of disability quite recently, and the general ethos among social researchers is that 'disability' is socially constructed.

According to Finklestein (1981), disabilities and the negative social associations has come about as a result of capitalism. Finklestein argues that prior to the industrial revolution, people with conditions now labelled as disabilities were looked after by their families, earned a living and contributed to the household income via the small-scale cottage industry.

However, it was the development of the manufacturing and machinery era that began to limit the contribution that could be made by those who were disabled. With the growth in industry through manufacturing, coal and steel and the movement of people to where work was plentiful, disabled people began to be viewed as incapable of working as quickly, and limited in terms of being able to move to areas where work was available. As such disabilities where perceived as 'shortcomings' or factors which prevented them from working.

The Medical Model of Disability

The medical model of disability is frequently rejected by disabled people as it regards an individual's disability as a problem or condition that needs to be 'cured' or 'fixed'. It views people with disabilities as needing to adapt to society as best they can. The 'problem' is therefore seen to lie with the disabled person.

The Social Model of Disability

The social model holds that disability is the result of the norms and values of society and as such disability is caused by social barriers and discrimination. People are not inherently disabled; they become 'disabled' when they are labelled as such and treated as second-class citizens. This only happens because the 'disabled' are viewed as 'disabled' in conventional society and by current social norms and values. The social model also looks at how stereotyping can present disable people as dependent and even 'tragic'. Barnes (1992) found that the media tended to present the disabled rather patronisingly as either tragic or brave. This perspective therefore, highlights the social constructionist notion of disability.

Activity 54 – Think of the portrayal of disabled people in the media; do you think Barnes's perspective could be applied?

The Sociology of the Body

The sociology of the body is also a fairly new topic in sociological research: it focuses on how social norms and values impact individual bodies and body image, and how images and perceptions of the body can contribute to what is seen as healthy.

Body image

Given the focus on dieting, weight loss and thinness in western society, body image has become a major area of social concern. Historically (and in many non-western cultures today), thinness has been associated with poverty and malnourishment. Now, in modern, western culture, women in particular are impacted by the celebrity or supermodel norms and standards portrayed by the media. As such, many women have developed eating disorders such as anorexia and bulimia. Of course, the mass media is not the only cause of this problem: eating disorders also result from biological, psychological and emotional causes. Eating disorders do not only affect women: 10 per cent of those suffering from eating disorders are men.

According to the Anorexia and Bulimia Care,[25] which is one of two UK national organisations that work with people with eating disorders:

- In England and Wales, approximately 269,000 females have a clinically diagnosed eating disorder
- Of all those identified as having an eating disorder, approximately ¼ affected are boys of school age
- Approximately 10% of recorded cases of anorexia and 15% bulimia are men

---

[25] http://www.anorexiabulimiacare.org.uk/

Feminist Perspectives on the Body

Some radical feminists believe that, as women are becoming more successful, myths of 'perfect' female bodies are used to 'control' them, causing excessive worry and focus on self-image. Andrea Dworkin, writes: "In our culture not one part of a women's body is left untouched, unaltered.... From head to toe, every feature of a woman's face, every section of her body, is subject to modification."[26] This has been termed a 'backlash' on the part of patriarchal culture, and an attempt to limit and control women just as women's independence, freedoms and equality to men (in modern western society, at least) have never been greater.

The Social Distribution of Health and Illness

Social class

Statistics show that higher social classes are generally healthier than those of lower social classes, and that morbidity and mortality (specifically infant mortality) rates are significantly higher among people of manual labour backgrounds.
Lower social classes tend to:

- Have higher infant mortality rates
- More likely to suffer from serious medical conditions
- More likely to die before retirement
- More likely to have unhealthy lifestyles
- Be less informed re: healthier lifestyle
- Experience cultural and social deprivation

---

[26] (1974, 113–4)

Several explanations have been posited for these contrasts:

- The Artefact Approach: This theory states that statistics about poor health in lowest class of society are misleading. Since the lowest social class is so small, the bottom two social classes have been combined to compare to the middle class. Only then can we see the stark contrasts in health conditions

- Theories of Natural and Social Selection: This approach is based on an almost Darwinian principle in terms of evolution and the notion of the 'survival of the fittest'. Based on this principle, it is inevitable that some individuals will do better than others. Within the social selection context, if the same principle were to be applied to class, it stands to reason that lower classes are more likely to be unhealthy do to a lack of resources when compared to the higher classes who do not have such limitations and/or restrictions. As such, individuals end up in specific social classes due to good or poor health conditions, and that good or poor health can lead to a propensity to a lower or higher class

- Behavioural and Cultural Explanations: This view points to lifestyle choices as causing poor health. For example, working class men are more likely to drink and smoke heavily than are, say, middle class women. However, some are critical of the idea that the working class create their own fates as it is like blaming the working classes for their health issues and as such not looking into the wider social factors, such as why they are smoking - statistics show that working class smokers are more likely to suffer health problems than are middle class smokers. Also, the challenging living conditions associated with unemployment may cause stress and anxiety, leading to more smoking and drinking in the working class

- Materialistic or Structural Factors: This view states that the working class suffers from poor health because of low income, poor housing and poor working conditions: all factors that are beyond personal control but invariably can have a negative impact on health

Activity 55 - Summarise four viewpoints on the link between social class and health.

Health and Gender

According to ONS statistics women outlive men, with an average life expectancy for women being 82.5 years and men 79.5. However, women are more likely to become ill (or at least, to visit the doctor and report symptoms) than are men. Women also take more medications and more sick days from work. Feminists argue that women are subject to more illness because of stress and anxiety due to the triple shift (particularly the stress that comes with raising young children). Also, women are more likely to experience poverty than are men because of single parenthood: this could make them more subject to illness, and also brings together the social categories of gender and class or poverty, reminding us that social factors often interlink. So why do women live longer? Some social factors include the following: women are more likely to seek medical help than are men. Women are less likely to smoke and drink in excess than are men; also, men tend to live more hazardous lives than women and are more likely to engage in risk-taking behaviour.

From the biological perspective, it also seems that men are actually more feeble as biological organisms than women. Since it is far more important (evolutionary speaking) that women survive times of scarcity (such as famine or disease outbreak) than men then it makes good adaptive sense that women have stronger immune systems and have a lower infant mortality rate. For every 100 live female births, there are in fact 106/7 live male births: but this is a fact of nature to allow for the fact that more boys than girls die in infancy (under normal conditions) and so by the time those boys and girls reach puberty, there is an equal sex ratio.

Health and Ethnicity

Statistics from the 2011 Census show that persistent health inequalities can be seen in certain ethnic groups. For example, in 2011 Pakistani and Bangladeshi women had a 10% higher rate of illness than White women. White Gypsy and/or Irish Travellers, who were included for the first time in the 2011 census, were found to have particularly poor health, and for both men and women they were twice as likely to have long-term illness when compared to White British rates. The Chinese are reported to have better health overall. Statistics vary further when factors such as age are taken into consideration.

There are many possible explanations for these incongruities. Biological researchers, for example, point out that African Caribbeans tend to have higher blood pressure levels, which can cause strokes and heart attacks. Also, sickle cell anaemia, a fatal blood disorder, has been known to affect African Caribbeans. Regarding Asian members of the population, cultural and behavioural researchers point to the use of ghee (a less healthy form of cooking fat) and higher carbohydrate foods as causing health problems.

Structural theorists view poor health as a result of poor living and working conditions among lower class groups e.g. Pakistani and Bangladeshi groups tend to live in poor housing conditions and generally suffer more health problems than Indian and Chinese groups, which tend to occupy middle class neighbourhoods. Lastly, many researchers think that racism and discrimination lead to unemployment or difficult working conditions, which have an impact on both mental and physical health.

Overall, factors to consider when looking at health and ethnicity are:

- Biological - related to age, sex, genetics etc.
- Education
- Social class
- Income
- Local Environment
- Discrimination and inequality

Health and Age

As the contingency of UK citizens aged over 65 continues to grow, so does the body of research linking health to age. Statistics show that the number of pensioners will continue to grow, and that people will continue to live longer in the coming years; not surprisingly, with the degeneration associated with aging, there are health implications. The healthiest members of the 65+ age group tend to be of white, middle class backgrounds.

Health and Region

Regarding region, statistics show that people from the north of the country tend to exhibit poorer health conditions than those from the south; also, suburban and rural areas that are populated by white and middle class citizens tend to be healthier than the poorer urban areas populated by ethnic minorities.

Health care in contemporary society

Health provision in the UK is free and has been since the NHS was established in 1945; however, many inequalities in the healthcare system still exist. For example, money is allocated to medical institutions differentially by region. In theory, poorer regions are supposed to receive more money but in actuality, the top hospitals are usually located in wealthier parts of the country, drawing in more advanced researchers, as well as the top-qualified practitioners (and thus more money).

In 1971, Dr Tudor Hart coined the concept of inverse care law, which states that those in society (usually the poorest) who need health care most receive less or poorer treatment than those in society who are more affluent and need it less. Research has shown that wealthier areas of the UK (e.g. Kingston and Surrey) have more GPs than do more deprived areas.

Some people do opt for private healthcare providers such as BUPA. This has caused much controversy as private insurance schemes (which presumably give people access to faster and better healthcare) are too expensive for poorer members of the country and take the top doctors out of the NHS system.

Healthcare and Gender

As we have discussed, women are more likely to visit the doctor to report themselves as ill than are men, despite the fact that women outlive men. Some think that women are not necessarily worse off than men; mothers have more time to visit doctors due to what could be perceived as more flexible or part-time working schedules, and they often visit the doctor frequently with their children anyway. Also, women are socialised into being more emotionally expressive and are less inhibited about communicating symptoms than are men.

Women also tend to be more aware of health issues through their use of health, beauty and fitness magazines and products and, as such, may be more aware of symptoms when they arise. Lastly, some would say that male doctors view women as more vulnerable or weaker than men and tend to diagnose women with illnesses more frequently, whereas they would perhaps tell a man with the same symptoms that he was not in fact 'really ill'.

Activity 56 – Why do think it is that women suffer from more illness and yet live longer lives than men?

Healthcare and Ethnicity

It has been suggested that the reasons that ethnic minorities experience worse healthcare than their white counterparts are many. Some researchers point to issues of linguistic and cultural difference; for example, Asian women may not want to see male doctors for religious or cultural reasons and may avoid preventative cervical and breast cancer screenings for reasons of modesty. Of course, language is also an issue: patients with poor English language skills may have trouble communicating symptoms and may be misdiagnosed by doctors. Lastly, in terms of socioeconomics ethnic minorities may be more likely to live in poor conditions, having working class jobs that prevent them from taking time off work to seek medical treatment.

Activity 57 – Why do some ethnic minority groups choose not to use healthcare services?

Research the link between healthcare and ethnicity further. You may like to use the following article as a starting point:

http://news.bbc.co.uk/1/hi/health/789302.stm

Healthcare and Age

As the sector of society aged 65+ grows, it seems that, unfortunately, the amounts of healthcare opportunities for this group do not. Many are concerned that one day the NHS will not be able to provide healthcare for all and thus will be forced to ration its services. It seems that this may have already been occurring for the 65+ age group. For example, women over 65 are not invited for routine breast cancer screenings and 20 per cent of heart units operate on age-related admissions policies. Also, rehab centres for brain injuries tend to focus on treating people that need to return to work, and cancer research often excludes the elderly.

Mental Illness

There is much controversy surrounding research on mental illness. Namely: does 'mental illness' even exist, or is it a social construct? This controversy becomes more apparent when we look at the fact that definitions of, and responses to, mental illness vary over time.

Many researchers would agree that mental illness is a serious problem that requires serious attention. Those of the predominantly western medical/psychiatric model would agree that people who exhibit 'abnormal' behaviour and/or symptoms of depression should be treated by a qualified medical practitioner. According to these medical specialists, the most common reasons for mental illness is, generally the result of the following:

- Troubling and traumatising childhood events (this is known as the psychoanalytic model)
- Chemical imbalances in the brain; usually treated with anti-depressants

The statistics regarding the broad allocation of anti-depressant drugs are disturbing: it is estimated that over 3.5 million people in the UK are taking some form of anti-depressant at any given time.

You may be thinking: are millions and millions of people really depressed or mentally ill? Is it necessary for so many people to alter the chemical balances in their brains? These are some questions that labelling theorists ask, and challenge.

For thinkers such as Scheff (1966) and Szasz (1971), mental illness is about social roles and labelling. Some may be 'labelled' as mentally ill because they do not adhere to, or act outside of, the social norms and basic rules of society. So, to label someone as mentally ill is to exert a certain level of social control and therefore maintain some form of social order.

According to labelling theorists, 'mental illness' is a social construct. There have always been people that society has chosen to categorise as 'abnormal': in the Middle Ages, they were often dubbed witches, and now, they are categorised as 'mentally ill'. Labelling theorists note that many people go through stages in their lives in which they feel miserable, but to label these individuals as 'clinically depressed' and prescribe them with anti-depressant medication is completely unnecessary. Once labelled by doctors (usually falsely) as 'mentally ill', people are often admitted to hospitals, where doctors tend to engage in spurious interaction with them due to this label and in some instances resulting in an individual becoming institutionalised in that they become dependent on the 'system' that has labelled them as mentally ill.

Goffman said the label mental illness was a stigma and that institutions and hospitals that labelled an individual as such were reinforcing negative labels and rather than enabling the individual to 'get better'. The system that treats them (such as psychiatric institutions) teaches an individual how to conform to the label given to them – 'mentally ill'. Eventually the mental illness becomes the individual's identity resulting in the loss of their real identity.

Some schools of thought are critical of labelling theory, claiming that mental illness is a very serious and real issue that must be addressed carefully and cannot simply be attributed to the process of labelling. As such, labelling theory would be seen as naïve or even dangerous by the majority of western medical practitioners.

Social Factors

Another cohort of people that disagree with labelling theorists think that mental illness is the result of social factors rather than solely of chemical imbalances or genetics. For example, statistics show that more women suffer from depression than do men: many social researchers think that this is caused by the stress of the 'triple shift' of paid employment, housework and emotional care giving, as well as gender role socialisation and the reality of the inequality that it causes. Working class women tend to suffer higher levels of depression than do middle class women, mostly because working class women experience harsher living conditions (poverty, ill health) as well as upsetting life events.

Activity 58 –
Discuss how social factors such as class, ethnicity and gender can influence rate of mental illness.

You may like to research this further by visiting the website of one of the largest mental health charities in the UK, Mind:

http://www.mind.org.uk

Ethnicity

According to the Mental Health Foundation,[27] mental illness in the UK affects different ethnic groups in different ways as socio-economic factors play a part in contributing to the type of mental illness experienced.

Irish people statistically have higher rates of depression and alcohol related issues when compared to other ethnic groups. They are also more likely than other ethnic groups to be admitted to hospital.

African Caribbeans have lower rates of what may be regarded as common mental disorders but are more likely to be diagnosed with severe mental illnesses such as schizophrenia. They are also more likely to be treated under a section of the Mental Health Act and subsequently institutionalised in some way, receiving medication and not being offered alternative talking treatments such as psychotherapy. Overall, people of African Caribbean backgrounds (particularly men) tend to experience higher rates of depression than do white people. Many think that this is due, in part, to high levels of unemployment, underachievement and racism.

For Asian people, statistics are a little patchy but it has been suggested that mental health problems are often unrecognised or not diagnosed in this ethnic group.

Social Class

Regarding social class; studies have shown that poorer people are more frequently diagnosed with mental illness than are middle class people. Relative deprivation can be a contributory factor when it comes to looking at mental illness and class. According to Krieger (2001), Graham (2004), and Regidor (2006) socioeconomic inequalities affect how people feel and how they feel can have an impact upon their mental well-being.

---

[27] http://www.mentalhealth.org.uk/

Age

It is generally accepted that the population is aging. According to the Institute for Health Metrics and Evaluation (2010), approximately 15% of adults ages 60 and over suffer from a mental illness. The conditions that are the most common forms of mental impairment for this age group is dementia, depression and Alzheimer's Many sociologists argue that elderly people are often unnecessarily labelled 'mentally ill', and thus face spurious interaction from staff in residential care homes and, as such, this is another factor to be considered when looking at age and mental illness.

What some sociological perspectives have to say about mental illness

For some schools of thought, mental illness is seen as a form of social control in that it is through labelling some people as mentally ill that it is a way of controlling non-conformist behaviour. Szasz (1971) for example argues that people, who are labelled as mentally ill, can be institutionalised against their will and treated accordingly. Some Feminists claim that women who are treated for depression are treated in a way that takes away their independence by controlling the diagnosis and treatment they receive.

Medicine, Medical Intervention and the Health Professions

Throughout history, medicine has been viewed by many as a progressive force that improves people's chances at fighting diseases and living for longer. For example, diseases that killed people in the nineteenth century (pneumonia, influenza, and bronchitis) are seen as much less threatening and treatable today, thanks to modern medicine. However, the sociologist, Illich (1975) says that medicine has gone too far in its attempts to eradicate pain, sickness and delay death. For Illich this is tantamount to 'playing God'. He uses the term 'iatrogenesis', meaning, illnesses caused by modern medicine.

Examples of these include ineffective treatments that cause more illnesses or complications (Clinical Iatrogenesis); illnesses caused by over diagnosis or over prescription (Social Iatrogenesis);[28] a move away from the traditional approaches of dealing with health and illness (Cultural Iatrogenesis) – as society has developed, aging has become taboo and for Illich, attitudes to this have become almost consumer like in nature, in that various means, medical and non-medical have been promoted in order to combat aging and delay death.

On the other hand, social researchers point out that social and economic developments in the nineteenth and twentieth centuries have led to better health conditions. Factors such as improvements in public hygiene, waste removal and sewage disposal systems, as well as declining family size and better diets have improved health conditions and prevented the spread of disease.

Different Models of Health

Biomedical Model – This model focuses on the physical and biological aspects of health and illness. It also looks at the processes associated with diagnosis and treatment as well as the practices of health care professionals.

Social Model – looks at the wider factors and influences that can be associated with health and illness, such as social, cultural and environmental factors beyond disease and injury. Rather than focusing on health care professionals, this model looks at policies, health promotion and health education.

You can see the application of both these models in the following scenario.

---

[28] We can see the consequences of this in terms of concerns regarding the over prescription of antibiotics, generating the emergence of conditions that are immune to antibiotics.

What would you do if you woke up tomorrow with symptoms of the flu?
Would you:

a) Say, "That's impossible - I can't get the flu. I've had the flu vaccine"
b) Visit your GP in hopes of obtaining antibiotics
c) Purchase vitamins and other herbal remedies
d) Go about your regular business to the best of your ability—it's your body's job to fight off illnesses and there's not much else you can do about it. You have already taken preventative health measures by eating well and exercising regularly, and you just can't afford to take the day off work because you've got a lot on at the moment and the kids need looking after this evening and you've got some friends coming round for dinner....

All of the above choices are likely or possible responses to illness today, though which one you would personally take is socially determined. In some instances your response to this would be based on a biomedical model, in that the symptom would be used to determine the physiological condition and, as such, diagnose the problem and the solution to the problem which could result in a medical diagnosis to confirm the illness and medical intervention to combat the illness. Another response could be social in that environmental factors could be attributable to the condition, and in taking the matter into your own hands by trying home based remedies, healthy eating etc, this would correspond with certain aspects of the social model.

Note that statistics suggest that it is far more likely that women rather than men would feel the need to 'struggle on' and so would be in choice D. On the other hand, seeking out natural or alternative remedies as in C is far more likely of those with the resources to pursue such options, and so is determined by class.

In terms of medical strategies, then each of these four choices also represents a different position, as follows:

So, in response to the scenario, if you answered A, you may be a supporter of conventional western medicine, which would advocate the prescription of minute doses of influenza virus in the form of a vaccination.

If you answered B, you are a supporter of aetiology, which is the branch of modern medicine that attempts to rid people of the virus or bacteria that caused the disease in the first place through drugs and specialised treatment.

If you answered C, you might be into multiple forms of alternative medicine such as acupuncture and aromatherapy.

If you answered C or D, you could be a supporter of iatrogenesis (which as addressed earlier in relation to Illich), which is the belief that modern medicine is actually detrimental to your well being e.g. antibiotics make the immune system weaker over time and can have harmful side-effects; hospitals and doctors are dangerous in that they expose people to bacteria and viruses or there is a risk of misdiagnosis.

There are supporting and critical arguments for each of these approaches.

Activity 59 – Research homeopathy, a popular form of alternative medicine. You may like to visit the website of the Society of Homeopaths in order to understand this medical approach:

http://www.homeopathy-soh.org/about-homeopathy/what-is-homeopathy/ Which social groups do you think would be likely to take up homeopathy, and why?

Globalised Health Industry – The Globalisation of Health

When looking at health and illness, due to the changing and evolving nature of society, we need to also look at the impact globalisation has had on health. Globalisation in this context focuses on global communication, cultural and demographic movements. These transitional processes means that there has been, to a certain extent, an improvement in health, with innovations in health being communicated from one part of the globe to the other, benefitting countries that otherwise would not have knowledge of or access to certain health resources. Different Sociological Perspectives on Health

Functionalist

When Functionalists look at society, they tend to look at the various elements of society as having an impact on how society is maintained and ordered, and how the various facets of society work together for the good of society overall. So, when it comes to health and illness, they look at the favourable condition of health - to be sick not only means that the 'sick' individual cannot fulfil their purpose and role within society, and as such can be regarded as deviant, but the individual can also be a burden to society as a whole. Functionalist thinker, Parsons, refers to the 'sick role' and in looking at this he argues that the sick role is not only biological but also social. There are rights and duties associated with the sick role if it is 'sanctioned'. The rights stem from the sick role if in fact the individual affected is actually sick and has been diagnosed as such by a socially approved medical professional. The duty stems from the individual's responsibility to take appropriate steps to get better by either taking the initiative or by taking steps to improve the situation by seeking medical attention. In this context the deviance of being sick, is excused, temporarily. However, those who use the sick role illegitimately in order to opt out of their societal duties and roles are frowned upon and classed as deviant, with appropriate sanctions being imposed as a result.

Activity 60 - Find out more about 'the sick role'. You may like to read the following article as a starting point:
http://en.wikipedia.org/wiki/Sick_role

Marxist Perspective

As we have seen in other units, when it comes to looking at the Marxist perspective in relation to any aspect of society, for the Marxists the emphasis in on the extent to which society reflects and reinforces the ideology of the ruling classes at the expense and to the detriment of the working or subject classes. Therefore, when looking at this perspective in relation to health, it is no surprise that health and illness is looked at in relation to factors such as:

- Unequal access to health care and resources
- Inequalities in terms of the medical profession
- The social causes of illness (e.g. poverty) – illnesses as a result of social inequalities
- Bad health being linked to cultural deprivation – working classes lead unhealthy lifestyles
- Two tiered health care system
- Doctors indirectly and probably unconsciously work for the capitalist system: their purpose is to get people (the working class in particular) back to work
- Doctors serve to promote the products of pharmaceutical industry = huge business. Thus the main purpose of health care is to ensure that the economy has plenty of able labourers

Feminism

Feminists are concerned with a variety of health-related issues, including the following:

- Seeing the medical profession as serving the interests of a patriarchal bias.
- It is through medicine that certain conditions have been medicalised in order to maintain the control of women. For example, Abbott and Wallace (1990) argue that women who are seen to deviate from what is considered to be the feminine norm are likely to be labelled as mentally ill in order to exercise control
- The medicalisation of child birth: e.g. male doctors view pregnancy and childbirth mechanically, as medical problems rather than as natural processes. Since they can have no direct or personal experience of childbirth themselves, then they are always divorced from the reality of their women patients' experience, and so they lack empathy or the ability to diagnose or treat appropriately. This puts women at a disadvantage in the medical establishment
- Contraception: as it is aimed primarily at women and can have harmful side effects. Contraception is thus socially constructed as a women's responsibility rather than a man's, and so is another responsibility that women must assume but men are freed from
- Status of nurses: they are mostly female and receive lower pay than doctors. Women are more likely to see themselves in the lower-status, lower pay role than men, and men are more likely to have the confidence and higher status that would enable them to become doctors
- Capitalism and women's health: e.g. profitable anti-ageing and weight loss industries, all of which are largely targeted at women. Also, women are necessary for producing next generation of workers and keeping working husbands fulfilled in a traditional capitalist schema where care-giving and nurturance (still largely a female gender role) is unpaid and unrecognised, though absolutely vital

Activity 61 - Compare and contrast two different sociological perspectives on health. Which one do you favour the most, and why is this?

Conclusion

As with education, there are many social and cultural factors at work in healthcare to stratify what is intended to be a neutral and national provision for all citizens. It is important that you begin to see the links and comparisons between the Sociology of Healthcare, and the Sociology of Education and can link this back to issues of culture, identity and socialisation.

Activity 62 – Imagine that you wanted to do research into how cultural and social factors can influence patients' recovery after an episode of major illness.

How would you go about designing a research programme to investigate this? What research methods would you choose, and why?

What issues would you have to consider in order to design an ethical and reliable project, and how would you ensure this?

4.2.4: Work, Poverty and Welfare - Optional

A Level 4.2.4

Key Areas:

- Different definitions and ways of measuring poverty, wealth and income
- The nature, existence and persistence of poverty on contemporary society
- The distribution of poverty, wealth and income between different social groups
- Different responses and solutions to poverty by the state, private, voluntary and informal welfare providers in contemporary society
- Organisation and control of the labour process, including the division of labour, the role of technology, skill and de-skilling
- The significance of work and worklessness for people's lives and life chances, including the effects of globalisation

Defining Poverty

Since 2008 we have been in the worst economic period that the world has experienced since the Great Depression; we are confronted directly with issues of poverty and welfare. Unemployment rates in the US and UK has risen and the UK's currency has depreciated in value. Burglaries are on the rise and people are feeling generally anxious, trying to stay afloat and to avoid losing their jobs, investments, pensions, and homes. Even if we are not experiencing poverty directly, we know that other people in nearby neighbourhoods and communities are. The social reality of poverty and the social construct of wealth and poverty are interlinked issues (along with that of social class) that many sociologists are keen to investigate.

Activity 63 - How would you define poverty?

Poverty is a tricky term to define. It is inherently problematic not only to define but also to measure. For example, being unemployed does not necessarily mean that one is 'living in poverty' - an investment banker who is hoping to be made redundant so he can use his severance pay to take an extended holiday to South America is not 'living in poverty' despite becoming unemployed. Also, working 'in the streets' is not necessarily synonymous with poverty: talented buskers, when given the right pitch, can make quite good money.

There are so many factors to be taken into consideration when trying to understand the concept of poverty and most significantly trying to define it; therefore, it is not surprising that poverty is regarded as being very much dependent upon the perspective it is being examined from and the definition being used. When looking at poverty, significantly, we have to think beyond our own society; looking at the bigger picture we see that citizens of developing countries are living in circumstances that are far worse than those that most of you taking this course will ever experience. For these reasons, whilst some sociologists look at poverty in terms of basic and fundamental human needs being met for survival, many sociologists opt to measure poverty comparatively, observing that what a society considers 'rich' and 'poor' respectively can vary greatly from place to place and over time .

According to a UN Statement made in June 1998, poverty was defined as follows:

"Fundamentally... a denial of choices and opportunities, a violation of human dignity. It means lack of basic capacity to participate effectively in society. It means not having enough to feed and clothe a family, not having a school or clinic to go to, not having the land on which to grow one's food or a job to earn one's living, not having access to credit. It means insecurity, powerlessness and exclusion of individuals, households and communities. It means susceptibility to violence, and it often implies living on marginal or fragile environments, without access to clean water or sanitation."

This definition does seem to incorporate many factors dealing with not only with basic human needs but also social needs as well. What follows are some of the general definitions used in terms of poverty:

Absolute Poverty: Some researchers have attempted to universalise the concept of poverty by developing the term absolute poverty. Absolute poverty is measured against the basic needs such as food, water and shelter - resources that people need in order to survive. In global terms, absolute poverty is defined as being living on less than $1 a day; a reality for many millions of the world's population.

Relative Poverty: It was Peter Townsend who is credited with applying a relative poverty approach in the investigation of the extent of poverty in the UK. Relative poverty is measured within the context of a given cultural or economic setting.

The relative poverty in Winchester, UK would be far different from the relative poverty in, say, Tegucigalpa, Honduras. When people receive an income that prevents them from obtaining these basic needs, they are said to live below the poverty line; therefore, they are considered as being poor in comparison to the majority of people in your society. In terms of relative poverty, one lives below the poverty line in the UK when he or she receives 60 per cent or less of average income.

Townsend (1979) said that;

"Poverty can be defined objectively and applied consistently only in terms of the concept of relative deprivation."[29]

---

[29] Townsend, P. (1979). *Poverty in the United Kingdom*. London: Penguin.

He also stated that:

"Individuals, families and groups in the population can be said to be in poverty when they lack the resources to obtain the types of diet, participate in the activities, and have the living conditions and amenities which are customary, or at least widely encouraged or approved, in the societies to which they belong. Their resources are so seriously below those commanded by the average individual or family that they are, in effect, excluded from ordinary patterns, customs and activities."[30]

For Townsend, poverty was equated with a deprived lifestyle and, as such, to look at poverty only in terms of income and financial resources was not sufficient enough to give us a true indication and sound understanding of the extent of poverty in society. Therefore, other factors such as social connections, decent living and working conditions and so on, were all key elements that contributed to deprivation that excluded individuals from their communities and, as such, would deem such individuals as experiencing poverty.

Tony Byrne (1990) saw relative poverty as a situation where people were able to survive adequately, in that their basic needs were being met, but they were either less well off than they used to be or that they were at a serious disadvantage "in their ability to experience or enjoy the standard of living of most people – for example, not being able to afford an annual holiday."[31]

According to The Rowntree Foundation poverty prevents people from engaging fully with society and should not be regarded as the fault of the individual/s experiencing it.

Subjective Poverty: here poverty is based on the individual's own perception of their situation/circumstances. The individual may have an adequate amount of financial resources to survive but when they look at their position in relation to others and being unable to have the same resources as others, subjectively they see themselves as being in poverty.

---

[30] Townsend, P. (1979). *Poverty in the United Kingdom*. London: Penguin.
[31] Social Services: Made Simple (1990)

Social exclusion: Social exclusion is commonly described as that which comes about as a result of poverty. Though this is true - poor people certainly do experience high degrees of social exclusion – we do need to bear in mind that there are many individuals and groups that are not living in poverty that are alienated from the social and decision-making activities in their societies (people may experience exclusion as a result of race or gender). Social exclusion therefore is beyond the individual's control. They may be excluded due to their inability to fully participate in society. This is often caused by low income, unemployment, poor neighbourhood, inadequate housing and so on. Mack and Lansley (1985)[32] introduced the concept of 'socially perceived necessities'. They distinguished between those who lacked necessities by choice and those who lacked the necessities because they could not afford them. For Mack and Lansley, poverty was the perception of an enforced lack of social necessities that was a significant factor.

A study by Gordon *et al* (2000) indicates that several factors can increase chances of social exclusion, including: unemployment, debt, poor health, dependence on state benefit, low educational achievement and loss of primary integration. Primary integration is defined as a 'feeling of belonging in society'; those who do not experience this sense of integration may be far more prone to committing crimes and to behaving in other socially deviant ways.

Lister (1996) looks at poverty in terms of social exclusion and not so much on income deprivation. Therefore, as a concept, poverty is multi-dimensional, and Lister therefore stresses the importance of looking at poverty in terms of deprivation in relation to societal structures, lack of choice and power, social attitudes and exclusion.

Activity 64 - Note how the definitions above could be incorporated into the definition given by the UN Statement (1998) definition.

---

[32] In Poor Britain(1985)

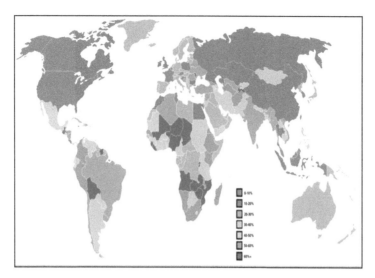

This map shows the percentage of the world's population that live in poverty in each country. This shows us that poverty varies globally.

Measuring Poverty

Gathering quantitative data on poverty is a complex, and often problem-ridden process. Firstly, governments and sociologists must work out a way to operationalise poverty as a concept that is universally recognised and measurable. In the early 1900s Charles Booth and Seebohm Rowntree[33] conducted two large scale and significant surveys on poverty in London and York. Booth reported that the main causes of poverty in London were old age and unemployment. Rowntree found that 20,000 people in York were in poverty. 28% of the population were poor due to low wages and therefore lacked sufficient provisions in the form of food, fuel and clothing, in order to keep them healthy. We have already talked of absolute poverty and how some sociologists define poverty based on the essential resources that one needs for a healthy life in a given social setting. Most recently, this way of measuring poverty has been titled the budget standards approach. This type of measurement identifies the minimum budget required for families and individuals to satisfy basic needs. However, the method has been criticised for discounting community and social activities that people wish to take part in: some researchers feel that measurements should take social exclusion into account. Thus, Townsend created the deprivation index, which is time and place-specific (e.g. incorporates relative poverty) and identifies 12 items (including both social activities and basic resources) that are necessary to the whole population.

---

[33] Booth, 'Life and Labour in East London (1889)
Rowntree's early studies of York 1899, 1936, 1950

The Persistence of Poverty

Despite a rise in UK living standards and several government reforms aimed at eliminating poverty, vast social inequalities still exist. In fact, recent research suggests that the gap between the rich and the poor is widening. There are two main explanations for this growing problem: dependency-based explanations and society-based explanations.

Dependency-based explanations

Dependency-based explanations are associated with conservative political thought, including the views of the New Right and of Margaret Thatcher and John Major. These types of explanations state that poverty is the result of a lack of individual initiative to break historical and family trends, as well as a lack of individual initiative to exit the comfort zones provided by welfare and unemployment benefits. For example, according to David Marsland (1989), research on poverty tends to exaggerate the extent of poverty in that the focus on relative poverty is often confused with inequality which, for Marsland, is a different issue all together. He argues that people will remain in poverty as long as we have an over-generous welfare system; welfare benefits have created a 'culture of dependency' in which people expect (and can become wholly dependent upon) government support.

For Marsland, if we look at poverty properly there has been a steady rise in living standards and poverty has been largely eradicated. In fact the universal welfare provision provided by the state in the form of benefits and the social welfare system has generated a culture of dependency and there is the expectation that the state with take care of society's members. Charles Murray (1980) takes this a step further, claiming that there is a growing over reliant 'underclass' that is a threat to the stability of society. He points to illegitimacy e.g. children being born to unmarried mothers are undisciplined, there are rising crime rates and the social acceptance of unemployment as proof of a growing underclass.

Society-based explanations

People who subscribe to society-based explanations tend to be more politically liberal. They view poverty as the result of the (unfair) structure of society. Marxists specifically point to the controlling, ruling class who dominate capitalist societies as the cause of social inequality. The ruling class, according to Marxists, actually benefits from poverty, and for thinkers like Westergaard and Resler (1974), poverty is symptomatic of wider structures of inequality. For Marxists those who control the means of production in a society can exploit labour and maximise profits. Marxists further state that welfare benefits are deliberately kept at low levels in order to encourage competitive, hard work in capitalist societies (note that dependency-based explanations state that welfare benefits are too high). For Ralph Milliband, poverty is a complex issue and a concept that goes beyond mere economics. For Milliband, status and power are significant factors, as a lack of both means a lack of bargaining power which means that the poor will have lower wages, lesser positions in the workplace, resulting in poverty.

Feminists argue that we live in a patriarchal society, in which men dominate women, placing them in economically dependent and thus inferior positions. A patriarchal society is fuelled by patriarchal ideology, and from a feminist perspective this ideology aims to justify male domination and the exploitation of women. As such inequalities can be exhibited by male wages earners receiving more than female. Women may experience stereotyping in the working environment and therefore receive lower wages as a result. It is factors like this, coupled with other demands, such as childcare responsibilities (particularly an issue for single parents) that had resulted in a situation where women are more likely to experience poverty than men. We do need to be aware, however, that the gap in terms of poverty levels between men and women has become significantly smaller. A Poverty and Social Exclusion survey found that in 1999, there was a 6% gap between the poverty rates of men and women. By 2012, the difference between men and women was not significant. From a Marxist perspective, they would agree that women are powerless in capitalist society and that the work that is done at home is unvalued and unpaid, though it is entirely necessary for ensuring men's economic independence and privilege. If we look at statistics from the Office of National Statistics, whilst the gap can be seen to have been narrowed slightly, there still appears to be a marked and therefore significant difference.

Office for National Statistics: Annual Survey of Hours and Earnings 2014 Gender pay gap based on median (average) hourly earnings not including overtime			
Year	2014	2013	1997
Full time only	9.4%	10.0%	17.4%
Full time and Part time	19.1%	19.8%	27.5%

In the light of the differences in pay and earnings, this is seen by some feminist thinkers as a significant contributory factor of poverty for women.

Some society-based perspectives are less radical. Functionalists, for example, would argue that inequality and poverty is inevitable due to the meritocratic structure of society. Meritocracy is based on the principle that people are rewarded within society according to the amount of work and effort they put in – you get out of something what you put into it. Also, as argued by Davis and Moore (1945), some roles are more 'functionally necessary' than others and require different skill levels, abilities and expertise, and therefore should be rewarded and valued accordingly in order to ensure that the best people fill the roles as needed. Davis and Moore (1945) followed up by saying that in order to motivate people, higher rewards should be given for higher levels of achievement. From this point of view there would be no point in offering a doctor the same amount of reward as someone who works in a factory. This means that rewards in our society are based on talent and effort and not on social background. Note, however, that this view is open to question by other schools of thought, as it seems not to consider other social and structural variables that can impact of levels of earnings, rewards, etc. From a functionalist perspective, poverty serves a function within society. For example, according to Gans (1972), poverty provides employment opportunities for those who work in welfare, as well as providing opportunities for generating income from second and third hand goods. Overall, from this perspective poverty is also a benchmark by which members of society can measure where they stand comparatively.

Another approach is that of the Social Democratics. This approach has elements within it that present not only a New Right influence, in terms of meritocracy, but a Marxist influence (in terms of social inequalities and capitalism). There is the view that poverty is the result of inequalities within society and too high a level of inequality is potentially damaging to society both at an individual and wider social level. However, this perspective does stress the value of a certain level of inequality based on merit, in that those who work hard should be rewarded accordingly and therefore differences in terms of hierarchy levels of income etc are inevitable. Marquand (1998) stated that:

"A meritocratic society is one in which the state takes action to raise the level of the talents – particularly the talents of the disadvantaged – which the market proceeds to reward. First, the state levels the playing field. Only then does the game commence."

There is the acceptance that there is the need for state intervention in order to redress any imbalances within society so as to ensure, according to Lister (2000) equality of opportunities.

Activity 65 –
How do society-based explanations account for poverty?
In particular, how do Marxists and feminists explain poverty?
Which account do you favour, and why?
Social class
The UK government uses a scale from 1-8 to determine class background on the grounds of employment. The details of this scale can be found on the Office of National Statistics website:
http://www.ons.gov.uk/about-statistics/classifications/current/soc2010/soc2010-volume-3-ns-sec--rebased-on-soc2010--user-manual/index.html

The New Right thinkers such as Murray (1991) suggest that the very poor constitute a class that stands aside from mainstream society, and they are referred to as the 'underclass'. They are at the very bottom of the class structure and consequently are excluded from mainstream society. The New Right perspective has been associated with referring to this class as the undeserving poor, whose own moral, economic and educational inadequacies have contributed to their position of poverty; as such, the underclass are seen as responsible for their own situation.

From a Weberian perspective, social class is not only about the extent income and wealth determine the class individuals fall into, but also about the extent to which people have power and status, which enables them to negotiate their position within society. Weber argues that prestige and status can be gained by ownership of property, as such the sick, elderly, unemployed, less educated are not likely to have prestige and power. If in poverty they are not in a position to negotiate or bring attention to their position in society. For some in society this works to their advantage as it helps to maintain the status quo, securing the position of those in power, but to the detriment of those who do not have power.

Activity 66 –

Research this scale of social class using the above website. Where would you place yourself on this scale?

Do you think this method of assessing social class is a good one? Why or why not?

The distribution of poverty, wealth and income

The way poverty, wealth and income[34] are distributed throughout UK society is an important topic of study for sociologists who research class. However, these aspects factors also tie into other social categories, such as gender, ethnicity, age, disability and family structure.

Gender

In looking at this particular aspect of this discussion you should refer back to the feminist perspective of poverty. It should come as no surprise that women are more likely to experience poverty than men, though studies are not exact because statistics on women and poverty are underestimated since most reports are based on entire households rather than on individuals. In 2005, women were 14 per cent more likely than men to be living in poverty, and since 2008 most jobs lost in the global recession have been women's jobs (which as we have discussed, are typically lower paid and in the '5 Cs'). Average female wages are lower than male wages, and because women tend to occupy a larger percentage of part-time and lower paid jobs than men (and do more unpaid domestic and child-care labour) their jobs are more expendable and are the first to be cut in times of recession or economic downturn.

Ethnicity

The Joseph Rowntree Foundation reports that, minority ethnic groups are twice as likely to live in poverty than white people. The Bangladeshi population experiences the most difficulties, followed by Pakistanis, Black Africans, African-Caribbeans and Indians. The reasons for these inequalities vary from group to group and may be seen in terms of levels of unemployment, inadequate housing, and educational achievements and so on.

---

[34] **Income**: It is important to distinguish between earnings and income. Earnings are the portion of household income that comes directly from paid work, whereas income includes things such as investments and savings. There are two types of income: **gross income**, or total income prior to tax and National Insurance deductions, as well as **disposable income**, or gross income minutes said deductions.

The Foundation found that in 2012/1013 the rate of poverty for White people was 18% compared to 39% for Black and Black British, 35% for Asian, 27% for Mixed and 39% for Other.[35]

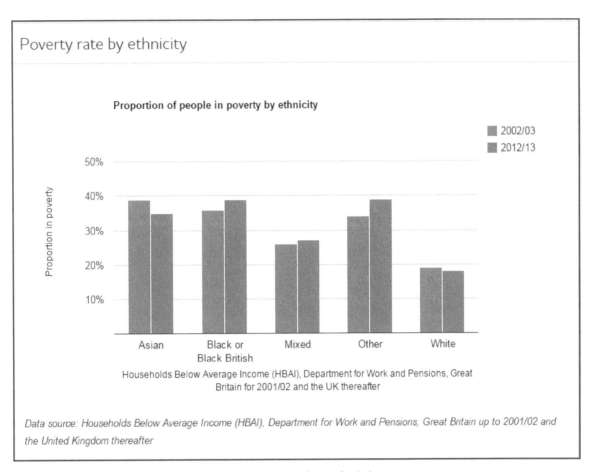

Poverty rates by ethnicity

Activity 67 – Which ethnic minority groups are most likely to live in poverty? Why do you think this is?

You may wish to further your research into ethnicity and poverty by using the website of the Institute of Race Relations. It can be found here: http://www.irr.org.uk/about/

You can also find out more about the UK demographic categorised by ethnicity by looking at census data. After March 2011, the most recent census data is available here: http://www.census.gov.uk/

[35] http://data.jrf.org.uk/data/poverty-rate-ethnicity/

Single Parents

Studies have indicated that single-parent families are, perhaps, the most economically disadvantaged group in society. According to the General Household Survey (2001), of the 25 per cent of households which are single-parent, the vast majority are run by single mothers, and it is Afro-Caribbeans who have far higher rates of single parent families than whites. This survey also shows that about half of single-parent families had a gross income of £150 per week (or less). This brings together the social categories of gender, ethnicity and class, and makes a compelling case for understanding how social disadvantage 'triangulates' across all these three categories. In 2004, it was estimated that 28 per cent of UK children lived in poverty and that many of these children lived in single-parent homes. However, note that according to findings from the Joseph Rowntree Foundation and data from the Department of Work and Pensions, 2014:

"Ten years ago there were 3.8 million children in low-income households. Since then, the number has fallen by about 100,000. The number of children in poverty in lone parent families has fallen by 300,000 while, for children in households with both parents, the number has increased by about 250,000."

Activity 68 – Why do you think single parent families experience poor living standards compared to two-parent families?

Age and Disability

Disabled children experience the highest risk of living in poverty throughout childhood and into adulthood, and certainly experience fewer job opportunities.

Elderly people are also at high risk of poverty. As with all social categories, there are many contributing factors that influence this, such as state versus private pensions, gender, marital status and ethnicity.

The consequences of being poor: the poverty cycle

The poverty cycle or the poverty trap is the name given to the sequence of events, circumstances and social conditions that tend to trap people in poverty, and make it hard for individuals to achieve social mobility. This phenomenon has often been observed in rich countries and has been researched by sociologists. The factors in the poverty cycle can include the following:

If someone has claimed state benefits or been on welfare, then they usually lose these payments once they get a job. Usually, the jobs that people might get who have been on benefits are not highly paid, so in fact individuals may be worse off through working rather than receiving benefits. This fact tends to encourage a culture of non-working, or of dependency on welfare payments, and traps individuals in lower incomes.

Sociologists have observed a poverty culture of an underclass culture among those who have been living for a long time on state welfare. This culture has behavioural norms, values, beliefs and ideologies different to that of the majority, mainstream culture. If an individual becomes thoroughly absorbed into the poverty culture, then they can find it hard to interact with anyone outside of it, and especially to gain a job and enter into mainstream culture.

A culture of dependence on state benefits could be seen as removing an individual's motivations or initiative to change. This could further prevent an individual from trying to gain a job if they have lost the motivation or confidence in their own personal qualities to make the efforts necessary. The poverty trap, or dependence on state welfare, can therefore be very hard to escape.

There can also be wider societal implications; some sociologists, researchers, economists and other thinkers have proposed that a heavily divided and unequal society is actually worse for everyone (not just for those who are in poverty). This could be because having just a few rich and many poor creates a sense of injustice in those who are excluded, and can lead to higher rates of crime, social unrest and instability which is worse for everyone since it leads to greater fear of crime, less social cohesion and higher financial costs (through insurance, taxation and so on) to compensate. For example, the popular sociological book The Spirit Level: Why equality is better for everyone (Pickett and Wilkinson, 2009) argues the case for this.

Social Responses to Poverty (Social Policy since the 1940s)

The Social Democratic Approach: 1940s – 1970s: The welfare state was introduced during the time of the Second World War when our nation was experiencing heightened levels of social solidarity and national identity. The Beveridge Report of 1942 was thought to be the official start of the welfare state: Beveridge identified what he referred to as the 'Five Giant Evils' of poverty:

- Squalor – poor living conditions
- Ignorance – lack of education
- Want – in terms of need and living conditions
- Idleness – work for all; addressing the issue of unemployment
- Disease – recognition that diseases could be linked to poverty

Beveridge in his report identified that state intervention was needed in order to combat the Five Evils. Beveridge's recommendations included:

- National Insurance - contributions from employees and employers
- National assistance or a means tested benefit 'back up' to national insurance.
- Universal family allowance. To help those with low wages
- NHS (1948) = Free healthcare for all. To reduce illness and the burden of claims due to illness and disability

Beveridge's reforms saw the introduction of the following legislation:

- Education Act 1944
- Family Allowances Act 1945
- National Health Service Act 1946
- National Assistance Act 1948

The idea behind these reforms was that people would make payments out of their wages and would in turn receive payments when they were unemployed.

This operated on the assumption that unemployment would be rare and short-term. In the short-term, Beveridge's reforms appeared to alleviate poverty. However, data reports that immediately followed his changes indicated that there were only marginal short-term changes in poverty levels.

Problems occurred when the demand for welfare provision outweighed the contributions that people made.

Criticisms of Beveridge's reforms:

- Insurance calculations for those 'in need' were based on flat rates and did not account for rent differences
- Single women had to pay into the insurance scheme; married women were marked as dependants on their husbands so were less motivated to get paying jobs. As a result sexual inequality in society was perpetuated since this reinforced and entrenched gender stereotypes

Conclusions and Outcomes:

The Government concluded in 1950s and 1960s that the welfare state was the best way to alleviate poverty and continued to follow the Beveridge report. In the 1970s, however, the Conservative government introduced a tax-funded family support scheme to benefit low income families and, in 1974, the Labour government expanded this policy by adding a child benefit scheme. Disability benefits were also introduced in the 1970s.

The New Right Approach: 1979 – 1997

As we noted in our discussion of dependency-based explanations, the New Right believes that the welfare state leads to unnecessary dependency issues and ignores individual accountability: As such, Margaret Thatcher made it one of her top priorities to cut government spending on welfare and to encourage a competitive economy, driven by individual initiative with an emphasis on individual freedom and responsibility and reduced spending by the state.

The New Right policies included:

- Benefit freezes and changes (typically decreases)
- Increased selectivity for benefit giving (increase in means tested benefits)
- Introduction of Child Support Agency (absent parents, not the government, responsible for supporting children)

Criticisms/Outcomes:

- Policies did not reduce poverty, but rather, expanded the gap between rich and poor
- Increase in means-tested benefits had negative implications: more stigma attached to being poor and also created and perpetuated poverty traps (as discussed)

Charles Murray (1989), in the Sunday Times referred to a crisis of the 'underclass'. In terms of the emerging underclass, Murray said that the 'underclass' refers to a type of poverty rather than the extent or degree of poverty. He said that the poor did not just lack just money but could be defined by their behaviour. For example, their homes were untidy and unkempt, the men in the family were unable to hold a job for more than a few weeks at a time, drunkenness and alcohol abuse was common, children were poorly behaved and were more likely to be juvenile delinquents, and that women who had children outside of marriage had 'contributed to' the increase in numbers of the underclass.

Not surprisingly Murray has been extensively criticised for his analysis of the underclass and poverty. Hutton (1996) argues that the idea of reducing welfare expenditure in a time of austerity are based on false assumptions about poverty and the underclasses. Hutton says that when compared to other countries, Britain runs the "...meanest, tightest, lowest cost social security system in the in EU."[36]

The New Labour Approach: 1997

Tony Blair, the new Labour Prime Minister, made it his mission to eradicate child poverty, and he attempted to do so by introducing educational programmes and employment laws that would make people more self-reliant and financially independent. For example, the Sure Start programme introduced new pre-school nurseries throughout Britain for underprivileged children; this freed up single mothers for employment opportunities and ensured greater educational equality. In addition, New Labour introduced the child tax credit and increased child benefits.

Furthermore, New Labour introduced the New Deal Policy, which required people aged 18-24, who had been unemployed for 6 months, to do one of the following: to enter job-related training schemes, to volunteer, or to go back into education. To facilitate this, they subsidised employers to take on people from this age bracket as trainees.

Overall, researchers feel that New Labour policies were more preventative in nature: they did not seem to provide immediate relief but rather attempted to make individuals more responsible and accountable for their finances. There has been debate over how effective these policies have been over the past decade. Some feel that the impact of New Labour policies are too difficult to assess and do not measure up to Tony Blair's predictions; others feel that his policies have made a significant difference.

---

[36] OECD Organisation for Economic Co-operation and Development

Comparison of different approaches to social welfare

As we discussed earlier, until the Conservative government took over in 1979, it was widely accepted that individual welfare was the responsibility of the government: it had been the government's job to ensure healthcare, educational and financial security during times of economic hardship.

The Conservative government completely turned this around by encouraging the privatisation of healthcare, education and pensions. They felt that the NHS had a monopoly on healthcare (they were the only service provider) and could, therefore, give sub-par services to 'customers' as there was no incentive for competition within the healthcare industry. As such, the government started encouraging people to invest in private medical insurance (thus emphasising the higher quality of private healthcare). Additionally, they took state education money and funnelled it into schemes that allowed underprivileged students to attend independent schools. Lastly, they pushed citizens to invest in private pensions rather than the National Insurance scheme.

The Brown years: Labour government 2007-2010:

The last years of the Labour government were marked by the global financial crisis of 2007-08, which put a great deal of pressure on social welfare spending. However, during this time Labour's spending plans and policy were largely the same as those pre-crash. In the run-up to the 2010 election, the Conservatives campaigned on a platform of austerity and social welfare reform, in the name of reducing the national debt: while the Conservatives did not win a majority in the 2010 election, and instead entered into a Coalition government, it was clear that many people at the time supported this change of social policy direction.

For your own research, a thorough analysis of the impact of Labour's social welfare spending and its effects on reducing wealthy inequality, from 1997-2010, is available here.[37]

---

[37] http://sticerd.lse.ac.uk/dps/case/spcc/rr01.pdf

Coalition Government 2010-2015

This was a major turning point, and the five years of the Coalition government was massive changes to social welfare policy and to organisations such as the NHS on all levels. For example:

- The NHS was restructured
- Introduction of Universal Credit
- Pension reforms
- Increase of non-state provision of key services (such as in education or health)
- Increasing local autonomy (such as in the case of Academies or free schools, which are more autonomous than local authority run schools)
- Changing the criteria for receiving benefits, essentially restricting those eligible

As a result of a package of reforms and changes known as Austerity or the Austerity programme, total public spending fell by 2.6% between 2010-2015, though this average masks a huge variation among different sectors, with some services taking much more of a hit than others. For example, some services were cut by around 33%, and spending per child on childcare, Sure Start and early years education fell by 25% between 2009-2010 and 2012-2013. Services for adult users of social care fell by 7% during 2013-2014, with poorer groups more affected by the cuts and by changes to taxation compared to richer groups. Some analysts predict that poverty will worse as a result of these changes from 2015-2020, while the current Conservative government remains in power.

A useful summary of the changes in social inequality from 2007-2013, which includes comparisons between the situation in 2017, 2010 and 2013 in particular, as well as discussion of the wealth inequality between men and women; ethnic groups and abled and disabled people can be found here.[38]

---

[38] http://sticerd.lse.ac.uk/dps/case/spcc/SRR05.pdf

Make sure that you can comment on changes to UK social policy over time, and also that you keep up to date with changes to legislation. By its very nature, government policy is constantly changing as society changes, with new laws coming into effect every year. You can research social welfare policies further by reading the website of the Department for Work and Pensions (DWP), the largest social spending government department. This department is responsible for the State pension, disability and ill health benefits for working age adults:

https://www.gov.uk/government/organisations/department-for-work-pensions

You can find a list of current DWP policies here, and you are strongly encouraged to check this site regularly and keep up to date with welfare and social spending changes and reforms while you study this A level Sociology course:

https://www.gov.uk/government/policies?organisations%5B%5D=department-for-work-pensions

Voluntary and Informal Welfare Provision

In this changed welfare climate, an increasing portion of welfare activities are provided by voluntary organisations such as non-profit charities, as well as informally, by family and friends. Many sociologists think that one of the reasons that the extended family has given way to the nuclear family is the welfare state; people have become reliant on the government for support that used to come informally from family members.

Many researchers have high hopes for voluntary organisations and charities, such as NSPCC and Shelter, which operate for specific causes and not for profits. In line with governmental concerns about self-sufficiency, some charities are dedicated to education and social integration. The Baytree Centre in South London, for example, provides career skills, development opportunities and language classes for migrant women, as well as after-school classes and activities for young girls. Their motto states:

Baytree's central aim is to help raise aspirations, enabling their beneficiaries to achieve their personal, professional and educational potential. By providing training and mentoring in a positive, encouraging environment, they offer practical routes into social inclusion and better opportunities.

(See the Baytree Centre's website): http://www.baytreecentre.org)

The government encourages such activities, as evidenced by their campaigns for community care. These campaigns encourage charities, extended families and local councils to provide welfare services. Supporters of these programmes argue that using the voluntary sector or encouraging family support networks is a much cheaper option, especially when it comes to caring for the elderly. Also, such practices facilitate social inclusion and create less social stigma when it comes to issues such as mental illnesses (e.g. living in an institution vs. being cared for by family).

Activity 69 –
What are the advantages of voluntary or informal welfare provision?

Research organisations such as the Baytree Centre. Do you think that there are any disadvantages to social care being provided through such means rather than directly from government?

Criticisms of a mixed economy of welfare

One of the main criticisms of private welfare is that it is only available to people that are privileged enough to afford it. Thus, some think that the encouragement of private education, medicine, pensions etc. expands the gap between the rich and the poor. For example, students in private schools experience smaller class sizes and better facilities, and retirees also experience inequalities in income. As such, Beveridge's initial intentions (to make welfare equally available for all) have been compromised. Many are worried that citizens will stop supporting state-funded resources and will take on individualistic attitudes similar to those held in America.

Criticisms of voluntary and informal provision

Many feel that the government is pushing local forms of welfare provision to save money rather than to promote social inclusion. Feminists also think that 'informal care' is unfairly left to women, who are not paid for the work and may already have full time jobs. Others point out that voluntary organisations are not enough: many people in need are still neglected and would benefit from more government support.

Activity 70 – Review your work and research on wealth and poverty.

You may like to continue thinking about the sociological dimensions of this subject by investigating some of the changes to the patterns of wealth and poverty across the UK by visiting the following, where you can read a short summary (or even the full report) on this:

http://www.jrf.org.uk/publications/poverty-and-wealth-across-britain-1968-2005

Poverty and Employment

It should be noted that not all who experience poverty are on state benefits, as statistics show that a large number of people who would be regarded as poor are actually employed but the income they receive from their employment is too low to meet their needs. There are a number of sociological explanations for this phenomenon.

Dean and Taylor-Gooby (1992) in their analysis of dependency culture argue that changes in the labour market (with the decline in certain industries and the lack of job security) has had a significantly negative impact on the most vulnerable within society by marginalising them and placing them in a negative light, resulting in poverty.

Globalisation, work and poverty

Globalisation refers to connections and integration that occurs on an international level and therefore can be seen on an individual social level (having exposure and access to other world cultures, from the food we eat to the clothes we wear) to macro impacts and connections through interconnected economies, trade and labour. It is the latter that is particularly significant in terms of the impact globalisation has had on work and subsequently poverty. Large industries, once the suppliers of employment opportunities are said to be utilising cheaper labour costs overseas; the result is, less secure employment that is often temporary and subsequently makes individuals more susceptible to poverty.

Option 2 (choose 1 from the following 4)

4.2.5: Beliefs in Society - Optional

Key Areas:

- Ideology, science and religion
- Social change and stability in relation to religious beliefs, practices and organisations
- Religious organisations, including cults, sects, denominations, churches and New Age movements, and their relationship to religious and spiritual belief and practice
- The relationship between different social groups and religious/spiritual organisations and movements, beliefs and practices
- The significance of religion and religiosity in the contemporary world, including the nature and extent of secularisation in a global context

Introduction

Perhaps you consider yourself to be a religious person. Perhaps you don't. Regardless of your affiliation, or lack thereof, with a religious institution, it is safe to say that you possess your own system of beliefs about the world; you may associate yourself with a particular religion, philosophy or political movement. Even atheism can be considered a type of belief.

Knowing that you and the rest of your peers taking this course will possess varying belief systems, you must now try to remove yourself from your personal views and affiliations in order to study beliefs in society objectively, as a social researcher.

We will explore in the following section how sociologists approach systems of belief as agents of and as barriers to social change. Also, we will examine to what degree belief systems influence society and social systems.

Ideology, Science and Religion

Belief systems do not necessarily entail solely religious (meaning spiritual or sacred) ideas. Belief systems are much broader: they can include anything from religious perspectives, to philosophies, to ideologies. Ideologies are described as non-religious, secular views that are politically or economically charged. Yet this concept gets more complicated; for example, whilst Marxism is an example of an ideology, Marx saw his own views as scientific fact: it was the ruling class that created false, distorted 'ideologies' and imposed them on the working class. We can thus see how necessary it is that we, as social researchers, examine belief systems from an objective (unbiased) distance as far as possible.

Belief and knowledge

Put simply, belief systems are created based on what people think but do not actually know for certain. You can believe that the man who you ask to watch your laptop in a café whilst you use the lavatory is 'good'; you can know that he is a thief when he disappears with it before you return. Religions, ideologies and philosophies are not based on fact; but rather, provide different ways of explaining the world when there is an absence of knowledge.

Science, Religion and Spirituality

Religion has been around since the dawn of humanity; anthropological research shows that even the earliest of pre-modern, hunter-gatherer societies engaged in some form of ritual or symbolic activity. Many groups practised animism, which is the belief that all humans, animals and plants possess spirits or souls. The Trobriand Islanders, for example, used to practise magic in order to influence the spirits before they went out to sea, an attempt to control their environments in what seemed like uncontrollable conditions. The Trobriand Islanders could explain dangerous weather conditions by relating them to the sea spirits' temperaments (Malinowski 1915).

This brings us to the key social idea that religion is based in the experience of the inexplicable or mysterious; this is known as the numinous. This was argued by Rudolf Otto, one of the most important writers on religion in the early twentieth century, in his book The Idea of the Holy.

However, if it were solely the case that religion served only to explain the mysterious, then science would have wholly replaced religion years ago. Religion further has a normative component: it gives people moral guidelines and promises rewards for those who live their lives morally; it provides a template for 'normal' and desirable human behaviour.

Science and knowledge

Prior to the development of science, people sought knowledge of the world in other ways, often turning to religion. However, since the Enlightenment, many people have turned to science as a source of knowledge. Many people think that science is a superior way of gaining knowledge about the world because it is objective and can be applied universally. These people would say that religion, on the other hand, is subjective (biased, based on personal views) and culture-specific.

There are two main schools of thought within science that examine the relationship of science to religion. They are rationalism and relativism:

Rationalist view: Science tells us things about the world that religion does not. Before the rise of science as a guiding philosophy in the Enlightenment, there were many religions, and they all had conflicting ideas. Science allows us to discover real knowledge about the world (e.g. Crick and Watson's 1953 study of DNA, which revealed the process of natural selection).

Relativist view: Scientists operate within their own paradigm and, as such, possess a subjective view on the world, much like any other religion. Atheists tend to disagree with relativists, claiming that they are just trying to appease powerful religious groups.

Atheism and science

It is important to recognise that in the Enlightenment, science was closely allied with religion. The quest to know more about the universe and how it operates was seen by many (for example, both Newton and Darwin) as essentially religious, because it was the attempt to know more about God's creation and to glory in its diversity and wonder.

However, in the modern era science has falsely come to be seen as tied to religion, though in fact science is a method rather than a pro or anti-religion viewpoint, despite the best interests of some famous public scientists to claim otherwise, such as Richard Dawkins.

Think of Richard Dawkins and his controversial publication The God Delusion. To atheists, to think that God exists is completely illogical and incorrect; there is scientific evidence that refutes claims made by world religions such as the in-depth historical research (complete with carbon dating and so on) on whether Noah's Ark could have actually, physically existed, and the scientific impossibility of many religious concepts, such as virgin birth (Christianity) or reincarnation (Buddhism or Hinduism).

However, other atheists are actually more agnostic than they are atheist: they are sceptical of religious doctrine and the existence of supernatural phenomena; they cannot 'prove' that God exists, but they cannot prove that God does not exist.

Spirituality and religion

The New Age movement has facilitated many outlets for people to become 'spiritual' without necessarily practising religious doctrine. Instead of looking to an external, divine being, a seeker of New Age 'spirituality' seeks the divine within himself or herself. New Age movements in the West often draw upon elements of the Far East religions e.g. Buddhism and may include anything from tarot to yoga. As noted by Bruce (1995), New Age thinking includes the following themes:

- Rejection of science as 'cold and hard fact' and as necessitating atheism as a philosophical outlook
- Rejection of organised religion, in particular dogma and intolerance
- Interest in ecology as a scientific discipline that is also amenable to spirituality or a sense of connection
- Scepticism of professional expertise as the expense of personal insight, personal experience and personal intuition

Social Change and Social Stability

Functionalists

Functionalists, note that the essential purpose of religion is to facilitate the collective conscience and to maintain the status quo. The basic underlying principles of all major religions serve the same purpose in that they encourage people to behave 'morally' or, in sociological terms, to abide by social norms. Durkheim (1912) claimed that religion serves a crucial, binding purpose in society. Religion, in producing a collective conscience ensures people join together to invest in the same values and principles. Religion also instils 'morality' in people, and in doing so, maintains social norms. For example, to avoid punishment by God, people do not steal. If nobody steals, then society will function more effectively. Thus, religion serves as an agent of secondary socialisation preventing chaos and encouraging social cohesion. Parsons took this a step further, claiming that religion provides guidelines for people in terms of 'core values' and so religion serves to help people deal with inexplicable 'life crises'. A funeral provides an important 'framework' for a group of people to deal with the loss of a human being. Without these frameworks, which allow people to manage crises more effectively, we would experience anomie (a chaotic society with no social norms).

Neo-functionalism

Neo-functionalists claim that religion serves as an important, cohesive force in modern multi-cultural society. They say that civil religion promotes social solidarity and collective consciousness.

For example, in America, the majority of school children will recite the following 'Pledge of Allegiance' to an American flag, which hangs at the front of the classroom, each morning:

I pledge allegiance to the flag of the United States of America, and to the Republic, for which it stands: one nation, under God, indivisible, with liberty and justice for all.

The words of this pledge demonstrate a fusion of religious faith and patriotism that is ingrained into children's minds from young ages, a phenomenon that seems much less present in Britain where the percentage of non-Christians and of non-believers is higher.

Neo-functionalists might take this comparison a step further, noting how this social solidarity created by civil religion can cause Americans to unite and support their newly elected presidents with enthusiasm and fervour.

Criticisms of Functionalists:

- Religion can actually cause conflict and make society more dysfunctional e.g., Catholics vs. Protestants in Northern Ireland, because they can create and highlight differences between people, exacerbate inequalities and lead to distrust and hate
- As Western societies become more secular, collective worship becomes less common and so would not have the same 'binding' effect that it once did. Indeed, this is in direct contrast to post-modernists who would claim that there is no one fixed monolithic truth, and to try and create or pretend otherwise is to miss the opportunity of multiple identities and meanings that we are otherwise afforded
- In some cases religion can be the source of oppression
- Modern societies are multi-faith; Durkheim spoke of a single, moral community, but this is hard to imagine in reality in a context where many different peoples from different cultures live side-by-side and bring with them diverse religious traditions
- Religion can also bring about social changes

Activity 70 –

To what extent do you think that faith in a multi-cultural society can facilitate social cohesion?

If you were researching this topic as a sociologist, how would you go about drawing up a research title and a robust research project that would give you reliable and valid data?

Make sure that you consider the stages of the research process and your work on research methods when you answer this question.

Marxism

Marxists most definitely do not see civil religion as a positive force in society. Marx holds that religion is an agent of social control, which allows the ruling class to maintain ideological dominance over the masses. Religion, in a sense, 'justifies' hardship and social inequality experienced by the masses, as heaven will be their ultimate reward for suffering during life. They see radical change as necessary in order for the working class to free itself from ruling class oppression, after which we would be able to enter a utopia of classless communism. Religion keeps the masses in order by perpetuating false consciousness: it legitimises ruling class domination and it brainwashes people into thinking that social inequalities are God-given and are therefore predetermined and impossible to change by any human agency.

But in certain circumstances religion can be a force for revolutionary change being the only allowable means of expression and communication and as such, a means of passing on revolutionary ideas e.g. the Southern Baptist Church Movement, headed by Martin Luther King Jr.

Neo-Marxism

Like Marx, Gramsci thought that the ruling class did use religion to assert control over the working class. He agreed that religion was a key element in the maintenance of social control and that the ruling class did, indeed, exercise ideological control over the masses in a process known as hegemony. However, Gramsci felt that religion, rather than conservatively preventing social change had the potential to benefit the working class. He argued that the working class was more than capable of rebelling against the status quo to free themselves from rebellion. Religious officials could combine forces with working class intellectuals to educate the working class about their plight. This type of collaboration could empower the working class to rebel. Religion thus has the potential to become a catalyst for social change.

Maduro (1982) further developed the idea that religion could lead to social change. He focused particularly on liberation theology as it pertained to Latin American countries. Practitioners of this theology felt that it was the church's duty to assist in the liberation of oppressed people; powerful Catholic leaders could side with the oppression in struggles against what they saw as corrupt regimes. For example, in South Africa, former Anglican Archbishop of Cape Town, Desmond Tutu, campaigned to overthrow the apartheid regime (a system of racial segregation in South Africa which oppressed the black majority), which was ultimately abolished in 1990. For Maduro, religion can be one of the main means available to "bring about a social revolution".

Criticisms of Marxism:

- The church does not always support the ruling class
- Marxism does not account for secularisation
- The concept of false consciousness could be nothing more than a biased assumption
- Some argue that religion would still be needed in a communist society

Feminism

There are many different types of feminists so it is difficult to generalise about 'the feminist' perspective on the relationship between religious belief and social change. That said, it is safe to say that many feminists would disagree with the functionalist notion that religions benefits society as a whole by maintaining the status quo. For many feminists, the status quo is based upon patriarchal principles. Feminists argue for social equality between men and women. Many feminists would argue that the patriarchal norms which people learn from religion cause further gender inequality in society, which is already male-dominated.

Many feminists think that religion asserts patriarchal ideology which subordinates females to universal male domination. For example, men dominate the upper positions in the hierarchy of the Catholic Church because women have been deliberately excluded from holding these positions (such as Pope or Bishop) by virtue of gender.

Even in the Protestant Anglican Church, the Church of England, women were also discriminated against until fairly recently. For example, in 1992 the Church of England voted (narrowly) in favour of women priests, with the first women being ordained to this position in 1994. You can read more about this event here:

http://news.bbc.co.uk/onthisday/hi/dates/stories/november/11/newsid_2518000/2518183.stm

More recently, the Church of England voted overwhelmingly in favour of women Bishops in 2014 (though there was a narrow defeat of the same motion in 2012), with the first woman Bishop named as Libby Lane in December 2014, and ordained in January 2015 at York Minster.

In various parts of Islam, Muslim women are also expected to dress in a very restricted manner whereas men are not; world religions therefore typically teach that women are inferior and subordinate to men, and that this state of unequal affairs is God-given and therefore cannot and should not be changed by any human means. For feminist thinker Simone de Beauvoir (1953) religion exploits and represses women, placing them in inferior positions to men.

Criticisms of the Feminist perspective:

- The status of women in religious organisations has improved in religious institutions, especially in the west. For example, although there is still a great deal of debate about women's ordination in the Church of England, this issue in 2012 received a great deal of support such that it looks likely that in the near future women will enjoy parity with men in terms of the positions of power and responsibility they can hold
- Many think that feminist views on religion are ethnocentric. For example, some Muslim women claim that wearing the hijab is quite liberating, and that it is only western women's perception that the hijab is misogynist or an example of patriarchal culture. On the other hand, some Muslim women have also spoken out about the crimes committed against women in Islamic society, such as honour killings, female genital mutilation or arranged marriages, and see the veil as an instrument of male oppression of women

Social Action Theories (Weber)

Weber (1905) famously argued that religion could have a changing, shaping influence on the economy in his study The Protestant Ethic and the Spirit of Capitalism. He pointed out how Calvinism, a type of Protestantism, led people to behave in ways that benefited the workforce and fuelled capitalism.

Calvinists believed in the doctrine of predestination and the ascetic Ideal. It was these two core principles that contributed to the growth of capitalism. With predestination, the belief was that whether or not someone was going to Heaven had already been predetermined by God, and this created what Weber referred to as salvation anxiety.

People would look to external signs that they were chosen. The ascetic ideal or working hard would also relieve salvation anxiety. Calvinists developed what Weber referred to as the Protestant work ethic, or religious devotion to their daily work. Furthermore, as Calvinism is an ascetic religion, in which people deny themselves luxury, profits were typically not consumed or invested in frivolous luxury, but rather, were re-invested in business ventures.

This led to the spirit of capitalism, a continuous cycle in which people pursued profit for the sake of pursuing profit again and so a self-justifying and legitimising system was created: their lives were guided by the notion that they had to earn their places in Heaven and that this could only be done by hard work.

Weber discussed how individuals use religion to justify inequalities in their daily lives e.g. how some people have wealth, power and status and others do not. He calls this explanation for inequality the theodicy of privilege or non-privilege.

He cites the Hindu caste system as an example, claiming that people of the lowest caste can even consider their lowly status as punishments due to bad behaviours in past lives, and people of the highest caste can justify continued discrimination against them for this reason.

Criticisms of Social Action Theory:

- Some feel that Weber only provided partial descriptions, ignoring how religion can shape 'big picture' social realities
- Some argue that capitalism came first and that Calvinists used it to their advantage
- Others claim that capitalism is just as likely to have resulted from other religions or places e.g. Judaism in Central Europe

Postmodernism

Postmodernist theorists note that there is a diversity of religions in society today to choose from. Ideas overlap, and people often create their own belief systems based on bits and pieces of different religions, ideologies and philosophies (Madeline Bunting refers to the process as creating a DIY cocktail). Since postmodernists hold that there is now no 'grand narrative', this is an appropriate response to the fragments of all the world's culture that are now available to us through the modern mass media.

Criticisms of Postmodernism:

- Postmodernists are often criticised in their implication that religions in multi-faith societies are treated with equal status
- Postmodernists do not recognise that religion continues to exercise control over many people's lives, and thus many are not free to play with their own identities and to pick and choose from narratives as they wish

Religious Organisations

Churches

According to Max Weber (1920) and Ernst Troeltsch (1931), a church has the following characteristics:

- Large, formal organisation
- Bureaucratic structure
- Hierarchy of paid (usually older, male and higher class) officials
- Automatic recruitment
- Tries to appeal to all members of society
- May have close relationship with the state
- Accepts wider society
- Claims monopoly on religious truth
- Integrated into mainstream society

A good example of this is the Church of England, which is part of the worldwide Anglican Church. Though the relationship between the Church and State is much weaker that it was in the Middle Ages, it still exists; the Queen is the head of the state and the head of the church. Troeltsch's definition, though based on western churches, can be applied to religions in non-western countries e.g. Islam in Iran.

Activity 71 –

To understand how religion operates as a social structure, social fact or social institution, research the Church of England in more detail.

What is the hierarchy of the Church of England and how is it organised?

You may like to use this website for your research:

www.churchofengland.org.uk

Denominations

Denominations are smaller, formal religious groups that 'broke away' from dominant religious groups. A good example would be Methodism, which was founded by John Wesley in the eighteenth century as an offshoot of the Church of England. According to Neibuhr (1929), denominations are like churches in that they are formal organisations with a hierarchy of officials and try to appeal to all members of society. However, denominations do not maintain close relationships with the State and do not claim a monopoly on religious truth. Also, they may not accept wider society or religious diversity. At the beginning of the twenty-first century, there were 250 Christian denominations in Britain.

Sects

Sects are religious groups that are usually born out of conflict and formulated in opposition to the church. Typically, churches represent the more formalised form of religion since they are institutionalised into society. The historian of religion Ernst Troeltsch's definition of sects claims that they:

- Are headed by a charismatic leader
- Have exclusive membership
- Have no automatic recruitment
- Are typically small organisations with no professional hierarchy?
- Require total commitment of members
- Are opposed to the state and wider society

Despite all of these differences, like churches, sects claim a monopoly on religious truth. As sects are usually headed by charismatic leaders and require voluntary membership by adults, most of them die out when the leader does. However, some sects, such as Methodism, expand and become denominations.

Cults

Whilst sects 'break away' from established churches, cults are formulated independent of past church affiliation. To this extent, they can resemble sects. Bruce (1995) described a cult as a movement with no fixed set of beliefs. Wallis (1985) describes cults as having the following characteristics:

- No claim to monopoly on religious truth
- No control over members' lives
- Emphasis on the individual and their 'inner power'
- Limited contact between members
- Little or no organisational structure; they are the loosest of any religious organisation
- Short-lived

Most cults do not operate under a defined, theological figure. They may include many mystical elements (for example, astrology and tarot) and may promise an increase in wealth and status. Like sects, cults tend to be short lived, particularly if they do not live up to their adherents' initial expectations.

New Religious Movements

There has been much confusion in recent years, particularly in the media, regarding what all of these new, small religious groups should be called: sects or cults. Though we have now established the difference between these terms, they can be confusing to the general public.

To solve this issue, Wallis (1985) coined the term New Religious Movements (NRMs). NRMs include:

- World-rejecting NRMs which are critical of the world and usually adopt communal lifestyle
- Politically radical and morally conservative
- World-accommodating NRMs which have usually have broken off of existing churches. Tend to be politically conservative

World-affirming NRMs which have no collective worship, usually conservative, offer people the opportunity to realise their fullest potentials and so to advance in society by discovering their inner, spiritual powers

The relationship between social change and social stability and religious beliefs, practices and organisations

You may be aware that there are some key structuralist theories that sociologists refer to frequently. Structuralist theories can be divided into two categories: consensus views, which tend to be more optimistic, as well as conflict views, which tend to focus on social inequality. These approaches share a common thread when it comes to religion. Generally speaking, most structuralist theorists see religion as a conservative force (meaning that it preserves the existing way of life and upholds existing norms and values).

The relationship between difference social groups

It is important that you can discuss the social trends of belief and participation in formal religious organisations such as churches, synagogues or mosques. For example, you need to know if and to what extent factors such as class, ethnicity and gender impact on the likelihood of an individual's involvement in religious expression, and of what type.

Moreover, it is important that you have an awareness of how religious behaviour and expression has changed over time in the UK, especially in the last fifty years of the twentieth century up to the present.

Gender

We have already touched on feminism, patriarchy, and the subordinate role of women within religious organisational frameworks. Though most of the main world faiths are monotheistic and headed by one god who is usually described in male-terms, most religions prior to the middle of the Bronze Age were polytheistic and included female goddesses that served essential purposes in ceremonies and rituals. Eventually, polytheism faded and the Hebrew god Yahweh became supreme, remaining the focal point of Judaism, Christianity and Islam today.

Male dominance in world religions

Here are some specific examples of how gender impacts one's abilities to participate in religious traditions (and thus, in many cases, society in general).

- In Catholicism, women cannot hold office. The most esteemed position for women in the Catholic Church is that of the nun, whose dress is much more restricted than that of the male clergy. Women are not allowed to be ordained as priest or Bishop within the Catholic Church
- In Hinduism, only men can become Brahmins
- Males and females can both hold religious offices in Buddhism, but male monks hold higher statuses than female nuns
- In some places, Muslim women cannot enter mosques for worship
- Orthodox Jewish women cannot participate fully in ceremonies

Why has religion evolved this way?

In many cultures, women's subordinate position is partly rooted in a taboo surrounding the female menstrual cycle. In patriarchal and misogynist cultures, the female is seen as 'not man' and as therefore inferior or subordinate. Therefore, anything specific to women is viewed with distrust, suspicion or condemnation. The menstruating woman is seen as 'dirty' or 'impure' and, as such, must be excluded from public areas and social or religious activities.

For example, in the famous Hindu epic the Mahābhārata, there is a moment in which the queen Drapudi, who has isolated herself and wrapped herself in cloth at the time of her menstruation, is publicly shamed. One of her (five) husbands has lost her in a gambling bet to their enemies; she is thus dragged out of seclusion and into public in the middle of her menstrual cycle: one of the most horrific and shameful of events imaginable to a Hindu woman. Even worse, the enemy party attempts to strip her naked by 'unravelling' her garments from her body. In a final, turning point in the story, the god Krishna preserves her dignity by making this piece of fabric endless. Drapudi is thus never fully exposed.

In other religious stories, women are depicted as evil demonesses and sinners. For example, the Hindu goddess Kali is associated with death and destruction and is sometimes referred to as 'Kali the Destroyer'. Also, in the Bible, it is Eve, not Adam, who engages in 'sinful' behaviour first, and further, many women in the Bible are depicted as 'evil' whores, though as many feminist theologians have commented, this is due to the patriarchal culture which produced the biblical texts, resulting in women being deliberately written out of religious history authored exclusively by men.

In conclusion, there are many examples from various Christian, Muslim, Hindu and Jewish texts in which women are victimised, excluded, or portrayed negatively, linking these examples to how women receive unequal treatment in real-world settings.

On the other hand, women increasingly have more options in some societies. For example, women can now become Jewish Rabbis in more progressive or liberal branches of Judaism. Also, the Presbyterian Church of Scotland ordains female ministers, and the Church of England has opened the priesthood and more recently, the Bishopric to women. Women are also more likely to attend church and belong to a religion being more inclined to be drawn to NRMs, many of which operate on principles of gender equality (e.g. Quakers and Unitarians). Some New Age movements have even taken interest in the goddess, and goddess worship is certainly a popular expression of the New Age and could be considered a NRM.

Gender and social class

Here are some trends which tie in gender and social class:

- Young, working class women are more likely to use New Age divination than well-being therapies like herbalism
- Middle class women are more likely to attend traditional churches but may well pick and choose from different holistic activities available in mainstream culture (without subscribing to the spiritual aspect)
- Most women involved in New Age movements are middle aged (men are younger)
- Men and women's interest in New Age therapies are usually 'middle class' e.g. yoga, reflexology, and meditation

Ethnicity

Statistical trends show that, generally speaking, over the past few decades, participation in predominantly white and Christian religious organisations has gone down, whereas participation in religious organisations by British minority ethnic groups has gone up. There are several reasons for this interesting sociological trend.

Reasons for the growth of minority ethnic faiths in the UK:

- Immigration and the maintenance of cultural identity: ethnic minority immigrants seek comfort and familiarity in their home religions. This facilitates a sense of community, social solidarity or collective conscience
- Racism: some groups turn to religion as a way to cope with racism. Through religious activities, people can reinforce their ethnic identities and achieve sense of status
- Degree of control: people's faiths tend to control their everyday actions or provide a comforting and reliable guideline (e.g., in terms of diet or dress), thus reinforcing their senses of identity

Second generation

Generally speaking, it seems that second generation Muslims follow Muslim customs and traditions less than their parents. For example, young Muslims in the UK might wish to break the 'no drinking' rule; also, young Muslim women may not wish to wear the hijab, opting to wear Western clothing whilst still following Islam. Muslim women may go further still and reject the sexual and social restrictions that Islam as a religion places on them.

Practices such as these exemplify Britain's cultural hybridity. However, to call Britain a 'multi-faith' or 'religiously plural' society would mean that all belief systems are viewed as equally valid. As it stands now, the majority of the religious population is Christian, and the Anglican Church (the Church of England) is considered the main religious organisation and is indeed the officially-sanctioned religion of the UK since it is the state religion.

Generation, belief and participation

Overall, it seems that younger people attend church less than older people. The lowest level of participation in church activities is among youths aged 15-19; however, there is a higher level of participation among the 15 and under. The people most likely to attend church are those over 65. Studies show that the proportion of groups attending church declines with each passing generation, and this is likely due to the increasingly secular nature of society.

Age and belief

People aged 15-34 are most likely to be non-believers, whereas moral conservatism and prayer activities are more common among older people. The Church has less of an influence on society today than it did prior to the Second World War.

Age, sects and cults

Middle aged, middle class people are most likely to join cults, given the tendency of cults to promise success and spiritual fulfilment and also due the fact that middle class people are more likely to have the resources and leisure available to them to investigate the alternatives and find out about NRMs. Unlike sects, cults do not require members to withdraw from the world and so suit adults with families.

Young adults are more likely to join sects. Unlike middle-aged people who are settled into families and careers, young people have greater chances of experiencing anomie, or feelings of purposelessness and so turn to the communal or moral support of sects. They also have no dependants and thus have time to participate in the (often) all-consuming activities of sects.

The Significance of Religion

Statistical studies have indicated that an increasing number of people are claiming to be non-believers; church attendance has declined from 11.1 per cent in 1980 to 6.6 per cent in 2005. The 2011 Census revealed that 59% of people identified as being 'Christian' in the UK, though the majority of those who do identify themselves in this way do not attend Church regularly, as can be seen from church attendance data. This was a decrease from 72% who identified as Christian in the 2001 Census (this was the last census – they take place every 10 years). As we have discussed, most researchers into the sociology of religion hold that this shift is a result of the increase in secular culture and the belief that scientific explanations and research take precedence or actively undermine religious viewpoints. Some researchers also feel that there is less of a taboo against atheism or agnosticism, and that it is far more acceptable to publicly state a lack of adherence to any religion. You can view an infographic on the religious landscape of the UK as revealed by the 2011 Census here.[39]

---

[39] http://www.ons.gov.uk/ons/rel/census/2011-census/detailed-characteristics-for-local-authorities-in-england-and-wales/sty-religion.html

Is the data reliable?

It is always crucial when examining secondary sources to analyse the reliability and validity of the information at hand. The data used to draw these conclusions about faith in the UK should be examined carefully. Bear in mind that just because someone attends church does not necessarily make him or her a 'believer'; it is important also to factor in people's self-categorisation and how they choose to define themselves. Also, churches may overestimate or underestimate their attendance figures. Anglican churches, for example, may overestimate their church attendance figures because they want to avoid church closures. Catholic churches, on the other hand, may undershoot their figures for tax purposes.

Researchers may not necessarily be as thorough as they can be; for example, Hadaway *et al* in their study of religious services in the US, counted cars in car parks to measure church attendance when they could not access church data, though obviously they would not have known how many people came in each car and how many used public transport.

Then there are the actual survey questions. You will see that on the YouGov Poll, people were asked if they believed in God, Heaven, Hell, etc. (though the concepts of Heaven and Hell do not exist in Buddhism and Hinduism, meaning that there is evident bias in the research method). In being Christian faith-focused, these surveys which indicate that the percentage of believers in the UK has decreased over the past 4-5 decades could be excluding a large portion of the population that is, indeed, religious but not Christian.

Even with much critical data analysis, it still appears that religiosity is indeed on the decline in the UK.

Activity 72 - Read the following article on religious or spiritual experience in modern Britain. Are you surprised by this? Do you think this presents good evidence for a decline in religiosity or a rise?

http://www.guardian.co.uk/commentisfree/belief/2009/nov/07/religious-experience-research-centre-lampeter

Explaining secularisation

By now, you have been introduced to the 'secularisation thesis', which is the idea that society becomes less religious as it undergoes certain social processes, such as secularisation and industrialisation. Auguste Comte (1798-1857), a key early functionalist theorist, divided human history into 3 stages:

- Theological (when religious beliefs were dominant)
- Metaphysical (philosophy was central)
- Positive (when society is characterised by science/rational thought)

Functionalists such as Durkheim predicted that society was a result of industrialisation and would undergo social fragmentation, which would lead to individualism. (Incidentally, many researchers point out how NRMs are secular and individualistic in nature.)

Marx felt that the capitalist societies, which resulted from industrialisation, would use religion to legitimise social class differentiation but that, ultimately, capitalist societies would shift to classless communist societies, in which religion would no longer be necessary.

Weber also agreed, claiming that as society became more rational, people would turn away from religion and tradition in a process known as de-sacralisation.

Multi-faith societies

Several researchers claim that because so many religions exist in society today, their messages are weakened by competition. How is one to choose a 'right' religion if so many exist?

Wilson (1982) notes that the ecumenical movement (in which Christian denominations have combined forces to offer joint services and to pool talents and resources) is a clear response to secularisation and the plurality of religions that 'compete' with Christianity today. Furthermore, people are increasingly seeing religion as a personal matter, rather than as a communal, institutional activity, and this further causes individualism.

Disengagement

In short, many researchers claim that as the church is no longer closely related to the state, the influence of religion is weakening.

Structural differentiation

On the other hand, Parsons argues that religion, like all social institutions, performs fewer functions as society develops.

As the state takes over many tasks that used to be executed by churches e.g., education, churches can focus more on religious doctrine, moral issues, and on strengthening religious beliefs in society in general.

The continuing importance of belief systems

Not all researchers think that religion is 'dying out' and that society is becoming more secular. It is important to note that much of the 'pro-secular' research on religion in the US is Christian-focussed and has thus been dubbed ethnocentric by several theorists.

Statistics on Muslim and Sikh faiths actually indicate an increase in religious practice in the UK and it is certainly the case that church attendance is also increasing amongst ethnic minorities and in urban areas. Also, if we consider non-Trinitarian religions e.g. Mormons, Jehovah's witnesses, as well as NRMs e.g. Unification Church or Scientology, we will see an increase in religious practice.

In addition the immigration into the UK from EU countries with a strong and recently repressed Catholic tradition, such as Poland, has resulted in a significant growth in church attendance.

Arguments against secularisation

Many researchers argue that the growth of NRMs does not reflect a shift towards individualism and secularisation. In fact, as Stark and Bainbridge point out, all of the major world religions started out as sects. NRMs thus indicate a continued interest in religion and in spirituality. Furthermore, many people have taken to alternative forms of worship such as through Televangelism.[40] Others engage in more personal types of worship without necessarily belonging to a religious organisation.

Explaining the religious revival

Several sociologists think that we have moved beyond the period of modernity in which science and rational thought over-shadow religion, into a period of postmodernity, in which people are exposed to new opportunities for religious activity and can pick and choose from several religions.

Giddens (1991), on the other hand, argues that we operate in a new, radical phase known as high modernity, in which we are always looking to improve society and to advance technology. As such, the existential questions about who we are and why we are here, have been separated from our day-to-day existences. In order to gain spiritual fulfilment, we will, once again, turn to religion.

The international context: Religious fundamentalism

We have already referred to the US a few times in this section. You are probably already aware of the continued popularity of Christianity in the US. Despite all arguments for secularisation, the US, which is one of the most rationalistic or individualistic societies in the world, still maintains a high degree of religiosity.

---

[40] Televangelism, Evangelism through religious programmes on television. Such programmes are usually hosted by a fundamentalist Protestant minister, who conducts services and often asks for donations. Billy Graham became known worldwide through his TV specials from the 1950s on. Other prominent televangelists have included Oral Roberts, Jerry Falwell, and Pat Robertson. Source: Encyclopaedia Britannica.

There are many possible explanations for this. Some think that Christianity and Judaism in the US have become inherently more secular in nature, so as to go along with overall societal shifts. Others think that a large percentage of people who practice Christianity are not doing it solely for religious reasons. Rather, they are partaking in 'Americanism', and it is considered highly un-American to be atheist.

On the other hand, conservative Protestantism is on the rise, and Christian fundamentalist groups continue to hold a lot of political power, meaning that they have the money and resource to maintain a noticeable presence and get their message across.

Religious fundamentalism

The rise in Christian fundamentalism can be linked to a growing global trend towards religious fundamentalism in general, e.g. Jewish fundamentalism in Israel and Islamic fundamentalism throughout the world.

According to Armstrong, religious fundamentalist groups feel threatened by the secular west and its liberal values and are thus reacting, and strengthening. Christian fundamentalists disapprove of abortion and homosexuality. Moreover, Muslim countries are reacting against western involvement in their economic and political issues, in particular those that relate to women's rights.

Activity 73 –
The French thinker Jean Baudrillard (a famous postmodernist) is associated with his work on religious fundamentalism.

You may wish to research his perspective further, and his interpretation of religious fundamentalism as a social phenomenon here:

http://plato.stanford.edu/entries/baudrillard/

Conclusion

Religious and social beliefs are often an emotive topic for sociological study. It is particularly important to start seeing the links between beliefs and ideas and sociological perspectives and research methods; you will study this further in Unit 4.

Option 2

4.2.6: Global Development

Key Areas:

- Development, underdevelopment and global inequality
- Globalisation and its influence on the cultural, political and economic relationships between societies
- The role of transnational corporations, nongovernmental organisations and international agencies in local and global strategies for development
- Development in relation to aid and trade, industrialisation, urbanisation, the environment, war and conflict
- Employment, education, health, demographic change and gender as aspects of development

Introduction

Right now, you are most likely sitting comfortably in your home, in a library or at a desk with your eyes fixed on a laptop or computer screen. Perhaps you have a take-away coffee in hand. You are immersing yourself in these descriptions of British society (or obsessively checking your email!). After completing this course, you may even carry on with university-level study, sipping more lattes, reading more books and staring at more high-definition laptop screens.

You are among the elite few.

The twentieth and twenty-first centuries have brought about rapid changes in our world, particularly in the last few decades, in which we've seen the global spread of ideas, technology, capital and commodities. To complete a specialised educational qualification, online and from the comfort of your home, would have been unimaginable during the years surrounding your birth. Today, we inhabit a society in which people can aspire to a high quality of life, enjoying luxuries such as high-speed Internet access and take-away coffee (the latter commodity, incidentally, typically reaching us through the process of globalisation, for example via a well-known American coffee chain).

Unfortunately, vast inequalities now exist in our world: nearly 1.3 billion people live on less than a dollar a day, or rather, on around a third of the cost of a take-away coffee which so many of us buy regularly without a second thought.

This section will discuss and analyse the sources of inequality in our world: not just in monetary terms, but also in terms of access to key resources, such as education and healthcare. We will discuss basic terminologies relating to the spread of Western industrialisation and other development strategies. We will also outline the theoretical perspectives that influence global aid, trade (and thus development) examining strengths and criticisms of each. Lastly, we will tackle how global development links to social issues surrounding gender, health, education, the environment and conflict.

Understanding Development: Describing and measuring development

You may have already read articles, overheard discussions, and even engaged in political debates about 'third world' countries, in which people experience poorer living conditions than we typically do here, in the first world. These classifications of 'first', 'second' and 'third world' are actually based on political, rather than economic, differences. A quick breakdown:

- First world – capitalist nations (which are consequently wealthy), such as the UK, USA and Japan
- Second world – communist nations, such as China. It is more common now to hear the emerging economies of former 'second world' nations described as BRICS: standing for Brazil, Russia, India, China and South Africa
- Third world – countries that did not align themselves after the Cold War. These countries, such as Bangladesh and Ghana, are often poor, and include a number of countries in South America, Asia and Africa

Some people are critical of these categorisations in that they imply that the first world is 'better' than the third world because of the implications of the terms, though it is certainly true that the first world is more developed and suffers from fewer of the problems of extreme poverty and deprivation that characterise third world countries.

A classification that people often use to divide the world in economic terms is that of the north/south divide. The northern hemisphere is considered much wealthier than the poor southern hemisphere, though of course there are exceptions. Although these terminologies are more politically correct than saying 'rich countries' and 'poor countries', the division is highly oversimplified (think, for example, about Australia and Romania). As such, there is yet another system of classification: the rich minority world and the poor majority world, which avoids geographical references altogether, and also makes the important point that most of the world's population do not enjoy the kinds of living standards of those in the UK, and that most of the world's population is in extreme poverty.

And finally, the most detailed classification regarding development is as follows:

- MEDCs – more economically developed countries (Britain, Japan, US)
- FCCs – former communist countries that have shifted to capitalism since the Cold War (Eastern Europe)
- NICs – newly industrialised countries (Mexico, Brazil) but now more commonly specified as BRICS (see above)
- LEDCs – less economically developed countries (Sierra Leone, Bangladesh)

This approach seems the most thorough and detailed, yet it was designed based on a western value system of measuring GDP and wealth.

Measuring development

There are many different ways through which development is currently measured. Perhaps the most common and well-known approach involves measuring the gross domestic product, or GDP, which accounts for the total value of all goods and services produced by a country. Though high GDPs indicate productive economies, in which a great deal of wealth is created, this is not always the case. In fact, people criticise the use of GDP measurements in that they do not account for the way that wealth is actually distributed in a country: wealth may only reside in the hands of the elite (the 1 per cent or 10 per cent in recent popular terms from the Occupy Movement) and may trickle 'up' rather than down, as anticipated.

Activity 74 - Do you think GDP is a good way to measure development?

Other ways of measuring development include:

- Gathering statistics that relate to the availability of basic human needs (clean water, food, infant mortality rates, etc.)
- Gathering statistics that relate to the provision of education and healthcare
- Gathering statistics that relate to human freedoms (there is a danger of ethnocentrism here, as 'human freedoms' are defined by the usually Western researchers that are measuring them)

Lastly, there are the composite indicators such as the United Nation's human development index (HDI), which combines statistical measurements of education, health and life expectancy.

Activity 75 –

Research the Human Development Index further.

Do you think this is a good way to measure development?

Read the latest HDI Report. Which countries rank highest, and which lowest? Does this surprise you? Is there anything else which surprises you?

You may like to use this website to start your research:

http://hdr.undp.org/en/statistics/hdi/

Modernisation theories

Explaining underdevelopment

Modernisation theories have been developed based on the notion that the majority world should become more like the minority world. Many of these theorists claim that certain countries are underdeveloped because they lack key resources, which would allow them to 'advance' from one 'stage' to the next along the following continuum, developed by Walt

Rostow

Rostow's cycle of societies:

- Stage 1 – Traditional society. Economies operate at subsistence level, meaning that people hunt, gather and grow food to feed their own (usually small) populations, leaving little product for trade (and thus little trade for profit)
- Stage 2 – When producers in traditional societies make technological advances, they become more efficient and can sell surpluses for profit
- Stage 3 – Entrepreneurs begin to reinvest profit from trade, expanding businesses to generate even more profits. This stage is the equivalent of industrialisation in the West
- Stage 4 – As societies become more industrialised, there is a greater need for certain logistical and social services. There becomes a demand for educated workers, transportation specialists and, eventually, a variety of specialised service industries. During this time, stable governments and taxation systems evolve
- Stage 5 – The stage of mass consumption. As wealth trickles down, raising people's salaries, people's lifestyles begin to improve and they begin to invest in goods beyond those which satisfy their basic needs. This stimulates demand and the consumer society, which also creates jobs and stimulates more production

Rostow felt that all societies resided in one of these categories; he claimed that it was the task of development researchers to work out why some societies e.g. majority-world countries, get 'stuck' at one stage, or locked into a cycle of poverty, and cannot progress to the next stage. He claims that usually it is because majority-world countries lack the technology and entrepreneurship necessary to break these cycles.

Activity 76 – Can you try to relate Rostow's cycle of societies to the development of the UK or to another country you are familiar with?

Talcott Parsons has further pointed out that cultural factors often prevent majority-world countries from progressing. Whereas capitalist nations are driven by entrepreneurship and individual achievement in a meritocracy (though of course other sociologists contend this), many majority-world cultures operate based on values of collectivism and ascribed status. People are often locked into small, rural and insular communities and, as such, are not contributing to industrial advances in urban centres. This makes it difficult for them to make the sweeping economic shifts necessary to 'progress' to the next stage. However, this view could also be criticised for ethnocentrism.

Promoting development

Modernisation theorists discuss many potential ways to promote development in majority-world countries. Most of these policies involve capital injections that are intended to boost technological processes and ultimately lead to the creation of industrial infrastructures. Money is given to the majority world in the form of aid (grants or loans) as well as through transnational corporations (TNCs) that set up business operations in the actual locations where development work is being done. Other investments are aimed at making major cultural changes, establishing modern educational institutions and mass media circuits.

Evaluating modernisation theories

Modernisation theories are among the macroeconomic theories that have been (up until the 1970s) greatly valued for their transformative implications. Modernisation theories intend to transform entire economies, thus improving lives of huge populations. They have been created based on thorough research of the history of development of countries, so seem promising in this aspect.

However, modernisation theories are quite ethnocentric. They assume that western capitalist societies offer the best way to live and often overlook a diversity of resources that are available in both poor and rich countries. Also, these theories often pinpoint local, isolated processes as the causes of impoverished living conditions, failing to account for inequalities in global trade as well as historical occurrences such as colonialism.

Neoliberalism

Neoliberalism has become the dominant perspective in development since the 1970s, and was developed in close association with the New Right movement of the 1980s (you will recall we discussed the New Right in the AS section of the course). Like modernisation theorists, neo-liberalist theorists think that the majority world should aspire to the economic structures of the developed minority world; however, neoliberalism claims that this transition should be done primarily through trade, rather than aid.

Neoliberals hold that development should be achieved through the encouragement of free trade, thus minimising government interference and allowing the laws of supply and demand to preside. However, in many countries the State heavily subsidises public services such as education and healthcare: this creates high taxes and thus prevents people from making entrepreneurial investments in private businesses. It is the private sector, according to neoliberals, that will create healthy competition, fuelling a productive economy and ultimately benefiting the consumer.

The government interferes by creating import tariffs (which make imported goods more expensive than domestically produced goods), and subsidies (which are payments given to domestic producers) in order to make them more competitive. Things that might seem on the surface helpful to the economy are really only bolstering domestic businesses artificially in the short term. These businesses will become dependent on the government and thus will have less incentive to improve or advance in order to become globally competitive. In the long term, the government thus prevents productivity (and development) by interfering with the economy.

Neoliberals are further critical of aid-centred policies. They claim that, by injecting capital into majority world countries, minority world governments are breeding a 'culture of reliance' and keeping these economies stagnant.

Promoting development

Neoliberals have created and implemented structural adjustment planning, which involves attaching terms and conditions to loans given by development agencies e.g. the World Bank and IMF. The basic stipulations are as follows:

- Focusing production on exports
- Allowing the private sector to provide public services
- Agreements not to subsidise producers
- Agreements to reduce import tariffs
- Deregulation – e.g. reducing labour and environmental laws, as well as business taxes

Evaluation

The neoliberal perspective has been lauded for its usefulness in promoting growth and self-sufficiency in majority world countries and it is one of the most dominant perspectives in modern economic theory. However, it has been criticised by many as having misguided views about the free market and about the sanity of liquidating natural assets (clean water, air, climate and soil) for the same of short-term economic gain.

For example, businesses from wealthy countries already have inherent advantages in the so-called 'free market'; they operate with more efficient processes and thus can reap greater benefits from economies of scale. Other people criticise structural adjustment planning specifically, noting that, for example, the privatisation of public services can exclude the poorest members of these societies.

Dependency Theory

Dependency theory is rooted in the Marxist movements and evolved in the late 1960s. Basically, dependency theorists think that poverty was caused by the exploitation of the majority world by the minority world.

Andre Frank (1967) created a historical model of exploitation, which claimed that the exploitative relationship between the minority world and the majority world evolved through 3 stages:

- Mercantile capitalism – when European merchant explorers, such as Columbus exploited closed economies of trade)
- Colonialism – when these informal exploitative practices were formalised in an 'era that wrought devastation on the majority world'. In the majority world, economies were reshaped, geopolitics were distorted, and cultures were undermined
- Neo-colonialism – decolonisation gave the illusion that exploitative practices were being stopped when, in fact, they were not. We are not in a stage of post-colonialism, but rather, neo-colonialism. Former colonies are now satellite nations that remain subservient to, and exploited by, former colonial administrators, or metropolis nations

Evaluation:

Dependency theory has been positively recognised in its portrayal of the world as interconnected, e.g. members of societies who are living in poverty are not blamed for their dispositions. That said, the theory is criticised for not providing any tangible solutions to global inequality, thus implying that development is not possible in the majority world. Also, dependency theory is criticised for making incorrect generalisations, e.g. the wealthy nation of Norway has never held colonies, and the former colonies of Canada and Australia hold considerable wealth.

Counter industrial movements

Up until now, all of the perspectives that we have discussed have agreed on one thing: that the western model of industrial development is the one that the world should aspire to. The following perspectives, however, would disagree with this statement:

Environmentalism

Environmentalists stress that the long-term, ecologically destructive effects of industrialisation are in no way justified by any short-term benefits that industrialisation may yield. Industrialisation results in the degradation of the biosphere, the loss of biodiversity and the over use of resources. Moreover, the economy is dependent on the environment - not the other way round. It makes little business sense, therefore, to destroy the very thing that provides vital services, in the form of crop pollination, soil fertility, biodiversity, clean air and water.

Neopopulism

Neopopulists claim that industrialisation causes social problems. The mechanisation of labour displaces factory workers and leaves people jobless. Industrialisation also destroys close social networks in communities by creating urban centres, which are socially alienating and often rampant with crime and illness, and also breeding grounds for mental illness, anomie and despair. Lastly, poor nations often become dependent on rich nations for technological materials and knowledge. Ernst Schumacher (1973) in his ground-breaking economic text Small Is Beautiful further claims that industrialisation is centred on the (false) idea that human beings are fulfilled by consumption.

People-centred approaches

These perspectives are rooted in microeconomics and sustainability. Perhaps the pioneering thinker behind people-centred approaches was Mohandas Gandhi (1924) who proposed the idea of swadeshi, or small, self-reliant communities as well as the idea of 'moral economics', which is much similar to the concepts behind contemporary sustainable development. In sustainable development things are created and constructed only to meet the needs of the present without jeopardising the availability of resources for future generations. The three types of sustainability are:

- Environmental sustainability – in which people do not use natural resources faster than they can be replenished
- Economic sustainability – in which people in communities to not rely on outside aid
- Social sustainability – in which everyone is included and no one is marginalised

Ernst Schumacher also created the concept of intermediate technology, in which producers in majority world countries are given technologies that improve their current ways of producing, rather than replacing them entirely with western alternatives. In his seminal work of alternative economics, Small is Beautiful, he proposed that small and localised, resilient economies were a better model of progress rather than large-scale and globalised ones.

Activity 77 –

Research the counter-industrial movements further. Do you think these movements offer a good model for global development? Why or why not?
You may like to start your research here:
http://www.ef-schumacher.org/
http://www.schumacher.org.uk/

Another important initiative has been microcredit, in which people in majority world countries are given access to small loans to be invested in businesses. A well-known example is the Grameen Bank in Bangladesh. Here is an excerpt from their website:

Grameen Bank (GB) has reversed conventional banking practice by removing the need for collateral and created a banking system based on mutual trust, accountability, participation and creativity. GB provides credit to the poorest of the poor in rural Bangladesh, without any collateral. At GB, credit is a cost effective weapon to fight poverty and it serves as a catalyst in the overall development of socio-economic conditions of the poor who have been kept outside the banking orbit on the ground that they are poor and hence not bankable. For more information on the Grameen Bank: www.grameen-info.org.

Activity 78 –
Research the Grameen Bank further and investigate the lending organisation Lend With Care:
http://www.lendwithcare.org/

Do you think this is a good model of development? Why or why not?

Evaluation of counter-industrial movements:

These approaches are useful in that they highlight the environmental and social costs of development. They are very long-term focused, aiming to preserve resources and enhance living conditions for our future generations as well as address pressing issues of inequality, such as that based on gender or disability. Also, these approaches can empower local communities to take control of aspects of development.

However, some people see the small-scale focus of these approaches as problematic and as having too limited an impact. Some people think that these counter-industrial theorists are too caught up in the short-term implications of industrialisation and they feel that any damages caused by industrialisation will fade over time.

Activity 79 - Do you think that small-scale, sustainable initiatives worth the effort and long-term benefits, even if they only impact on a limited number of people?

Or do you think that majority world countries reap more benefits from larger, short-term capital injections?

Research the debate on international aid further, making sure that you understand different perspectives and that you form your own opinion.

You may like to start your research by reading some blogs written by people who work for the Department for International Development (DFID)

http://blogs.dfid.gov.uk/

Globalisation

The chances are that you have already taken part in the process of globalisation (at least indirectly) at some point today. Are you wearing clothing which is not handmade? Did you have a cup of coffee this morning? These might sound like silly questions, but you have probably never sat down to research where, exactly, the fibres in your jumper were spun, or where the coffee beans, from which your derived your morning dose of caffeine, were grown.

Globalisation is a process that has an impact on our daily lives more and more as each day passes. Nations which were once isolated are now interconnected through rapid means of communication and transportation, as well as complex economic networks. With a simple Google search, you can access commodities from, and information about, locations around the world.

Causes of globalisation:

- Economic development – trade liberalisation (increased by the neoliberalism movement) decreased barriers to free trade. Also, transportation technologies have made the shipment of goods easier and more cost-effective
- Political factors – e.g. organisations such as the United Nations and the European Union engaging in dialogue; also, large-scale crises, such as global warming, that necessitate global cooperation
- Sociocultural factors – e.g., the Internet, which makes social interaction and commerce possible in even more ways and so expands the process of globalisation

Effects of globalisation:

- Diffusion of supply chains – products are now manufactured in multiple countries
- Corporations can now exist as powerful, autonomous entities, free from the nation state
- National economies have been integrated into a global system. This is particularly evident right now; as the US experiences its worst economic crisis since the 1930s, so are an increasing number of countries around the world
- Political implications – e.g. the shift of power from nation states to TNCs
- Diversity – e.g. a multitude of food, religion, clothing, and entertainment from different parts of the world available in one place. At the same time, homogeneity, as certain cultural artefacts can be found almost anywhere (e.g. McDonald's, Hollywood films – is this just a part of cultural imperialisation?)
- Interpersonal networks become extended through online social networking (Facebook, My Space)

Positive views on globalisation:

- Neoliberalists think that globalisation provides vast and important opportunities for trade
- TNCs use these global markets to spread wealth
- When nations have an economic interest in one another, governments are more likely to address or solve political problems
- Cultural effects are seen as positive in that they increase freedom of individual choice

Negative views on globalisation:

- Neoliberalism has forced free market politics on areas of the majority world that do not have the capacity to abide by this system
- Neoliberalism = (destructive) capitalism. Large, profit-driven corporations operate without considering environmental and social implications
- Many argue that globalisation increases inequality by increasing the power of minority world countries; also disproportionately benefits the wealthiest consumers, who exercise greater choice over consumption patterns
- It has not increased positive, inter-cultural dialogue, but rather, has created cultural imperialism (e.g. Americanisation)

Activity 80 - Reflect on globalisation now. What is your initial opinion: are you in favour or against?

Is globalisation new?

The Transformationalists would argue that it is: we live in time of outstanding globalisation which is serving to transform political institutions in a process that is certainly not uni-directional. This means that it is impossible to view globalisation as the project of just one powerful country (such as America) or just one driving force. Instead, globalisation is a decentred force that works in many different directions.

However, one of the most notable trends in globalisation is that the power of nation states is being remade under globalisation, to include the new powers that TNCs now have and the new reality of global communications and media. This position in the globalisation debate is often seen as a mid-way point between the globalisation sceptics and the hyperglobalisers.

The Hyperglobalisers are of the opinion that globalisation is a modern and happening process whose effects can be felt everywhere. For example, in the modern west, we notice the outcomes of globalisation when we visit a modern shopping centre where we can acquire goods made and imported from all over the world. The hyperglobalisers therefore see globalisation as a trend that is indifferent to national borders, with the most prominent trend being the increasing power of market forces at the expense of democratic government. This leads to a world without borders which is the characteristic state of globalisation.

Finally, when hyperglobalisers analyse globalisation they pay particular attention to the role of the nation state in an increasingly interconnected world. An important point is that national governments no longer have much control over their own economics due to the power of international trade, and that each national economy is now subject to the shocks and changes that are being felt within the global economy. As a result, there is a corresponding knock-on effect on democratic government: politicians no longer have the power to take on TNCs, and citizens in each nation state can see that governments are weak. This leads to a despondency and despair about any individual's power to change anything, and so to a characteristic powerlessness of the individual that is typical in a globalised economy.

The Sceptics (as their name suggests) argue that globalisation is certainly not as an important a trend or process as the hyperglobalisers or the transformationalists would argue. In particular, sceptics doubt whether globalisation is all that modern a trend and without any other historical precedent. Sceptics say that in fact, in the past there was also significant globalisation.

Moreover, the sceptics say that as a trend, globalisation is confined to certain groups of countries. As such, we do not yet have a truly global economy: in Europe, North America or Asia-Pacific, most of the trade that takes place is between countries within these regional blocks rather than between each regional block. Therefore, the local or regional (rather than the global) is still an important dimension and must not be overlooked.

With this in mind, sceptics focus on a process they have called regionalisation. This is the trend outlined above: countries can trade with ease within a geographical region (e.g. Europe) due to modern technology and communications, but so far trade between regions does not seem to have become as important, even though hyperglobalists would claim otherwise. In fact, the regionalisation of the economy is actually a trend away from a true globalisation, and compared with trade networks of the nineteenth century which were truly global, the truth of modernisation is that regions are becoming ever more important.

Finally, sceptics do not think that globalisation as a trend is overturning the strength of the nation state, and it would therefore be a mistake to think that the power of national governments is in decline. Since national governments are often key players in international trade agreements and policies, the nation state still has a large role to play in shaping national economies and decisions about international trade.

Activity 81 - Consider the three perspectives on globalisation given above. Which one do you think you agree with the most, and why is this?

Processes and Influences – Aid

Types of aid

Aid can consist of many things, including money, food, medicine, technology, materials, knowledge, expertise, or weapons, and is usually offered by a gift or a loan. Government aid can be given for different purposes; for example, relief aid is usually given to countries following large-scale disasters (man-made or natural, such as the 2005 Tsunami), as a short-term way of preventing a situation from worsening. Development aid, on the other hand, has more long-term implications and attempts to improve and advance knowledge and infrastructure over time. Aid is distributed bilaterally (directly from one nation to another) and multilaterally (when multiple governments contribute to a common pool of money that is then redistributed e.g. through the World Bank). In addition to government aid, NGOs, or non-governmental organisations (such as charities) also deliver aid and communal banks give loans.

Models of development aid:

We already touched on this topic in the previous section, and there are several theoretical perspectives on how, where, and to what degree aid should be distributed.

Modernisation theory – For modernisation theorists, aid is best distributed directly and now. Modernisation theorists support large-scale, rapid transformations to the economies and infrastructures of majority-world countries.

People-centred perspectives – For people-centred theorists, aid should be small-scale and local, aiming for long-term sustainable benefits to the economies of majority world countries (think: intermediate technologies, microcredit schemes, investments to support local teachers and doctors and to reduce gender inequality by educating girls and empowering women).

Critical perspectives on aid:

Many theorists are out to counter the misconception that aid is always a positive measure with positive implications. Specifically, dependency theorists say that aid-giving governments often have hidden, political agendas. For example, in what is known as tied aid, governments give 'aid' to the countries that house their most prized producers, in turn benefitting themselves but also ensuring long-term commercial interests. Also, 'aid' was given to oppressive, right wing governments during the Cold War to hold back communism. Neoliberalists hold that aid is counterproductive, leading to false, short-lived economic buoyancy and cultural reliance on hand outs. This actually prevents majority world economies from developing.

Loans and debt

Some Theorists support loans as the best forms of aid, in that they will eventually be repaid so that they money can be used again. However, dependency theorists disagree, pointing out that nations can, and will, often take out loans to service the interest of previous loans without reducing the amount that they have borrowed.

Trade

Many theorists feel that trade has the potential to boost the economies and fuel the infrastructures of majority-world countries more so than aid. Neoliberals, for example, argue that with a free market that is now slowed down by subsidies, high taxation, import tariffs etc. majority-world countries could benefit, buying and selling goods without restriction. Neoliberals have taken two key measures to promote and maintain this free market:

- Negotiations with organisations such as the World Trade Organisation, which eliminate protectionist policies to open markets to global competition
- Implementations of structural adjustment policies to accompany World Bank loans, encouraging recipients to incorporate free market principles into their economies

Criticisms:

Dependency theorists, on the other hand, argue that such theoretical ideals are intangible and impractical: trade has been distorted, benefitting the wealthiest of nations and capitalising on the poorest of nations, since colonial times. For example, once imperial powers took over certain countries, they manipulated production in these countries to serve, what they felt at the time were, their best interests. This meant that colonies had to stop producing a diversity of crops and materials, focusing on just a few cash crops and primary resources. As such, the majority world continues to be reliant on the production of crop monocultures, and when these fail, they have no 'back up plan' of sorts; also, the oversupply of these crops can lead to over-competition, which drives down prices in the global market.

There are further contemporary processes which skew the global market to favour the rich. For example, the structural adjustment policies created by neoliberals cause majority world countries to cease protectionist policies, which many minority world countries continue to implement. As such, rich countries can afford to price their goods more cheaply and to sell surplus goods at cost in majority world countries in a process known as dumping. This drives majority world countries out of both global and domestic markets.

Fair trade

People have responded to unfairness in the global market with people-centred trade initiatives, such as fair trade. Fair trade initiatives are centred around the formulation of co-operatives, or collectives of producers who work together to produce exports, thus eliminating competition. By generating more produce, they can trade directly without losing profits to middlemen.

They also operate with a set minimum price and set rules for environmental and social responsibility. Often, a premium is factored into prices that can be spent locally on medical and educational services.

Many are sceptical of fair trade, noting that large corporations such as Nestle seem to take advantage of the fair trade label to appear socially responsible. Neoliberals argue that, in distorting the market, free trade is not beneficial in the long term. For example, there are a limited number of free trade products e.g. bananas, cocoa, coffee; many groups are encouraged to specialise, and this creates over-competition.

Activity 82 –

Research fair trade further. Make sure you understand the key principles and can discuss some facts, figures and case studies in relation to how it operates.

Do you think this offers a good alternative model of global development? Can you see any drawbacks? If so, what are these?

You may like to start your research here:

http://www.fairtrade.org.uk/

A History of Industrialisation

As discussed, the process of industrialisation, through which economies shift to mechanised, mass production, is often considered the key marker of progress, separating western from non-western, minority from majority. Modernisation theorists in particular emphasise the centrality of industrialisation in the process of development.

The Industrial Revolution began with Great Britain, followed by Western Europe and the US, in the eighteenth and nineteenth centuries. These nations had access to crucial resources (e.g. colonial riches, technological innovations, and an artisan class) which made industrialisation possible. Also, in Japan, the state pushed for similar shifts to mass production with different degrees of success. Lastly, several East Asian countries, such as Taiwan, Singapore, and South Korea, have more recently adopted export-focused methods of industrialisation, forming what are known as tiger economies.

Reasons why industrialisation is key to development:

- Efficient, profitable production techniques
- More affordable products
- Political change = freer and more democratic societies

Economic policies used to manage industrialisation:

1. Import substitution industrialisation (modernisation):

This policy, advocated by modernisation theorists, protects local producers with subsidies, replacing imports with domestic produce. Modernisation theorists emphasise the importance of protecting and fostering local industries so that they may, one day, be competitive in the global market. Neoliberals argue that such protectionist policies distort the free market, causing businesses to be overly reliant, only artificially successful in the short-term and, ultimately, not competitive in the global market.

2. Export-oriented industrialisation (neoliberalism):

This policy aims for healthy competition in a global market by pushing economies to export and import goods with no distorting barriers e.g. protectionist policies, taxes and subsidies. Supporters of export-oriented industrialisation cite the tiger economies as key examples of how their approach can be successful. However, others argue that these economies would not have survived market fluctuations without government subsidies.

Activity 83 –
Research the neo-liberal perspective on international development further. This is sometimes also known as the 'Washington Consensus'.

You can find an article here that gives an overview:

http://www.cid.harvard.edu/cidtrade/issues/washington.html

Do you think the neo-liberal model of development is a good one? Why or why not?

Criticisms:

Some, of course, do not feel that industrialisation is a positive societal advancement, noting several environmental and social consequences. Dependency theorists also argue that industrialisation often only secures the needs of the rich, and in fact on serves to polarise and concentrate wealth, leaving many in both 'first' and 'third' world countries who are poor, marginalised and exploited.

Urbanisation is the process whereby people migrate from rural areas to cities; with over 50 per cent of the world's population living in cities today, researchers are concerned with the social implications of this process, particularly as it relates to development.

Causes of urbanisation:

- Introduction of agribusiness, which took business away from local farmers
- Limited job opportunities in rural areas
- Lack of infrastructure in rural areas can mean poor transportation and sewage systems, as well as inadequate healthcare
- Appeal of cities to young people

Positive aspects of urbanisation:

Modernisation theorists think that the development of urban centres, especially in the majority world, is a positive thing. It shows that majority world nations are progressing along the lines of minority world nations; urbanisation can lead to development and trigger more industrial growth. Furthermore, cities serve important purposes in the global economic sphere by housing the large numbers of workers needed to produce export goods. Cities also tend to be progressive, more open-minded centres for change, entrepreneurialism and development.

Negative aspects:

Others are not so positive about the impact of urbanisation. For example, in the southern hemisphere, urbanisation has led to urban sprawl, or the haphazard spread of cities in unplanned, often dangerous, ways. Often, these rapidly expanding cities are not equipped with basic needs for their inhabitants, e.g. running water, sewage systems, and electricity. This leads to the formation of overpopulated slums: Also, dual-sector economies will often develop in which a large portion of the population are unable to procure legal or regulated jobs and consequently enter informal economies where work can often be illegal. This leads to a variety of social problems such as violence, drug abuse and gang cultures.

Education

If there is one universal, cultural fact that the majority of the world can agree on, it is that of the importance of a good education. Western cultures particularly emphasise how education is key to, and can have transformative effects on, majority world economies.

Activity 84 –
Research the charity Camfed. What does this charity do, and how does it see education as key to international development? Why is this?

You can start by visiting Camfed's website here:
http://uk.camfed.org/site/PageServer?pagename=home_index

Education as a development strategy

1. Modernisation theory:

In line with most of their arguments, modernisation theorists think that, in order for majority world countries to develop, it is necessary for them to imitate the educational systems of the minority world countries. Education is key to industrial development, providing able, specialised workers to enter the workforce.

Also, they feel that education helps the majority world to develop culturally, shifting away from folklore and superstition to more rational, scientific thought. It is also a key lever of gender equality; at present, more girls than boys are not in primary or secondary education globally, and so widening access will ensure that girls have better life chances and more equality of opportunity. Furthermore, the western model of education transmits values of meritocracy and individualism, both of which are necessary for entrepreneurialism.

2. People-centred approaches:

People-centred approaches also see education as key to development; however, they disagree with the notion that the western model of education should be applied universally to the majority world. Indigenous knowledge systems and traditions need be preserved, and people should be educated to avoid exploitation, rather than for the purposes of economic prosperity. They feel that education systems should be improved and not replaced, and that curriculum must incorporate pre-existing, local knowledge systems.

Critical perspectives:

1. Neoliberalism

Neoliberalists acknowledge that education does serve an important purpose in society; however, they are critical of the state administering any public services (education included) as this raises taxes and thus discourages entrepreneurialism. Neoliberalists suggest that public services be funded by the private sector, encouraging entrepreneurialism and investments by corporations.

2. Dependency Theory

Dependency theory is also critical of the perspective that education should be central to development. They argue that many majority world countries are still experiencing setbacks caused during colonialism, when the imperial powers stifled local cultural traditions and knowledge systems, establishing their intellectual models as superior. As such, the majority world has remained dependent on the minority world as a source of knowledge and truth. Furthermore, neo-colonialism has kept education from growing in majority world countries with the imposition of structural adjustment plans: governments are already in debt and, on top of this, must limit their spending on public services.

Population and demography

Malthusianism

We have seen and acknowledged the population explosion that occurred in the twentieth century, when the world's population quadrupled in 80 only years, reaching 6 billion in 1999. It was demographer Thomas Malthus who prophesised, back in 1798, that the world was on the path to outgrowing its natural resources. According to Malthus, the world's population could be measured and predicted with a mathematical model: it would reproduce at a geometric rate (e.g. 2, 4, 8, 16, 32), whereas agricultural production would generate outputs at an arithmetic rate (e.g. 1, 2, 3, 4, 5). Eventually, the day would come when the world would surpass its carrying capacity by counteracting the forces of nature with high rates of reproduction, as well as relief efforts and medical advancements that allow impoverished, dense populations to grow. Ultimately, overpopulation would lead to starvation, poverty, disease and even riots, resulting in the death of many people.

Therefore, a man-made or natural disaster that brings down the population as such is called by some a Malthusian check. As a result, whilst relief efforts provided by, for example, the welfare state, intend to help poor and starving people, they can also allow populations to grow to even more dangerous sizes, leading to the same problem all over again.

Neo-Malthusianism

More recent neo-Malthusian theorists have taken into account a variety of global concerns (unlike Malthus, whose research was rooted in a primarily western context). In 1972, Paul Ehrlrich, in his publication The Population Bomb, addressed issues such as the human need not just for food, but also for other natural resources such as water, oil, metals and minerals. He also discussed population checks beyond those of disease and starvation, including natural disasters and desertification.   More recently, researchers have discussed how overpopulation can result in political violence such as in Palestine, and genocide as in Rwanda in 1994.

Many contemporary social researchers have grasped elements of Neo-Malthusianism to provide interventions that lower birth rates e.g. birth control and health education which gives family planning advice. In this, gender equality is also key since discrimination against women results in a society where women do not have the power or education to limit their family size and choose to have fewer children.

Counter-Malthusian perspectives

Agricultural developments

Some researchers have argued that Malthusian's notion that the world's population would run out of food resources is not true. The current agricultural output is about 110 per cent of that which is needed to feed the world's population: starvation still exists today not because of a lack of available food but because of corruption, poverty and deeply ingrained inequality.

Ester Boserup has specifically argued that food will never be a problem because agricultural technologies advance in line with population growth. She notes that as populations expand, people do run out of the vast spaces that are required for crop rotations and intermittent production methods, which keep soil healthy and fertile. However, they compensate for this with technological advancements, machinery and fertilisers that allow them to produce mass quantities of food in a process known as agricultural intensification.

However, other commentators (such as the eminent Indian environmentalist Vandana Shiva) have noted that agricultural intensification exacerbates environmental problems such as soil degradation and loss of fertility and so leads to long-term problems with food supply which have a negative impact on development in the long-term.

Activity 85 –
Research Vandana Shiva's environmental and social work further. You may like to start by reading this article:

http://www.guardian.co.uk/world/2011/mar/08/vandana-shiva-100-women

The demographic transition model

Many researchers disagree with the Malthusian notion that overpopulation is inevitable and destructive. For example, Warren Thompson (1929) and later Frank Norstein (1945) developed the demographic transition model, which held that societies would transition through 4 stages of development, beginning with a stable, young population and followed by a population explosion that results from advancements in medicine, food production and basic social infrastructure.

Eventually, people will experience lower infant mortality and also resort to means of contraception, so birth rates will fall. And lastly, the birth and death rates would reach equilibrium, stabilising the population once again. This model is, of course, based on minority world countries as they have experienced, and surpassed, industrialisation. Some argue that such wealthy nations have entered a fifth stage, in which birth rates fall and elderly demographics increase to a degree that can lead to pension crises.

People criticise the fact that the demographic transition model does not ring true for rapid population changes in majority world countries, which are not accommodated by a parallel expansion resource provision.

Overconsumption:

A final set of critics of Malthusianism point out that our planet does possess enough resources to support all of its inhabitants: the resources are just distributed highly disproportionately. Studies indicate that the richest 20 per cent of the world consume about 80 per cent of the world's resources.

Some researchers examine lifestyle factors in order to gauge the amount of land and sea needed to sustain one person: this measurement is known as an ecological footprint. In a balanced world, where everyone consumed equally, each ecological footprint would measure 2 ha (hectares). In reality, the average North American has a footprint of 10 ha, the average European has a footprint of 5 ha and the average Indian has a footprint of 2 ha.

Actors and Outcomes

This section explores the specific institutions that contribute to the processes explored above, highlighting some key political issues surrounding these institutions.

Transnational organisations

We have mentioned transnational organisations (TNOs) several times throughout this section. Now, it is time to examine some different types of TNOs in detail.

Intergovernmental organisations:

Intergovernmental organisations (IGOs) address the interests of nation states on regional and national levels, with varying degrees of specificity. They can be broken down as follows:

- Legal-political institutions – represent countries on a range of issues – e.g. the United Nations, the European Union and the African Union
- Economic organisations – focus on monetary policy – e.g. the Organisation of Petroleum Exporting Countries (OPEC) and the Bretton Woods institutions (below)
- Special-remit organisations – serve specific purposes – e.g. the World Health Organisation (WHO), Interpol, and the International Organisation for Standardisation

Bretton Woods institutions:

The Bretton Woods institutions are perhaps the most notable and controversial of the IGOs. The institutions, which aim to provide centralised development strategies for the majority world, exhibit a strong commitment to neoliberal ideals of free market and trade liberalisation.

They are as follows:

- World Bank Group – provides financial advice and assistance (loans) to developing countries in aid of poverty reduction
- International Monetary Fund (IMF) – international organisation that oversees the global financial system. The IMF is concerned with how the economic policies of countries impact the global economy, particularly exchange rates and the balance of payments
- World Trade Organisation (WTO) – handles the rules of trade between nations. The WTO intends to establish a free market by removing barriers to trade

The Bretton Woods institutions have been criticised for catering to the economic interests of the minority world. In terms of their voting systems, those who contribute more dollars e.g. usually rich, industrialised nations, tend have more of a say over what these organisations do.

Activity 86 –

Choose one of either of these Bretton Woods institutions to research further:

The International Monetary Fund

http://www.imf.org/external/index.htm

The World Trade Organisation

http://www.wto.org/

What are their main roles and functions, and how do they operate?

Non-governmental organisations

Non-governmental organisations operate independently of the state at local, regional, national and international levels. They can be classified according to their activities:

- Operational NGOs usually focus on development and relief projects. Examples are Oxfam, Wateraid, Christian Aid and Islamic Aid
- Advocacy NGOs usually defend or promote a political cause. Examples include Greenpeace and Amnesty International

Activity 87 –

Research an operational NGO that interests you by visiting the websites of any of the ones listed above. What are the organisation's objectives? How do they raise money? What have they accomplished? What model of development do they follow, and what are their long-term aims?

Now compare and contrast the work of an advocacy NGO which interests you by doing the same.

Transnational corporations

Transnational corporations (TNCs) are currently the most controversial forms of international organisations: There has been a rapid growth in the number of TNCs in the past century, leading to much debate on their effectiveness versus their tendencies toward exploitation.

Positive views:

Neoliberals support the non-aid approach of foreign direct investment which ensures that corporate capital and expertise is invested in particular facilities in the majority world. TNCs also create employment so that people might earn and reinvest into their economies. The implementation of modern employment practices also introduces cultural values (e.g. competition, achievement) that are necessary to development.

Negative views:

Many think that TNCs are exploitative, claiming that they often abuse labour markets in majority world countries. Also, some theorists argue that TNCs are too neo-liberalist-dominated, transmitting market fundamentalism and uncontrolled capitalism; they feel that people's lives should not be dictated by the whims of the free market. Majority world economies become dependent on TNCs, giving corporations too much power over law-making and enforcement. On a final note, many feel that corporations have capitalised on differentiations in legal systems. For example, Nestle has mis-sold baby formula powder to majority world countries, using manipulative advertising strategies (showing images of nurses on packets to suggest that its product was baby-friendly and healthy; these kinds of tactics would have been illegal in the producers' home countries), and giving away samples until parents became dependent on the product, which they then continued to dilute with unsafe water. This led to an increase in infant mortality rates.

Gender

Whilst the development strategies discussed above may sound effective on paper, they do not cure social inequality. Gender equality is a particular area of focus for many development strategists. Some think that industrialisation is the 'cure' for gender inequality; others feel that it is the cause. The economist Amartya Sen (1992) has categorised the ways in which women experience inequality during the process of development as follows:

- Mortality – Higher mortality rates for women in China, Asia and North Africa
- Nationality – Patriarchal culture marginalises women. Female babies are victims of infanticide, sex-selective abortion and abandonment. This has led to a skewed global demographic: there are currently 117 MILLION women missing from the world's population (though the problem is largely confined to India and China) due to the marginalisation of girls at the expense of boys. This has been termed a 'gendercide' and is certainly a cause for concern, as well as being the largest genocide in human history, far outweighing the casualties of the horrors of twentieth century atrocities such as the Holocaust
- Basic facilities – Little or no access to education and other institutions necessary to develop profitable skills and to limit family size due to better information about fertility and contraception
- Special opportunities – No access to higher education and specialised training
- Professional – Segregation and underrepresentation of women in the workplace due to discrimination and sexism
- Ownership – Assets shared unevenly, further restricting women's participation in business and commerce. For example, only 1 per cent of all the land titles in the world are owned by women, and women earn only a fraction of the world's pay despite working the majority of the world's working hours
- Household – Women are often relegated to housework duties and childcare whilst men exercise power, control and decision-making duties. This benefits men because it allows them to have a comfortable home and family life while holding positions of power, but prevents women from being active in public life and attaining the same prestige themselves

Explanations of gender inequality

Modernisation theory

Modernisation theorists feel that industrialisation will eventually lead to gender equality by slowly changing the patriarchal values that are already in place in majority world cultures. With industrialisation and modernisation, women will be integrated into local, and global, economies.

Dependency theory

Dependency theorists essentially argue the opposite. They feel that the industrial West is rife with patriarchy, which they then impose on traditional societies in the majority world. This has been happening since the dawn of colonialism, when imperial powers introduced cash economies to their colonies, which were dependent on male labour, leaving women at home. Capitalism was born out of patriarchy and depends on it to exist: in the classical Marxist interpretation, the unwaged labour of women as housewives makes possible the exploited male labour of the industrial working class.

So, how do we solve this?

Modernisation theory

Modernisation theorists, put simply, say: "keep doing what we're doing!" Their research indicates that economic development will lead to cultural and political change, albeit with generational lags. They thus advocate the implementation of media and educational resources, as well as TNCs, which will introduce modern employment practices, in which women are incorporated.

People-centred approaches

People-centred solutions, as usual, are much more small-scale. They tend to work directly with communities and individual women, implementing sustainable development programmes that incorporate all members of a society, aiming for long-term social inclusion. Education, healthcare and trade schemes ensure the inclusion of women. Microcredit schemes, for example, target women, giving them opportunities to improve their lives through investment and enterprise.

Health

Development also influences patterns in health. Historically, in the minority world, ill health and death were caused primarily by communicable diseases, or diseases that can be caught e.g. typhoid, malaria. Now, the predominant causes of sickness and death are diseases of consumption, such as heart disease, diabetes and cancers. These are especially prevalent in the western world where sedentary lifestyles and excessive consumption of rich fatty foods as a result of industrialisation leads to these sorts of health problems.

The majority-world primarily still battles traditional diseases such as HIV/AIDS which has an impact not only an enormous number of people, but also the most economically productive demographic. Globally, 70 per cent of all cases are located in Sub-Saharan Africa, and 36 per cent of all Botswanan adults are affected. As development continues, the majority world increasingly faces illnesses associated with the minority world.

Activity 88 -
Research global healthcare and inequalities of distribution of disease and health in more detail.

Make sure that you can discuss some case study countries and explain what the key issues are with regards to healthcare, patterns of transmission of disease and global poverty.

The World Health Organisation is a good place to start your research:
http://www.who.int/en/

Explanations of health inequalities

Modernisation theory

Modernisation theorists think that these inequalities and changes in health in the majority world are an inevitable part of the process of development. According to Abdel Omran (1971), health changes occur in a specific pattern that parallels shifts towards industrialisation. This is known as the epidemiologic transition model, as follows:

- Pestilence and famine: High death and infant mortality rates as parasitic and infectious diseases are widespread
- Receding pandemics: Following the development of infrastructure, particularly sewage disposal, clean water and food production systems, communicable disease becomes less of a problem. People become more educated, and technology advances
- Degenerative and man-made diseases: With medical advancements, people die less and less from communicable diseases; instead, people die from long-term diseases caused by lifestyle choices. Industrialisation turns people into consumers and harms the atmosphere; overconsumption of unhealthy foods, harmful drugs and UV rays leads to heart disease, cancers, etc.

Dependency theory

Dependency theorists see things much differently. They do not see health 'changes' as inherent cultural problems that will eventually rectify themselves when societies 'transition' to the next stage of development. Conversely, they think that health problems have been imposed on the majority world since colonial times, when imperial powers wiped out indigenous populations by introducing diseases from their home countries. Dependency theorists hold that neo-colonial processes continue to have a negative impact on health in the majority world. The neoliberal implementation of structural adjustment planning, for example, trumps spending on public services: most notably healthcare. Also, profit-driven pharmaceutical companies have kept majority world countries from producing cheap, generic versions of antiretroviral that could be used to treat HIV.

Addressing health inequalities:

- Modernisation theory - Modernisation theorists, once again, claim that the way forward is to continue introducing Western medical practices and health-care technologies in the majority world. They aim to reach large numbers of people with centralised health-care systems, usually introducing GP practices and hospitals into urban centres. This approach has been criticised in that rural populations are usually excluded
- People-centred approaches - Instead of introducing brand new health-care systems, people-centred approaches aim to improve upon existing systems by, for example, providing resources, education and training to health-care workers. These development schemes are community-focussed, reaching far beyond urban centres into the most rural of areas. They are usually quite effective on a small-scale; however, many are critical of the fact that people-centred approaches do not produce large-scale changes

Environment

There is an ongoing debate regarding the relationship between development and environmental damage. Many people recognise what would seem to be the most straightforward argument: increasing development leads to increasing environmental damage. The solution, then, would be for the world to cut back on development initiatives. However, the debate on this topic becomes much more complex.

The origins of environmental damage

The key issue dividing those who debate about the origins of environmental damage: is capitalist environmental damage a product of demand or supply? Is it people's consuming lifestyles or the dominance of corporations that deplete the earth's resources? Is it a combination of the two? Many people think that the western capitalist industrial model of development leads to societies that are centred around consumption. This, in turn, leads to a need for mass production. Others argue that TNCs, for example, are profit-driven and environmentally destructive. Others point out that it is not always the minority world that is exploiting majority world resources. Often, people in the majority world must exploit their own resources in order to survive, and this also leads to environmental degradation.

Environmental management

1. Top-down strategies

With top-down strategies, international organisations attempt to develop universal rules and regulations that will protect environmental resources on a wide scale. This practice has been problematic in the past, as countries struggle to agree on universal policies and, further, to enforce them. Some are critical of these initiatives, as they block economic growth. One example of a top-down environmental approach is emissions trading.

2. Bottom-up approaches

Those who employ bottom-up strategies attempt to empower local people to take control of their resource usages and to contribute to the overall protection of the environment by making changes to their lifestyles. Some people have taken this a step further with sustainable tourism initiative. These strategies have proven effective at preserving local biodiversity and at bettering local lifestyles. However, people criticise bottom-up approaches for being too small-scale and for not impacting global warming.

Activity 89 – Through your own research, can you find one example of a top-down and another of a bottom-up approach to environmental management?

Employment

Modernisation theory

Much like their views on other development-related social issues, modernisation theories argue that the evolution of employment practices occurs in line with the predictable stages of development. In pre-modern societies, people shared resources in an informal economy, hunting and gathering without much of an organisational structure, much less a conception of 'employment'. As people developed agricultural harvesting or nomadic herding practices, as well as more organised social structures, there still was not much of a distinction between 'home' and 'work' life. All harvesting and herding activities were intended for subsistence, rather than profit-making, purposes.

Eventually, people begin to specialise in certain products, creating small, home-based enterprises, usually for local trade purposes. These are known as cottage industries. Still, their work and home activities are not distinguished from one another; employment does become necessary, but tasks are usually shared by family members inside the home. With industrialisation, 'work life' finally exists in a distinct sphere, separate from 'home life'. People increasingly specialise in different elements of production. This, in turn, leads to a need for universal education.

Employment and globalisation

Over the past 40 years, globalisation has led to shifts in employment in both the majority and minority worlds. First and foremost, manual labour jobs, formally completed in minority world countries, are now completed in the majority world. TNCs find majority world labour to be much cheaper and thus opt for this strategy to drive up profits. As such, majority world countries experience a surge of employment opportunities, drawing people away from rural lifestyles and into urban centres. Minority-world countries, on the other hand, have experienced de-industrialisation, with fewer and fewer (traditionally working class) manual labour jobs available. With these changes, we have also seen an increase in service industry jobs in minority-world countries.

Neoliberals are quite positive about these changes: they feel that the global shifts in labour reflect a successful free market. Employment markets cater to skills that they can market more successfully. Others are angered by the scarcity of job opportunities for minority world, working-class labourers.

War and conflict

Research has indicated that war and conflict are very much linked to inequalities in power and wealth. As such, many researchers think that tackling development issues will also lead to a safer planet.

Colonial Legacies

Many conflicts are rooted in colonialism. For example, German and Belgian colonial interventions partially contributed to the Rwandan genocide acts of 1994. Both colonial powers had given preference to the Tutsi people over their Hutu neighbours, thus pitting the groups against one another. Another example is that of the religious partition of India into India, Pakistan and Bangladesh, which occurred at the end of British rule in 1947.

Environment

Many conflicts have arisen over the way in which environmental resources are used such as oil. Some feel that these conflicts are an example of a Malthusian check: an inevitable outcome of overpopulation. Others feel that overconsumption of natural resources by the rich world leads to conflict.

Climate change also fuels conflict. For example, the desertification of arable land is one of the reasons behind the conflict in Darfur. This natural change led to competition between herding and agricultural communities.

Globalisation

Many different facets of the process of globalisation have led to conflicts. For example, migration can lead to conflicts between existing communities and new immigrants. Also, terrorist groups such as Al-Qaeda are able to have transnational, decentralised operations to global communication technologies. Neoliberal agendas have also led to conflict in majority world countries when TNCs have privatised public services and driven up prices. This has led to the discontent (and sometimes violent outrage) of local people.

The impact of war and conflict

War and conflict can obviously be major barriers to development. Civil wars draw governmental attention to the funding and management of arms rather than the production of trade exports. Conflict can destroy infrastructure and leave countries unsafe to live in and thus severely hamper develop. People are often dislocated: work populations break up, children are orphaned, and government funding is diverted to caring for the war-injured and traumatised.

Debt boomerang

Some sociologists have argued that it is a debt-based economic system that is set up to favour rich countries at the expense of the poorer ones that creates poverty in the global south. Therefore, debt can be seen as the root cause of poverty and inequality because it creates various debt boomerangs. These are so-called because the negative consequences of taking on more debt are always returned.

Activity 90 –
You can read more about debt boomerangs and how they relate to global inequality here:
http://www.newint.org/features/1993/05/05/keynote/

The patterns and trends in global urbanisation

Conclusion

Don't forget to link your work on poverty and wealth in the UK and sociological research methods with this topic. If you were a sociologist studying global aid and the links between rich and poor countries, which kinds of research methods do you think would be most useful, and why?

Option 2

4.2.7: The Media

Key Areas:

- The new media and their significance for an understanding of the role of the media in contemporary society
- The relationship between ownership and control of the media
- The media, globalisation and popular culture
- The processes of selection and presentation of the content of the news
- Media representations of age, social class, ethnicity, gender, sexuality and disability
- The relationship between the media, their content and presentation and audiences

Introduction

This topic is an examination of contemporary culture and communication through reference to the influence of the mass media. In an increasingly globalised world, heavily reliant on information and communications technology, the mass media is an ever important area of sociological research.

Social media have quickly become an everyday part of many people's lives in contemporary society. But what has been the impact on society of this?

What are the mass media?

The term mass media means any form of communications ['medium', plural 'media'] that are able to reach a mass [widespread or global] audience. Due to the rapid advancements in communications technology, there are many forms of the mass media today, for example:

Traditional media

- The press. The widespread cheap availability of the print media was first established in the nineteenth century. Governments used to exercise control over the content, but the freedom of the press (the freedom to publish and print whatever journalists wanted) was later established as an important part of a healthy democracy. In the early twentieth century, several national newspapers emerged (such as the Daily Mail, Daily Express or the Mirror)

- Film: the first film shown to paying customers was in 1895 in Paris. The first cinema in the UK was built in 1896. By 1914 there were over 500 cinemas in London alone. In the USA, a flourishing and vibrant film industry established itself over the first half of the twentieth century. By 1925, for example, 95 per cent of films were American

- Radio: The first radio broadcast was in 1906. By the 1920s, radio broadcasts of news and entertainment had become far more common, partly because during World War 1, radio communications technology was used by both sides to broadcast information, and this helped develop the medium further. The Golden Age of radio was from roughly the mid-1930s to the mid-1950s (before television and film because more widespread) when most households in America and Europe owned a set and listened regularly as an important medium of news and entertainment

- Television: this grew rapidly and came to take the place of cinema because it can be experienced more immediately in the home. In the 1950s commercial TV was introduced, and TV since then has been dependent on commercial revenues (apart from publically funded TV channels such as the BBC). In the UK, 85 per cent of all adults watch TV every day, and teenagers and children watch a very high proportion: on average around 25 hours a week[41]

New Media

---

[41] It is worth checking these figures, particularly for younger people, as they constantly change with the advent of social media and BBC iPlayer, for example.

New Media is a term used to define all forms of electronic communication and interaction through digital technologies, the internet etc.

- Digital TV: this has taken over from analogue. Sound and pictures are digitised and received via cable, satellite dish or TV aerial and decoder. This has expanded both the range available and the possibilities for interaction
- Internet: in 1969, the Pentagon Advanced Research Projects Agency (PARPA) developed a system which would allow scientists involved in military research to pool resources. A messaging function ('email') was added as an afterthought. The technology spread to universities in the late 1980s. After that came the spread of Internet Service Providers (ISPs) which provided dial up and broadband, allowing people to access the internet in their homes. There has now been widespread and rapid take up of the internet in the west, and the technology has afforded opportunities to spread knowledge and to make connections on an unprecedented scale

Interactive or social media: Facebook and twitter are both examples of this. Social media is a big growth area in the internet, and is any form of (online) media where people can interact with each other in real time. On Facebook, for example, people can connect with friends and can share personal information, such as pictures, video clips, website links or information about what they are doing as they do it. In real time, people can see and comment on this information. In effect, a virtual environment of communication is created, which can feel, in many ways, like face-to-face and 'real world' communication.

Activity 91 –
Read this article:
http://www.seomoz.org/blog/a-bad-day-for-search-engines-how-news-of-michael-jacksons-death-traveled-across-the-web

What does this article tell you about the process of mass communications today? How quickly did this news spread? Why do you think this is the case?

Interpretation

This event demonstrates very well the global mass media in action: there were so many people who were editing the Michael Jackson Wikipedia page during such a short window of time that Wikipedia actually had to freeze the page for protection purposes.

The first official news website to confirm Michael Jackson's death in public was MSNBC.com. However, this was one hour after TMZ posted their article, and by internet standards that was a long time indeed. By then, a great number of people around the world had already read the news, or received it in a phone call, email or text from a friend.

To compare, when John Wilkes Booth assassinated US President Abraham Lincoln in 1865, it took twelve days for the news to reach London.

Therefore, we can see that the degree to which we access and experience the global media can have a huge impact on our lives. The global mass media allows people around the world to experience the unfolding of events together, as if in a 'global village.' A good example of this was the funeral of Michael Jackson. Although it was attended by thousands in person, it was viewed on television or online by over 30 million people.

The Relationship between Ownership and Control of the Media

Activity 92 - Find out who really owns the media through doing some research of your own.
Rupert Murdoch is a famous media magnate. Find out which TV companies, newspapers and other forms of the media he owns. You may like to start your research here:
http://en.wikipedia.org/wiki/Rupert_Murdoch

You could then read the following excellent overview of media ownership (Under Concepts: Ownership):
http://www.cemp.ismysite.co.uk/culture/

Analysis

Although it may seem that there is a lot of variety in the traditional media, it is often the case that only a few people own many of the TV companies or newspapers. The largest media corporation which is owned and controlled by Rupert Murdoch is News Corp whose UK branch owns The Sun, Sunday Times, Times and a large proportion of Sky T.V. They also own media companies in American and Australia, as well as publishing companies and magazines.

Even though Murdoch is an example of private ownership in terms of the media, there is some indirect state involvement; for example the BBC is owned by the state and funded by taxpayers.

Sociologists often ask: who owns the media? Who controls the media? They ask these questions because if we know the answers, then we can start to know a little more about the media itself: what is in our news, and why? What is left out, and why? Why do we have this kind of entertainment and not that? In other words, knowing about ownership and control of the mass media helps us to find out more about the content of the media.

It is certainly still the case that the majority of newspapers, magazines commercial TV stations, radio stations and other forms of media are owned, published, edited and otherwise controlled by white, middle-class men. Therefore, some sociologists who research the media argue that sexist and racist messages are reproduced through the mass media, so the mass media reflect the agenda of those who own and control the media, and also create and help perpetuate gender and racial stereotypes.

For example:

In TV advertising, cleaning or domestic products (such as washing or laundry liquid, floor or bath room cleaners) typically portray a woman (as a housewife and mother) doing the housework and as the one ultimately responsible for keeping the home clean and tidy and the family safe, well-cared for, protected and nurtured. This is the stereotypical gender role.

In TV advertising and elsewhere (in entertainment and even in the news), young and beautiful women are used to sell products (such as cars, food products, alcohol and other consumer items) or to make news and entertainment more attractive and enticing. For example, it is often a young and attractive woman who reads the weather forecast; young and attractive women may co-present shows (often alongside older and less attractive men), and young and attractive women are often featured in the pictures in newspapers.

Many feminist sociologists would argue that this sends the message to women that beauty and attractiveness, being young and attracting a man are all important (more so than they are for men), and that women's beauty and women's bodies are commercialised and 'public property', for male consumption, in a way that men's bodies are not. This is another gender stereotype, and one that is clearly socially constructed.

Activity 93 –
Research advertising in particular further. You may like to collect examples of print or video advertising, for example.

Examine how gender, class, ethnicity and disability are portrayed in these idealised versions of the world.

What stereotypes or messages do you think these are sending about gender, class, ethnicity or disability?

Explanations of Media, Ownership and Control

Concerns have been raised by many sociologists about the concentration of power that is held by the few in terms of the media.

Melody (1978) argued that the concentration of ownership by the few means that the media becomes "standardised" and "the messages communicated are constrained and directed in both quantity and quality to meet the economic imperatives of the process". Further to this view, Doyle (2002) suggests that a concentration of power in the media will inevitably have a significant impact on public opinion in that the views, opinions and biases of those who control the media will be portrayed at the potential expense of the democratic process. In 1999 Giddens went as far as to say that:

"...television and other media tend to destroy the very public space of dialogue they open up, through relentless trivialising and personalising of political issues. Moreover, the growth of giant multination media corporations means that unelected business tycoons can hold enormous power."

This view is very much in keeping with the idea that media ownership by the few has an impact upon the democratic processes as referred to earlier in relation to Doyle (2002). This is also significant as it undervalues diversity in the media and can result in a potential abuse of power.

According to Curran (2003), there is evidence to suggest that ownership and the views of the owner are strongly reflected, particularly in the British press. So, despite the perception of investigative reporting, for example, owner bias is evident.

Marxist perspectives on the issue of ownership and control are, not surprisingly, cautious about the extent to which the few (who own the media) use the media to transmit certain values that the Marxist perspective associates with ruling class ideology. Miliband (1973) argued that the role of the media is to influence and shape how we see the world and how we live in it, downplaying the true extent of inequalities within it.

The Glasgow University Media Group (GUMG), apply what is referred to as a hegemonic approach, seeing the media as being in the hands of the few and power being maintained by constructed ideologies that are promoted by the mass media. Therefore, they accept that the media portrays and supports the views and interests of the capitalist system and the ruling classes. However, they suggest that this is unintentional because journalists and broadcasters tend to be from social backgrounds that have similar views and ideologies, and this is reflected in what they present and how they present it. Overall the domination of the media by giant, multinational corporations is such that according to researchers such as Edwards and Cromwell (2006):

"...the media system reporting on the world is itself made up of giant corporations. Indeed, media entities are often owned by the same giant corporations they are tasked with covering."

In terms of what has been addressed above, we are talking about media in the general sense of the word, but we do need to be aware of some of the sociological perspectives that have been put forward in terms of New Media, as this form of media in itself has had a significant impact on contemporary society. With this in mind Curran and Seaton (2003) identified two perspectives in terms of new media, Neophiliac and Cultural Pessimistic:

Neophiliac	Cultural Pessimistic
In favour of New Media because: It increases consumer choice It enhances democracy by offering access to alternative views – revitalising democracy It is an indicator of progress	Not so keen on New Media because: It decreases choice – decisions made by the few; poor quality and repetitive Major corporations dominate so their views are presented and reinforced The positive view of new media, in terms of things like progress is over exaggerated. According to Cornford and Robins (1999) new media is not so new; rather it's old media but just faster and more accessible.

Marxism and the media

The media is a tool, owned and used by the ruling classes to indoctrinate the subordinate classes and as such is used to reinforce ruling class ideology. Marxists hold that the content of mass media is controlled by its owners: the powerful, capitalist elite. These media moguls (owners) can manipulate the masses through media, conveying capitalist values and biased portrayals of political movements.

Neo-Marxism and the media

Neo-Marxists agree that the mass media propagates certain ideologies, in particular the values associated with capitalism. However, they are more sceptical of the direct influence of media owners. They rather recognise the mass media as just one part of the 'ideological state apparatus'. This is a collection of social institutions, including education, the family and religion which spread the values of capitalism and these norms and beliefs throughout society.

Pluralism

This is a liberal theory which states that different social groups should respect and tolerate each other. With regard to the media, this means that the media should be used as a space which is plural: different social groups and subcultures should be able to use the media as a way to communicate with each other and to explain their own viewpoints. This is an interactive model of the media; different groups can produce their own media (such as publish books, produce music or put on plays) which can then be viewed and enjoyed by other groups.

Activity 94 – Read the following article on pluralism in the media here (under Concepts: Pluralism):
http://www.cemp.ismysite.co.uk/culture/

Do you think that the media is pluralistic or not?

Post-Modernism

From this perspective the media has, in various shapes and forms, become more influential in all aspects of our lives, private and public. Because of this, the lines between media and reality has become somewhat blurred, and what is considered to be 'the truth' is now only a matter of different or competing claims being made, with the one that is most popular or makes the 'winning' claim is the one that stands. Through media such as Facebook, Twitter and other forms of social networking, people's sense of identity and choices in terms of lifestyles and opinions are being shaped, so traditional influences such as family, culture, communities etc. become slowly eroded and less influential and significant. According to Strinati (1995), the media influences and shapes identities.

People are now more ingrained in 'virtual communities and networks' (proto-communities) with the globalisations of the media - globalisation meaning that people are becoming more and more exposed to other social and identity forming choices. Note, however, from this perspective, overall this is a good thing as it offers global choices that were not available before. As far as this perspective is concerned, no one media product or format is more influential or greater than another.

Baudrillard (1983), argues that society has become so caught up in the media that this has resulted in what he refers to as 'simulacra' – a replacement of something real or reality, with a representation or likeness of what has been replaced - where the real world is lost e.g. Disneyland, whilst in a real country, is an example of simulacra, bearing some resemblances to the real world but in fact not being real at all:

"The Disneyland imaginary is neither true nor false: it is a deterrence machine set up in order to rejuvenate in reverse the fiction of the real."

Activity 95 - What criticisms could be made of the post modernist perspective?

What is the relationship between the mass media and the state?

Especially in authoritarian regimes, the media are usually repressive and manipulative. They distort and are biased. This is because there is no freedom of the media: instead, the media are owned and controlled by the dictator. The dictator ensures that no news or articles which are critical of the regime are published. Any dissenting voice is silenced, and the truth is not allowed to be told. There is no fairness of reporting; if the dictator commits a crime then it is not reported and the people do not really know what is happening from the official media.

Propaganda is a form of media bias: it is a form of political media which is intended to persuade. It is not fair or impartial. Rather, it is uncritical and is designed to indoctrinate. This means that the intention of propaganda is to impose a particular viewpoint on people by unfair means; this indoctrination. Propaganda is most usually associated with authoritarian regimes, and not with democracies.

Media, globalisation and popular culture

Giddens(1990) and Harvey(1989) described globalisation as:

"...the widening, deepening and speeding up of global interconnectedness."
It has been described as "accelerating inter-dependence", "action at a distance" and "time space compression". So generally we can define globalisation as a condition where the connections between nations and the operations within them e.g. trade, culture, economy, and goods and so on, become interconnected and increased. Within this context the media is seen to have a significant part to play in this process as well as being influenced by it.

Activity 96 - What do you think is the connection between media and globalisation?

With the world becoming 'smaller' due to globalisation, we are seeing the globalisation of the media e.g. satellite television, entertainment and programming, from other parts of the world through internet access and ownership of global media organisations.

In the light of the above we need to ask the question:

Is globalisation in this context a good thing?

Yes	No
McLuhan (1982) – 'Global Village' - Globalisation of the media has generated mutual understandings; broken down barriers; allowed for communication and interaction across the globe in real time. Flew (2002) – 'Global Popular Culture' – the media has generated a mass culture and mass consumption that is identifiable globally. Pluralists – 'Variety of choice' – consumers of the media can control what and how they consume; positive exposure to high culture therefore, being able to access areas that were once only accessible by certain classes e.g. people can have access to the ballet without necessarily going to the theatre.	Marxist – ownership in the hands of the few globally, promotes a particular viewpoint or ideology. Individuals are being assimilated into global culture, cultural homogenisation restricts choice. Fenton (1999) – many cultures have become Westernised or Americanised (Cultural imperialism). Thompson – causing tensions with some cultures feel as if traditional practices and beliefs are being eroded e.g. in China attempts have been made to control global media access. Ownership by the few is a threat to democracy. Diminishing face to face social interaction and generating exploitation. For those who do not have the same level of access, if they have any access at all, they are excluded or experience global inequality e.g. third world countries=digital divide Inadequate regulation.

Selection and Presentation of News Content

When looking at the selection and presentation of news content we need to consider and examine issues such as:

- Ownership and ideology
- Who decides
- World news and global impact
- Moral panics
- The audience
- News value – is it news worthy?
- Is it T.V news or press news?

Galtung and Ruge (1965) identified a number of features that would determine whether or not a story was news worthy. What is considered to be newsworthy would invariably be different according to who was making the final decision, which medium was going to be used to relay the story, who the audience were likely to be and so on. They also included factors such as:

- Frequency – if the event occurred over a short period of time e.g. a homicide - this sort of story fits in with news schedules
- Threshold – the bigger the event the better the story e.g. natural disasters
- Unambiguity (simplicity) – a straightforward, easy to understand story
- Composition – does the story fit in with the style and make-up of the newspaper or TV presentation?
- Elitism – the story refers to or involves celebrities or involves people where English is the first language and they bear cultural similarities
- Meaningfulness/Human interest – A story the audience can relate to and which focusses on telling a person's story from their perspective
- Continuity – if the story is likely to have a continuous impact on the audience in terms of maintaining interest e.g. specialist sporting events such as Wimbledon or something serious such as war or conflicts
- Negativity – bad news makes news, particularly if it is dramatic, tragic, and extreme - they will usually trump positive, feel good stories

Taking into account the above, it is clear that 'news' is, as McQuail (1992) suggests, socially constructed. There is no real objectivity as news is 'selected', so biased choices are made.

Note, once it has been decided what is news, how it is presented, can add to the credibility of the story. On TV, newsreaders are presented as neutral and authoritative. Their appearances are smart and their way of speaking is articulate but friendly – as such 'they must be relaying factual truths'.

Media influence

The 'power' of the media in terms of how it influences how we see the world can be seen in the work of Stanley Cohen (1972). Not only does his study show what constitutes what may be considered newsworthy, but it also shows the extent to which the media can influence our opinions and views of certain things (in this case a particular social group) to the extent that it creates what he referred to as a moral panic.

Daily Mirror front cover 1964

In 1964 it was reported that there were clashes between rival groups called the Mods and the Rockers at a resort in Margate, the result of which was significant disturbances in the area, with fights and violence breaking out. The news headlines and reporting content used terms, phrases and subheadings such as:

- "Wild ones"
- "40 arrested"
- "All day clashes"
- "Blood"
- "Shouting"
- "Girls fight it out"

The front cover of the newspaper included pictures of youths fighting and being taken away by the police. Cohen wanted to examine these disturbances further and try to establish the true extent of the clashes that was being presented by the media. The extent of the reporting was such that it created, as referred to by Cohen, a moral panic, stemming from the folk devils being created by the media. Folk devils refer to those who have been labelled as a threat to social order, norms and values. The moral panic being that, certain groups were then identified as being a threat to society regardless of whether or not they had actually done anything to warrant such negative responses.[42] When looking into the incident further Cohen found that the reports by the media were significantly exaggerated, and in fact eye witness accounts suggested that the gangs involved were not actually the Mods and Rockers but rather, local groups who had rivalries with each other. The consequence of this was:

- Certain groups with similar identifiable characteristics being negatively labelled
- The media suggesting that there would be further clashes and incidences of this nature
- Increased police surveillance
- Increased arrests
- Validation of the moral panic and folk devil labelling as a result of points 1 to 4 above

---

[42] This will be addressed in more detail when you come to the Crime and Deviance unit (4.3.1)

So what is clear from Cohen's work here is that the media, through agenda setting, has a significant amount of influence on how we see the world and others within it.

Agenda setting is the process by which those who hold power within the media (such as owners or journalises) set the content of the media. It is journalists, for example, and the owners of newspaper, who decide whether a story is 'newsworthy' or not. They decide what to report, and how to present it to the public. This is certainly still the case with more traditional media (such as print media).

Activity 97 – What criticisms do you think can be made of the research presented by Cohen in his analysis of the influence of the media?

Newer forms of social media have allowed members of the public who are not trained journalists to create and shape the news agenda also. For example, any member of the public can publish or broadcast news, as long as they have access to the internet.

They can write an article about an event they witnessed or took part in, or they can discuss their own political or other beliefs online with others. This trend is sometimes called the democratisation of the media, whereby media broadcasting is opened up to non-professionals (non-journalists) by virtue of internet access to social networking sites such as YouTube, Twitter or Facebook and the freedom of online content (at least, outside of countries such as China were there is more media censorship) to self-publish material, for example on a personal blog. This has both positives and negatives.

Activity 98 -
What do you think are the advantages and disadvantages of the democratisation of the media?

Why do you think it might be a good thing to have non-journalists publish or broadcast media? Why do you think it may not be so good? Think about these questions and make a note of your ideas and answers.

You might like to investigate 'citizen journalism' by finding out about the first citizen journalism organisation, Indymedia:
http://www.indymedia.org/en/index.shtml

The Arab Spring

The Arab Spring of late 2010 is often discussed as an example of the power social media can grant to ordinary citizens. This is because it was seen as a collection of popular mass uprisings against undemocratic, corrupt or authoritarian regimes across the Arab world, facilitated by ordinary people taking pictures of what was going on to publicise the movement or to protest against state sanctioned police brutality and crackdowns, or else tweeting live updates and breaking events as they witnessed them. You can read more about the power of social media here in the Arab Spring here: http://www.theguardian.com/world/2011/feb/25/twitter-facebook-uprisings-arab-libya

Citizen journalism

Sociologists who analyse the media have discussed the pros and cons of media democratisation. On the one hand, access to the internet means that anyone with the appropriate technology can tell their story, report on events as they happen or make their opinions and feelings known. This should be a non-elite process, and one in which ordinary people's voices can be heard in a way that was never possible historically, when it was only the opinions of the powerful elites which were recorded.

On the other hand, access to the internet technology necessary to take part in this kind of global debate is by no means itself unproblematic; it still depends on access to the wealth or social background necessary to make internet access easy, convenient and familiar.

Also, the democratisation of the media has led to some concerns about journalistic standards: if anyone can comment on a story, report or cover an important event (so long as they have internet access), then why do we even need professional journalists or professional members of the media? What about the future of professional news media, such as newspapers or news television channels, when we have blogs or social media to cover events and news as they happen, by ordinary people? If we think that anyone can report an event, then why bother with journalists?

Some media commentators would argue that this would lead to a lack of professional journalistic standards: good reporting, unbiased content, credible and fair representation of people and opinions. After all, we mostly still believe in the necessity for professional teachers, legal personnel and medical staff, so why do we find it easier to discredit journalism? No one would seriously argue that 'anyone should be able to perform a medical operation' – and yet we are reaching a similar state of affairs in journalism, where anyone is free to report an event or their story despite their lack of formal training or approval and accreditation from a professional body.

Consequences of media (mis)reporting

News broadcasting can create or widespread fear regarding (perceived) deviant behaviour, by sensationalising information about criminal activity as we have seen in Cohen's analysis of the media. In particular, the established and formal media tends to portray working class and minority ethnic young men very negatively. Often, they are stereotyped and labelled as society's most threatening criminals.

This is the process of selection: journalists select news stories from a wide pool of possibilities: there are many thousands of different things that happen each day, so why do some end up as news and others do not? Why do some crimes, for example, get reported, whereas other crimes which could be equally shocking or troubling, not? The answer is selection: journalists decide why this particular event, and not that, should be published in traditional media forms (such as newspaper).

Distribution is the process of how the media is broadcast or published or publicised. This is how we access and consume media; whether we can afford to access the internet, for example, or if we live near a shop which stocks the newspapers we would like to read. Social factors, such as where we live or how much money we have all shape our media consumption and are part of the question of media distribution.

Media bias is media distortion: this could be a bias against ethnic minorities, for example, or a gender bias. Therefore, any stories or media involving people from these backgrounds could be more vulnerable to biased or misrepresentative reporting.

The technical term media culture describes the values, beliefs, norms and ideals that are conveyed by the media. The media culture - what is valued or presented as normal, and what is not - can be seen by looking closely at the content of the media. The mass media create and then reinforce this culture, which is then broadcast to the rest of society who pick up on these messages.

The mass media is still dominated by a few middle class, white men who own many of the important media outlets, and traditional media are heavily professionalised: journalists and those who help create the news and entertainment shows behind the scenes all come from a similar background and profession. This helps to make sure that the media is all kept and sustained within the same kind of culture.

The Media and Ethics

Sometimes the lengths to which the media, particularly the press will go, to get a story, raises questions with regard to the ethical principles applied, if applied at all. In November 2012, the Leveson Enquiry, published their findings following concerns regarding the "...culture, practices and ethics of the press".

One of the main instigators for the report surrounded controversy concerning phone hacking and it was found that the News of the World newspaper had intercepted/hacked the phones of murder victim Milly Dowler and a number of prominent public figures and celebrities. This flagged up the whole issue of ethics in terms of reporting practices and the lengths reporters were prepared to go to "get the story" or "exclusive". This emphasised the need for the press to be regulated.

The enquiry also raised concerns regarding the press's attitude toward those in the public eye, treating them as if they were: "... public property with little, if any, entitlement to any sort of private life or respect for dignity" as such there is no "public interest" element that could justify it.

Media representations of age, class, ethnicity, gender, sexuality and disability

Age

Representation of age in the media can be split into three age group 'stereotypes':

Childhood	Generally presented in a positive light – innocent, cheeky, cute, 'bright eyed and bushy tailed'
Youth	Problematic, deviant, challenging (e.g. see Cohen's Mods and Rockers). Wayne et al (2008) found in content analysis research, that young people were often portrayed in a negative way and seen as a problem for the wider society.
Older People	Generally seen as interfering, mentally challenged, gullible, a burden. If, however, the older person is of a higher class (as opposed to working class) they may be seen in a positive light, often able to make contributions that are valued and respected (Newman, 2006).

Social Class

Classes are often presented in a stereotypical manner with the working class being presented as down-trodden and experiencing difficulties, usually financial. Class conflict or clashes are down-played, even though this is a significant factor within society. As stated, previously, in terms of age, according to Newman (2006), higher classes are presented positively, with lavish and enviable lifestyles. There is a tendency to focus on the extent to which they consume services and goods.

Nairn (1988) argues that if we look at the Royal Family for instance, generally they are seen in a positive light, with their lives playing out like a soap opera, but still having a level of respect associated with them representing the nation – part of the national identity.

Newspapers are generally associated with certain classes according to Curran and Seaton (2003). The class association is found in the content, so newspapers like the Sun focus more on celebrity news and gossip, which are seen to be topics that appeal more to working class interests. Papers like the Guardian tend to have content that is more likely to focus on current affairs, politics, financial affairs etc., and as such this is seen to be more in keeping with middle and upper class interests.

Ethnicity

The media does have a history of presenting ethnic minority groups as a 'problem'. Van Dijk (1991) between 1985 and 1989 looked at the reporting of ethnic minorities, particularly Afro-Caribbeans and found they were reported on negatively e.g. as criminals, involved in gang violence, drug dealing and so on. He suggested that this was partly due to the press being predominantly controlled by white people. Hall in the 1970s, argued that the 'moral panic' generated by the media in terms of muggings and its being associated with certain ethnic minority groups, was perpetuated by the media. Watson (2008) said that in particular, Afro-Caribbean people have been stereotyped as criminal by the media.

When looking at the 'face' of the media, such as news presenters and journalists, ethnic minorities are significantly under represented.

Gender

Gender is often presented in the media, generally, in the following ways:

Femininity	Masculinity
Tunstall (2000) – women are presented as sexual, domestic and focused on marriage related concerns. So, they tend to be seen as housewives, mothers and sexual objects. Working women – selfish, self-absorbed, unattractive, emotionally detached, sacrificing their family and femininity. Images of women are presented as sexual objects. Wolf (1990) suggests that the images of women presented in the media are based on something that is unrealistic and unobtainable for real women, but, nevertheless, they are encouraged to aspire to e.g. trying to be a size zero. Tuchman et al (1978) use the term 'symbolic annihilation' to describe how the media downplays women's achievements and, even if reported, the focus soon shifts to the woman's sexuality. As recently as 2012, the Leveson Enquiry stated that newspapers "...often failed to show consistent respect for the dignity and equality of women generally." However, there have been some positive developments. According to Gill (2008), images of women used in advertising are presenting women as more independent, confident and powerful.	Traditionally the media presented men as strong, active, unemotional, competitive and this was perpetuated by the media from entertainment (in films) to news stories (talking about 'heroes'). However, the 1980s saw the introduction of the 'New Man' and the 'Metro-sexual male' who was emotionally available, in touch with his feelings, treated women as equals, took pride in his appearance, saw fatherhood and being a husband as more than just providing and being the bread winner. However, Whannel (2002) suggests that the message is mixed, with on the one hand men being portrayed as New Men and Metro-sexual and on the other hand, still being expected to be strong, skilled and 'manly'. Whannel refers to David Beckham who is often in the media, as being an example of this 'contradiction'.

Sexuality

When we use the term 'sexuality' we are referring to a person's sexual character and sexual behaviour. In terms of sexuality and the media the normative presentation is that of heterosexuality with homosexuality being portrayed, negatively, stereotypically and at times comically, with gay men particularly, being presented as 'camp', flamboyant or very macho, and gay women being presented as 'butch', masculine and aggressive.

In the 1980s, the stereotyping of homosexual men was such that news coverage of AIDS created folk devils of gay men by referring to AIDS as a 'gay plague', this subsequently led to a moral panic.

Disability

The disability has an interesting relationship with the media. However, unfortunately this relationship has not been positive. Often disability has been presented in a negative light. According to Barnes (1992), disability is often seen in one of the following ways:

- A source of ridicule – physical disability has sometimes been used for comedic weight
- Someone to be pitied – in need of help and assistance
- Devoid of 'normal' feelings and emotions – there is the assumption that physical impairment equates with emotional instability
- Sinister – portrayed as the villain, vengeful or having sinister motives
- Non-sexual – lacking sexual feelings or not sexual at all
- 'Super cripples' – has amazing abilities or shows feats of heroics despite the disability e.g. as presented in some films and dramas, a blind person having psychic abilities

The relationship between the media, their content and presentation and audiences Whilst we have examined many aspects of the media generally, sociology also examines and seeks to explain the effects of the media on their audience.

We will now look at the four models regarding the relationship between the mass media and its audience and patterns of media use:

- The Hypodermic Model
- Two-flow Model
- Uses and gratifications model
- Cultural Effects Model

Hypodermic model

This is a model that suggests that the media transmits certain ideas into the minds of the audience. The audience submissively receives this information or the ideas presented to them. This being the case, this model suggests that there is a direct link between media violence and violent behaviour exhibited particularly, by children and young people. Therefore, according to this approach, the media destroys viewers' abilities to think independently or critically.

Bandura et al (1963) conducted an experiment where he exposed young children to films and cartoons depicting violence, and concluded that the children imitated some of what they had seen. McCabe and Martin (2005) went a bit further in their analysis and found that exposure to media resulted in some children being dis-inhibited ('dis-inhibition effect'), where the response to real life conflict is violence rather than discussion.

Activity 99 - What kind of criticisms can be made of the Hypodermic Syringe Model?

The hypodermic model has been widely criticised for its fairly narrow interpretation of audience behaviour. Most media researchers today would agree that audiences are not completely passive or homogenous as the hypodermic model would suggest.

Two-Flow Model

Some media theorists argue that audience responses are formed through a 'two-step' flow. The first step is the one through which the media reaches the audience via opinion leaders, and the second step is the one through which the opinion leaders' interpretation is passed onto others.

Katz and Lazarsfeld (1955) suggested that 'opinion leaders' are anyone who holds significant status among a group (e.g. peer group, work colleagues, family). They get the information from the media and then pass on their interpretation to others and thereby influence the views of others. Because opinion leaders' views are valued, they can have an impact upon the views held by others. For example, a teacher, who relays to her students what she saw on the news last night may pass on her views and opinions to her students who may well take it on board and change their own opinion because the students see the teacher as an opinion leader.

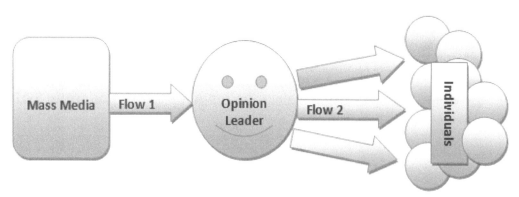

Figure13: Two-flow model

Within these social networks (these could be face-to-face, such as peer groups) or online (such as internet discussion boards) opinion leaders and formers who have the dominant voice or presence tend to strongly influence audience interpretations and responses to what is in the media.

Uses and Gratification Model

Also referred to as an interpretative model, this approach according to Blumler and McQuail (1968) suggests that media audiences are active participants rather than acting like empty vessels waiting to be filled as suggested by the Hypodermic model. In this model, the audience has a great degree of agency. For example, audience members can choose either to engage with or reject media content and output. Especially in the internet age, any internet user can create their own media (whether video, film, websites, blogs, music or any other type of content) and then can publish and publicise this online. The audience can actually choose to use the media to:

- Escape from every day, routine lives – the media provides entertainment
- Form and develop personal identities. People can use various media to present themselves in a certain light or use the media to modify the identity they already have
- Get information and news about things that interest them
- Have personal relationships and companionship by connecting and identifying with fictional communities and characters

As the media have developed, potentially, any ordinary internet user can become famous or achieve recognition, honour or other prestige through their media creations.

This grants a huge amount of freedom and agency to individuals who are no longer bound to accept passively media content which comes from external and remote authorities. Instead, audience members are actively shaping the media through their empowerment to create their own media forms e.g. many people post videos on YouTube.

Cultural Effects Model

This Neo-Marxist perspective suggests that the media's influence on its audience is not immediate but happens over a period of time. This has been referred to as the 'drip, drip effect'.

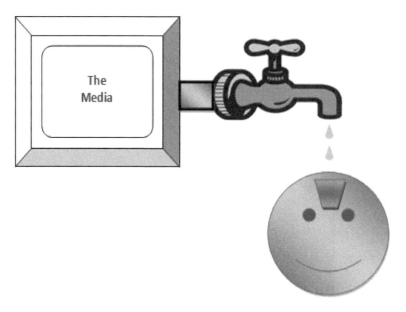

Cultural Effects Model

From a Marxist perspective this makes the media a very powerful ideological mechanism, particularly in terms of transmitting dominant the norms and values of the ruling classes.

Other perspectives

Reception theory

This theory was originally presented by Hans-Robert Jauss in the late 1960s, looking at how readers received and responded to literary text. Later research developed on this by looking at how people of different class or cultural backgrounds interpret or use the media in different ways. Stuart Hall, a reception theorist, views the media as 'texts' which can be read in different ways. In particular, media viewers might accept the intended message or the preferred reading or if a viewer's cultural or class backgrounds clash with the message being presented by the media text, he or she may take an oppositional reading.

Research Methods and the Media

Quantitative

Approaches used when looking at the media in Sociology tend to use methods such as content analysis, where the researcher will examine and analyse, for example, the type of news items in newspapers at a particular time, the distribution and sales of the press, the type of coverage given to certain stories and so on. In terms of television, sociologists may look at advertising during certain times of the day or the scheduling of advertising in relation to overall programming and audience figures in relation to this. This could be done over a short period of time allowing for categorisation and quantification of media content.

Qualitative

This methodological approach is often associated with Semiotics, which is the study of symbols and signs used in order to portray or present a particular meaning, whether overt or covert. So the meaning behind words, images and presentations can be an indication of the agenda being set by those who are in a position to determine media content. An example of this approach can be seen in the work of Cohen, who, as we saw earlier, looked at how clashes between Mods and Rockers were depicted in the media (primarily the press), exaggerating the extent of the clash, creating what he referred to as folk devils. Using such terms as 'crisis' portrayed the Mods and Rockers as potential threats to the very fabric of society generating a moral panic.

What is the relationship between the media and ideology?

The issue of freedom and censorship in the media is an important one for sociologists who research the media. Censorship is the deliberate policy of excluding some topics, journalists or other items from the news for political or moral reasons.

Many, but not all, forms of media also contain advertising. This is not a neutral factor: advertising also helps shape and create the media.

But what is advertising? It is any commercial piece of media (such as a print advert or TV commercial) which is designed to sell a product or service. It is geared around sales and consumption. There can be many different forms of media advertising, and everyone who uses the modern media on a daily basis is likely to be exposed to some forms of these regularly.

Sociologists who research the media are interested in the question of how far media advertising shapes, controls and regulates cultural values and norms.

Activity 100 – Choose your favourite media, or one you use regularly. This could be print media (newspapers and magazines) or it could be TV, radio or the internet. Have a closer look at this form of media, and think about the following questions:

What forms of advertising do you notice in your favourite media? What are they trying to sell? Are they effective? How do they affect the media context in which they are placed? For example, how do you think print adverts affect the rest of the content of the magazine or newspaper in which they are found?

What are the social trends of media consumption?

Choose one of the following social factors: age, social class or gender. How does media consumption vary according to this factor? For example, do men watch more TV than women, or vice versa? Do older people use the internet as much as younger people? Does social class impact on the type of media you are more likely to use or enjoy?

Activity 101 –

In the UK, OFCOM is the name of the regulatory body whose job it is to watch and regulate the media. They produced a detailed report on media usage in the UK. You may like to use this as a starting point for your research into the social trends of media consumption:

http://stakeholders.ofcom.org.uk/market-data-research/market-data/communications-market-reports/cmr08/

Mobile phone technology has progressed rapidly in recent years; but what about the environmental costs of such obsolescence? And how does mass and affordable communication change the way people interact with other and with society?

What impact do the mass media have on behaviour?

Sociologists are certainly interested in the extent to which people are influenced by the behavioural patterns they see represented in the media.

Activity 102 –

Read this article:
http://web.dailycamera.com/shooting/27acult.html

And this one here:
http://www.nytimes.com/1993/10/10/us/cartoon-on-mtv-blamed-for-fire.html
What do these articles tell you about the impact the media can have on behaviour, such as on violence?

Hamleys top 10 toys for Christmas 2010;

- Jet Pack Buzz Lightyear
- Ferrari F1 Electric Ride-On
- Stinky The Garbage Truck
- PaperJamz Guitar
- Vtech Kidizoom Video Camera
- Barbie Video Girl
- Ben10 Ultimate Alien Disc Ultimatrix
- Kung Zhu Hamsters
- Dave the Funky Monkey
- Beyblade Metal Fusion Super Vortex Battle Set

Advertising in the mass media can certainly influence shopping trends and consumer habits, as this list shows.

The New Media

Many sociologists and technologists think that the new media (in particular, social networking trends and peer-to-peer buying) are changing society in fundamental ways, in particular how people relate to each other and shape their personal relationships. For example, it is notable that now a substantial number of relationships start on the internet; people may use dating websites or use social networking sites such as Facebook to meet people. Clearly, this trend is in stark contrast to as recently as 10-15 years ago, and for that reason sociologists are interested in studying people's relationship to the media and how it is changing society.

Activity 103 – Research the changing relationship between people, new media and society.

You may like to read some new social sciences and media studies research in this area; you can do this by downloading copies of the journal New Media and Society here:

http://nms.sagepub.com/

Option 2

4.2.8 Stratification and Differentiation

Key Areas:

- Sociological explanations of stratification and differentiation in relation to social class, gender, ethnicity, age and disability
- Dimensions of inequality: class, status and power; differences in life-chances by social class, gender, ethnicity, age and disability
- The problems of defining and measuring social class; occupation, gender, and social class
- Changes in structures of inequality, and the implications of these changes
- The nature, extent and significance of patterns of social mobility

Stratification and Differentiation

Introduction

We use the term stratification to refer to hierarchical segments (or strata) of society, some of which experience higher degrees of social status and greater cultural and economic privileges than others. Social strata cannot be described simply in terms of income and wealth, but also in terms of cultural factors, such as accents, leisure activities and areas of residence. Differentiation within sociology refers to the differences that are exhibited within society looking at social and cultural differences in terms of factors such as class, gender, and ethnicity and so on. Therefore, when we look at issues such as social inequality, on the other hand, refers to relative differences in life chances, or opportunities that people have to improve their quality of life. Having access to basic resources (e.g. food, clothing, shelter, and education) betters one's life chances, as does having wealth, social status and power. Social inequality in relation to differentiation and social stratification are thus very closely related.

An overview of different systems of stratification

Systems of stratification (slavery, estate, caste, class, age, ethnicity and sex) have the following three features in common:

- The groupings or stratifications (for example, women or older people) are made up of individuals who are not all personally known to each other, but are rather identified by a characteristic such as age, sex or ethnicity
- These stratifications directly impact on an individual's life experiences and opportunities. In a heavily stratified society (such as one that practises slavery, for example) a member of the enslaved class will have a very different experience of life as compared to a privileged member. This is entirely due to their membership of a particular ethnicity, religion or other social group
- The definitions of these social stratifications change very slowly indeed, since powerful and entrenched elites are usually not quick to share power or to change the unfairness of the system from which they benefit directly

Slavery

Slavery, alongside gender discrimination, is most likely the oldest form of social stratification. Slavery was practised in both Ancient Greece and Rome, and in America more recently (until as late as the nineteenth century). The British also took part in the slave trade (the transportation of Africans from Africa to America) and made a great deal of money from this.

Slavery is the ownership of one human by another. A slave is an owned human; the property of another human. Usually, the owner has the power of life and death over the slave, and a slave is forced to do manual work for long hours with no pay, no rights, no education and no freedom.

There are modern forms of slavery still in existence, the biggest probably being sexual slavery or sex slave trafficking. Women from poorer countries are tricked with the promise of a job or lifestyle in a richer country, and are then forced to work as prostitutes or sex workers for little or no money once they arrive. They are essentially slaves because they are owned by the men who have trafficked them, have no freedom and find it hard to escape.

Estate

This type of stratification is also an older form, and is also sometimes called feudalism. It was found in Europe in the Middle Ages, and was based on a system of landownership that was heavily stratified. The king, at the top of the social system, owned a great deal of land and in return for services and loyalty from the aristocratic class, he lent this land to them to be used for hunting or for living.

The aristocratic class then lived on this land and the ordinary workers or peasants who lived there too did the majority of the work and had few rights, power or wealth themselves. They were land workers, for example, and they lived as part of the aristocrat's estate. It is from this that the name is derived.

Caste

This form of social stratification is associated mainly with India, and especially with the Hindu majority of the Indian subcontinent. In the Hindu system, individuals are born into different social classes or castes, which they usually inherit from their parents. Some castes have a great deal of social prestige and rank, while others have much less. At the bottom are the lowest group of 'untouchables'. People who are untouchables do the worst jobs and receive the least money, prestige or social honour (as their name suggests). In the Hindu system, it is thought that the caste one is born into is dependent on the extent of religious merit that has been achieved in a previous life. Therefore, if an individual has lived a good life, the thinking is that they will be born into a higher social caste in their next life.

Class

This is one of the major forms of social stratification in the UK today, and many sociologists argue that UK society is heavily divided along class lines, or along lines of wealth, income and status. The extent of wealth inequality in the UK has been the subject of earlier topics in this course.

Ethnicity

However, other sociologists dispute this to some extent, and argue that racism and discrimination against ethnic minorities is the major form of social stratification in the UK. The ethnicity of an individual, in their thinking, is the major way in which society is divided between those who have access to wealth, power and status and those who do not.

Sex

Feminist sociologists argue differently that sex is still the major form of social stratification. Women still receive less pay then men, are under-represented at the top levels of law, politics, business and finance, still do the majority of the housework and child care, and still suffer domestic violence, the fear of domestic violence, sexual assault and other forms of sex-based violence to a far greater degree than men.

Theories of social class

Functionalist theory of social class and inequality

Functionalists argue that all parts of society contribute to a working whole; social strata are no exception to this rule; they are interdependent and necessary. Each stratum has an important function, and if one did not, it would cease to exist.

Functionalists hold that inequalities in society are justified by value consensus, e.g. there is a consensus in western societies that doctors are very valuable contributors, and as such, they receive higher salaries. Parsons argued that power inequalities are necessary and an inevitable result of the fact that some are more capable of managing working lives than others.

Davis and Moore (1967) argued that society's functional prerequisites inevitably result in stratification.

Activity 104 - Ensure that you can explain the functionalist theory of social class and inequality.

Criticisms of functionalism

Marxist theory of social stratification

Unlike Functionalists, Marxists think that social structure is born out of struggle and conflict (rather than value consensus). Stratification benefits only the rich and powerful, or the ruling class, which uses its status to exploit the subject class. The ruling class owns and controls the capital, land, and industry in society whereas the subject class depends on the ruling class for survival.

All social structures and institutions serve to maintain the status quo, or the unequal power relationships in society. The media, law, and politics all define and control social values and the dominant ideology.

Activity 105 - Make sure that you understand the Marxist perspective on social stratification, especially as this relates to class.

Weberian theory of stratification

Weber was similar to Marx in that he felt that social classes were based largely on economic relationships. And like functionalists, he felt that people with skills that are in high demand will hold higher positions in the market. Overall though, he did not feel that stratification resulted from constant exploitation or aspirations to maintain value consensus. He felt that society was much more complex, and that social hierarchy was based not only on differences in economic power, but also on social prestige and political power. He discussed the concept of status groupings whereby people with social prestige and political power ally themselves to create powerful elites, though these are not necessarily related to economic power also.

Activity 106 - Make sure you understand the Weberian perspective on social stratification.

Postmodern theory and social class

Postmodern theory is more individual-focussed, as the theorists think that social class as a sociological category and as a key component of identity has become obsolete. Unlike the other theorists, postmodernists think that people can shape their own social identities, based on their own choices and perceptions about society. One's status in society is no longer dictated by social class, wealth, or power, but rather, is strongly influenced by lifestyle and personal values and choices.

Criticisms

Professional and economic power

According to Marx, society was defined and unequally divided because of power differentiation. He discussed power in terms of ownership of production, e.g., the bourgeoisie use their dominant position in society to control and exploit the proletariat.

Weber, on the other hand, discusses economic power in terms of job skill marketability. Those with highly marketable job skills will acquire more power and higher degrees of status in society. This accounts for differentiations in influence and power among members of the middle class.

Runciman (1990) argued that economic power was defined by many factors beyond occupational roles, including social status of immediate family members. He also devised a classification system to describe different elements of economic power:

- Ownership – e.g. people who own the means of production and industry have power
- Control – e.g. people that direct or control production and service provision within a trade or industry (ex: managers)
- Marketability – e.g. people with certain skills, qualifications or experience that can attract high prices for their labour

Personal power

In day-to-day social relationships, people usually experience inequalities in power. Weber described three such sources of authority.

- Charismatic authority – when people possess qualities that inspire others to submit to their authority. This is the only type of authority not linked to social class
- Legal authority – positions of authority that are acknowledged and widely accepted because of a society's legal system—e.g. police officers, judges.
- Traditional authority – inherited positions of power and status—e.g. the ruling monarch

Most people do not neatly fall under one of these three categories, but rather, a combination of categories.

Stratification and gender

There has been a considerable amount of concern and debate among sociologists over whether or not gender should be factored into studies that relate social class to stratification. Some feel that women should be categorised according to their social class background rather than their gender: it is social class that will directly impact a woman's social status and life chances. However, many argue that women are still disadvantaged in the work place. For example, there are twice as many men than women in higher professional and managerial occupations despite the fact that there are now more women graduates then men, and women outperform men in university.

Women often face glass ceilings and vertical segregation in the work place. Women also experience horizontal segregation within their own social classes: for example, conducting a disproportionate amount of care work (such as childcare and elder care) or housework and domestic tasks regardless of their class. If women are more likely to take time away from their careers to focus on domestic work and care giving, then this obviously impedes career development. It is thus necessary to incorporate gender into studies of stratification.

Theories of gender and inequality

Human capital theory

Human capital theory basically claims that women are disadvantaged in the workplace due to choice: they are simply less committed to their careers, usually due to a break that occurs during years of childbearing and childcare.

Many people have countered this argument, claiming that, for example, women who do not take career breaks still face troubles with climbing corporate ladders. Also, statistics show that women still earn less than men, indicating that women are still discriminated against in the workplace on the grounds of gender.

Reserve army of labour

Marx argued that women comprise a 'reserve army of labour' in capitalist societies that require more and fewer labourers respectively during booms and recessions. Women can flood the workforce when needed and retreat to their home lives when there are enough male labourers to satisfy the economy's needs. Whereas some argue that women take up part time work by choice, due to their lifestyles as care givers, Marx would argue that women are exploited as part-time workers, earning lower, hourly rates than full-time workers.

Feminism

Some feminists focus on women's inequality due to their relationships with men; others focus on the relationship of women to the labour market.

Radical feminists feel that men endeavour to control women in the workplace; women are often sexually harassed and can do nothing to retaliate without compromising their careers. Walby discusses public patriarchy, or the dominance of men in public life and the workforce (versus private patriarchy, or the dominance of men in the home), as the reason that women are disadvantaged in the workplace. Trade unions especially disadvantage women by using male power to exclude women from high status jobs.

Although she recognises that capitalism does contribute to gender inequality, she thinks that male dominance and unequal gender relations are the primary causes. In her book 'Theorising Patriarchy', Walby calls patriarchy:

"...a system of social structures and practices in which men dominate, oppress and exploit women" (1990).

She also states that:

"...patriarchal structures....restrict women and help to maintain male domination."

Attitudinal research into gender inequalities

A recent study indicated that a smaller number of people disapproved of unequal pay than had done so in the past. Both women and men felt that unequal pay is unfair, but women were angrier about the issue than men.

Research into the causes of pay inequality

Grimshaw and Rubery researched the causes of pay inequality in 2001.
They concluded that:

- Women tend to work in care jobs and public sector jobs that are typically lower paid than private sector jobs
- More women are in part-time employment compared to men, and part-time, hourly wages are, on average, only 60 per cent of full time wages
- When employers award workers based on merit and performance, they can often end up favouring men, yet masking unfair practices such as gender stereotyping (women don't make good leaders – so we won't promote a woman to a senior position)
- There has been an increase in the use of subcontracting and franchising. This has brought down wages in traditionally female jobs. For example, contracted cleaners are paid less than permanent cleaners

Radical Feminist Shulamith Firestone argues that patriarchy is an unnatural state that is oppressive and this oppression stems from biology. By virtue of being able to have children, women are oppressed by a patriarchal system that focuses on a woman's reproductive function and this biological distinction is one of the factors that maintain gender inequalities in society. She goes as far as to say:

"….family structure is the source of psychological, economic and political oppression."

Firestone also argues that generally the role played by men within society is given greater importance and significance when compared to women.

Stratification and ethnicity

As mentioned above, one's ethnicity can directly have an impact on his or her life chances. Though the UK is an incredibly diverse nation, ethnic minorities can and do often face poorer life chances than white people.

Stereotyping, prejudice and discrimination

It is important to differentiate between stereotyping, prejudice and discrimination. Stereotyping occurs when one's attitude toward a particular segment of society is based on oversimplified preconceptions. Stereotypes are often recognised by entire social groups or by all members of a society. Often, people use stereotypes to classify people and to make quick judgements on whether to enter certain social situations. A prejudice is a judgement that is based on stereotyped beliefs. Prejudices can be positive or negative. For example, someone might judge a white middle class woman in her mid-30s as a 'safe' person to pass by on the street at night. Even though this is, essentially, a positive judgement, it is still a stereotype. Lastly, discrimination occurs when people treat others differentially because of stereotyped beliefs. For example, people of black and minority ethnic backgrounds often experience discrimination in educational and workplace environments, thus having lower success and income levels and higher rates of unemployment. Studies have indicated that because of institutional racism, people of black and minority ethnic backgrounds are more likely to be unemployed or to work in low-paid and low-skilled jobs.

Sociological explanations of ethnicity and inequality

Many sociologists point to racism as one of the primary causes of social inequality in educational and work settings. There are several different theories of racism and inequality:

- Weber – points to power and status inequalities as causes of racism. Power is in the hands of the white majority; the interests of black and minority ethnic groups are often not represented, and thus they experience status inequality
- Rex and Tomlinson – supported the dual labour market theory. Basically, they argued that ethnic minorities are relegated to a secondary labour market, which has lower wages and poorer working conditions than the white-dominated primary labour market. An overrepresentation of immigrant workers in the secondary labour market has led to the formation of a black underclass
- Cox (working from Marx) – argued that racism is caused by colonisation, a mechanism which serves to justify capitalist exploitation
- Many sociologists refuse to stick to one theory—they think that racism is the result of a multitude of social events
- Pilkington – agrees that racial discrimination exists but disagrees with the notion of a black underclass. He feels that ethnic groups 'overlap' and that there are some minority ethnics that do have high-status careers

Definition:

Dual labour market theory: in this economic theory, the economy is divided into two parts. These are the primary and secondary sectors. The primary sector is that of professional labour and wages, while the secondary sector is that of low wages and short term job contracts in low-skilled labour.

On a final note, it is important to recognise that people from different minority ethnic backgrounds will have vastly different experiences from one another. Often, people of white or majority ethnic backgrounds wrongly assume that different minority ethnic groups have more similarities than differences. This is an example of ethnocentrism.

Age, Disability and Inequality

Whereas many researchers have discussed unequal treatment of women and minority ethnic groups (particularly in work environments), age discrimination has become so entrenched in society that it is often overlooked. The two segments of society that suffer the most from age discrimination are youths and elderly people. Elderly people are often stereotyped as incompetent; young people are often negatively viewed in response to social issues such as youth crime.

With life expectancy on the rise, the elderly segment of the population continues to expand; studies suggest that the high unemployment rates of people 50+ have become a major financial burden on the British economy, costing up to £30 billion per year. Some businesses have recognised the usefulness of employing people of diverse ages, thus abandoning mandatory retirement age policies and targeting older workers. Elderly people, comprising a large portion of the population, now exert an increasing amount of social and political influence.

Disability

Sociologists have also researched how disabled people are stigmatised and discriminated against; they use the term 'disableism' to describe this common social occurrence. Studies indicate that disabled people are much more likely to live in poverty and to experience lower life chances than able-bodied people.

Activity 107 –

Why do you think that disabled people more likely to live in poverty? Consider the relationship between disability and life chances.

You may like to research the link between disability, social exclusion and life chances further by looking at these statistics:
http://news.bbc.co.uk/1/hi/uk/4790438.stm

Dimensions of Inequality – Life Chances

The term and concept of 'life chances' was first introduced by Weber who defined it as:

"A person's power to obtain a supply of goods, external living conditions and personal life experiences."

Weber also suggests that 'life chances' can be characterised by three core elements:

- Class – economic relationships
- Status – social standing
- Parity – power and ownership through groups and organisations
- Of the three, class was the one that Weber considered to be the most significant

Overall then, life chances can be described as specific types of opportunities that one has, from birth, to improve his or her quality of life.

With the above definitions in mind we will now go onto examine what impact class, gender, ethnicity, age and disability have on life chances.

Life Chances and Class

Social class studies suggest that the higher an individual's social class, the greater their life chances. According to Westergaard and Restler (1976) class is the primary source of inequality. People who are born into lower social classes tend to be worse off, experiencing poorer health, educational opportunities, social exclusion and thus fewer non-manual job and job promotion prospects. People that are born into lower social classes also tend to experience higher infant mortality rates and shorter life-spans due to lack of access to certain resources such as health care or the opportunity to live a healthy lifestyle.

Even though there was an increase in social mobility (and thus an improvement in life chances) in the post-war period, middle and upper-class boys still had far greater chances of securing high-status jobs than working-class boys.

According to Walter and Saggers (2007):

"Social class impacts upon life chances, which are the opportunities available to people throughout their lives. These include: everything from the chance to stay alive during the first year after birth to the chance to view fine are, the chance to remain healthy and grow tall and if sick to get well again quickly, the chance to avoid becoming a juvenile delinquent and very crucially, the chance to complete an intermediary and higher educational grade."

Activity 108 –

Do you agree with the definition of 'life chance' given?
Has your 'social class' affected your life chances?

Differentiation: dimensions of inequality

Besides class, ethnicity and dis/ability, age and gender are also major contributing factors to one's life chances. For example, women, particularly those of lower class backgrounds, will experience disadvantages in the work place.

Life chances and Gender

When looking at life chances in relation to gender, there are three core areas that tend to be the focus of any sociological analysis and discussion (note, there are others but we will be focusing on three). They are:

Domestic arrangements	Studies show that men spend more time in paid work and women in domestic work. However, many feminist perspectives argue that in actuality women perform dual roles, working both inside and outside the home.
Educational achievement and experiences	Statistically girls do better than boys academically. However, inequality can be seen in the areas of study and training that girls choose when compared to boys – certain subjects and professions may be promoted according to gender bias. In terms of classroom interaction the dominance of males over females due to disruption and attention-seeking behaviour exhibited by boys at the expense of girls.
Health	Whilst women tend to live longer than men, they are likely to experience poor health over a longer period of time.

Duncombe and Marsden (1995), in their work on looking at households, argue that in reality women perform what they call 'Women's Triple Shift':

- Domestic labour/housework

- Emotional work – supporting partners and family, and keeping other people happy
- Paid employment

So, in the light of this, women are in paid employment as well as doing housework and they are also doing more emotional work, being responsible for the emotional well-being of the household.

Activity 109 –

It is important that you have an understanding of how levels of social mobility have an impact on society at large.

You may like to start your research into levels of social mobility in different countries here:

http://www.equalitytrust.org.uk/

Life Chances and Ethnicity

Ethnicity can be defined as characteristics shared by a group based on factors such as culture, heritage, ancestry, history, language, religion, nationality, shared norms and values, customs and practices and so on. Generally it can be regarded as a socially constructed thing that is sometimes connected to race, race being associated with distinctive physical characteristics that can distinguish one race from another e.g. skin colour.

The sociological discussions around race and ethnicity are complex. For example, some sociologists argue that race is a myth as there are very few significant genetic differences between races, and emphasis on the physical differences acts as a social tool for discrimination.

For the purpose of this part of the course, we will operate on the basis of the definition of ethnicity referred to above, whilst being aware there are many facets to this discussion.

Ethnicity like class and gender can be used as the basis for social discrimination and therefore a form of stratification. As with other social groups, ethnicity can impact upon life chances when we look at inequalities that can be experienced in terms of factors such as income and employment, education and health.

Barron and Norris suggest that there are two labour markets (Dual Labour Market Theory):

- The Primary Labour Market – good pay, good work conditions, job security, and opportunities for promotion, male dominated
- The Secondary Labour Market – low pay if paid at all, poor work conditions, lack of recognition, little or no opportunity for progression

According to Barron and Norris, ethnic minorities tend to be over represented in the secondary group. Rex and Tomlinson (1979) not only referred to the Dual Labour Market but also referred to what they saw as a 'Black Underclass' where people experienced racism in the job market – not being able to get a job or job security leading to unemployment and poverty, which invariably has an impact upon life chances.

According to the Parliamentary Office of Science and Technology (2007), Black and Minority Ethnic (BME) groups have "…worse health than the overall population…." They go on to say that, "Evidence suggests that the poorer socio-economic position of BME groups is the main factor driving ethnic health inequalities."[43]
The report goes on to point out that:

- South Asian men are more likely to suffer from heart disease
- Caribbean men are more likely to die from strokes
- BME groups are more likely to be diagnosed with mental health issues

Why these groups are more prone to the aforementioned conditions cannot be fully explained by simply looking at socio-economic factors, therefore some researchers have suggested that there could be a biological disposition to such conditions. It should also be noted that in terms of mental illness the reports suggests that:

"Black Caribbean and African people are more likely to enter psychiatric care through the criminal justice system than through contact with health services."
This, it could be argued by some, is more a result of discrimination within the criminal justice system and less to do with a predisposition to mental illness for certain ethnic groups.

---

[43] See www.parliament.uk/documents/post/postpn276.pdf for the full report.

Life Chances and Gender

When looking at life chances in relation to gender, there are three core areas that tend to be the focus for any sociological analysis.[44] They are:

- Domestic arrangements - Studies show that men spend more time in paid work, and women in domestic work. However, some feminist perspectives argue that in actuality women perform dual roles, working both inside and outside the home. Duncombe and Marsden (1995), when looking at households found that in reality women performed three roles known as the 'Women's Triple Shift' (as discussed):
    - ➢ Housework/domestic labour
    - ➢ Emotional work/supporting and keeping the household happy
    - ➢ Paid employment/Work outside the household
- Educational achievement and experiences - Statistically girls now do better than boys academically, though there are still gendered divisions in subject choice at A-level and degree level. This means that inequality exists through the areas of study and training girls choose when compared to boys – certain subjects and professions are promoted according to gender. Research by Swann and Graddol (1994) found that boys would get more attention due to their behaviour, being more boisterous than girls. They also found that boys would dominate class-based discussion.
- Health - Whilst women tend to live longer than men, they are likely to experience poor health over a longer period of time.
- Life Chances and Age - In order to address this aspect of this discussion we need to be clear about what we mean by age. The concept of age is a social construct in that what is considered to be old, young, and youthful, aged and in-between, is not just restricted to physiology but also by how society as a whole views certain age groups. Therefore, age and what constitutes a certain age group will change over time according to how society develops. So, age can be:
- Chronological – how old are you in terms of age, based on your actual date of birth

---

[44] There are others but we will focus on three.

- Biological – your chronological age may be 25 but due to some physical condition your physical age is 50
- Legal – as defined by the law in terms of certain rights and obligations
- Social – interaction with other members of society and how they perceive the individual in terms of their age
- Subjective – the individual's own perception and attitude toward age

Activity 110 - What do you think are some of the challenges older people face within society today?

In terms of society's understanding of age, age can fall into one of the following categories:

- Childhood
- Youth
- Middle Age
- Old Age

The age of childhood

According to Wagg (1992), childhood is a socially constructed concept. This view is born out when we look at childhood through the ages. In pre-industrial and industrial societies child labour was the norm, with children working from the age of 7 and younger if they were considered able to. Aries (1960) suggests that at this time, particularly in the Middle Ages, "the idea of childhood did not exist". In fact children were treated as smaller versions of adults with the law applying to them in the same way as adults.

Today, many aspects of this attitude to children would be considered to be child abuse and neglect. Shorter (1975) found that the death rates of children were high, and there was a high level of indifference that would never be seen as acceptable in today's society. Life chances in these circumstances therefore were not positive and could not be associated with any real level of longevity.

Childhood - When did the attitudes of the past change?

According to Aries, the 20th century saw families becoming more child focused and attitudes toward childhood being more positive and child centred. This for sociologists has come about because of changes in the law, smaller family units, compulsory education, the welfare state, improved healthcare and lifestyle resulting in a decrease in mortality rates, increased affluence, changes to the ages of consent and so on.

Despite the changes in attitudes toward childhood over time, Postman (1994) suggests that the age of childhood is disappearing fast, with children being given the same or similar rights and responsibilities as adults. He also suggests that because of the age of improved literacy and increased access to information, in that the children can access the adult world through things like the media, that the line between the adult world and childhood has become somewhat blurred and therefore the golden age of innocence is becoming a thing of the past.

So in the worst possible and extreme cases children are committing offences such as murder, one particularly high profile example of this is the murder of the toddler James Bulger by two boys aged 10. Also they are experiencing emotional and psychological problems that were once considered to be adult issues. Childline, for example, receives approximately 20,000 calls per year. According to the NSPCC in 2014, 48,000 children in England were identified as needing protection from abuse. All of these elements invariably will have an impact on life chances.

Activity 111 - What criticisms do you think can be made of the views put forward by Aries and Postman?

Old Age

In terms of stratification and age, it is argued that younger people carry a higher status within society than older ones and as such are valued more. This is often seen in the world of work where statistics illustrate the differences between age groups. For example, according to the Annual Survey of Hours and Earnings (2008), over 60s in full time employment received on average £22,611, when compared to those in their 50s received £26,191 and those in their 40s who received £27,951. The ONS in 2008 found that if an individual is unemployed, the older the person the longer they are likely to stay unemployed when compared to a younger person e.g. In 2008, 33% of unemployed over 50s had been unemployed for a year or more when compared to 29% of 25-59 years old. Older people are likely to experience a drop in their income over time. This, not surprisingly, can have an impact on the quality of living e.g. being able to afford basic living expenses. What is clear is that the older population is growing and that people are living for longer. Statistics from Age UK London make the following observations with regard to age in the UK:

- There are over 21 million people aged 50 years and over which is over a third of the total UK population
- There are over 12 million people of state pension age
- There are 10.3 million people aged 65 or over
- There are over 1.4 million people aged 85 or over
- Each year, approximately 650,000 people turn 65
- There are now more people in the UK aged 60 and above than there are under 18
- There are more pensioners than there are children under 16
- The numbers of people reaching the age of 100 has nearly quadrupled since 1981, from 2,600 to almost 12,000 in 2009
- Approximately 3.8 million older people live alone of which 70% of these are women over 65
- Over 2 million people over 75 live alone of which 1.5 million of these are women.
- 62% of widows are aged 75 and over

Population projections

- The number of people aged 60 or over is expected to pass the 20 million mark by 2031
- The percentage of the total population who are over 60 is predicted to rise from 22% at present to nearly 29% in 2033 and 31% in 2058
- The number of people aged 60 or over is projected to rise by nearly 50 per cent in the next 25 years
- The number of people aged 65 years and over is expected to rise by 65% in the next 25 years to over 16.4 million in 2033
- The population over 75 is projected to double in the next 30 years
- The number of people over 85 in the UK is predicted to double in the next 20 years and nearly treble in the next 30
- By 2083, about one in three people in the UK will be over 60
- Nearly one in five people currently in the UK will live to see their 100th birthday
- However, according to the National Statistician, the UK's population is ageing more slowly than other comparable countries

With an increasingly aging population, there are increasing health issues that will be experienced by older people from serious life altering conditions to those that are not considered as serious but may be associated with the aging process such as needing glasses.

Whilst we have looked at the childhood and old age, we must remember that statistics such as those presented by the ONS 2011/2012, show that the young, particularly young males between the ages of 16-24 are more likely than other age groups to be victims of crime.

Life Chances and Disability

As with ethnicity, social class and age, it is generally accepted within Sociology that disability is socially defined and constructed and our understanding of it has changed over time. Therefore, we have to look at it within a social context in order to apply a definition of what constitutes disability. However, according to the Equality Act 2010 a person is disabled if they have a "physical or mental impairment" and that "impairment has a substantial and long term adverse effect" on their "ability to carry our normal day to day activities." Even with this definition, we do need to remember the social construction of disability in that there are those who would argue that it is not the person who has limitations in terms of their ability but rather the circumstances and situations and the way society is set up that causes limitations and therefore affects life chances.

According to Oliver and Barnes (1998), disability can be the basis of social exclusion and oppression. Oliver argues that the definitions of disability with its focus on impairment, fails to take into account that a lot of the impairment and restrictions experienced by those classed as disabled experience impairment because the environment an individual has to operate within does not lend itself to the requirements of that individual.

"...In our view, it is society which disables physically impaired people. Disability is something imposed on top of our impairments by the way we are unnecessarily isolated and excluded from full participation in society. Disabled people are therefore an oppressed group in society. To understand this it is necessary to grasp the distinction between the physical impairment and the social situation, called 'disability', of people with such impairment. Thus we define impairment as lacking all or part of a limb, or having a defective limb, organism or mechanism of the body and disability as the disadvantage or restriction of activity caused by a contemporary social organisation which takes little or no account of people who have physical impairments and thus excludes them 4 from participation in the mainstream of social activities." (Oliver 1996)

Statistics from the Department for Work and Pensions (DWP) and Office for Disability Issues (ODI) show significant differences in areas such as education, work, living standards etc. for those identified as being disabled. A summary of their findings is as follows:[45]

Facts	Year	Disabled	Non-disabled
Families with at least one disabled person experiencing relative poverty			
Living standards	2011-2012	19%	15%
Working age in employment			
Employment	2012	46.3%	76.4%
End of Key Stage 4 achieving 5 or more GCSEs at grades A* to C			
Education	2010-2011	59.2% without a statement 24.9% with a statement	88.9%
Does not have any formal qualifications			
Post-19 Education	2012	19.2%	6.5%
Degree Level	2012	14.9%	28.1%
Discrimination			
Experiences of unfair treatment at work	2008	19%	13%
Justice System			
Likelihood of being a victim of a crime (16-34 years old)	2010-2011	39%	28%

According to the Family Resources Survey 2011/12 "...there are over 11 million people with a limiting long term illness, impairment or disability." And "The prevalence of disability rises with age. Around 6% of children are disabled, completed to 16% of working age adults and 45% of adults over State Pension age."[46]

---

[45] Complete 'Disability Facts and Figures' can be found at: https://www.gov.uk/government/publications/disability-facts-and-figures/disability-facts-and-figures#about-these-statistics
[46] Source: Family Resources Survey 2010/11

Social Class

The general (often unspoken) understanding that people have about social class is that three, distinct classes exist within British society: upper, middle and working. Many sociologists abide by this division in their discussions, also including a fourth class: the underclass.

The Upper class

Sociologists differ as to whether they still think there is a distinctive upper class or elite, based on ownership of wealth, land and property. In estates or feudalistic societies, there is a distinctive and powerful elite who control large amounts of land, money and labour. This is the aristocratic or ruling class.

However, in modern society, there is perhaps not quite the same distinctive elite who are visible and also highly powerful, though some sociologists argue that there is nevertheless still an upper class but they remain largely invisible to the public gaze. The modern upper class is instead the wealthy elite who have made a great deal of money from the financial system. In which case, one method to determine whether or not there is an upper class is to assess how far money and power are concentrated in the hands of an elite in society.

The Middle class

This is a very diverse and varied class grouping, and in fact can be further subdivided into: lower middle class, middle class and upper middle class. The middle class covers a range of white collar professions (such as education, the law or the medical profession) and service industries (such as tourism and catering).

Most of the British population can be considered middle class due to the relative minority of the upper class and the increasing decline of traditional blue collar working class jobs (such as mining or manufacturing). For this reason alone, it is problematic to talk about the middle class as a homogenous group since it is so broad and diverse.

The working class

Traditionally, the working class were those employed in blue collar industries such as mining, ship building, steelworks or manufacturing. In Marxist analysis, the working class was seen as the only class that had the potential and power to create revolution, by virtue of being the class with the least to lose and the most to gain, and having the powerful motivation of suffering from oppression and injustice.

Indeed, one hallmark of modernity in British society is the decline of traditional working class jobs as manufacturing locates abroad to follow the lower wage labour markets in countries such as China or India. This has meant that the traditional culture of the working class has changed dramatically as the traditional work of the working classes has changed in availability.

The underclass

Many sociologists now debate whether or not there is such a thing as an underclass. This term refers to the section of society at the bottom in terms of healthcare, education, living standards and life expectations. They are seen as being an excluded class, living outside of the norms and standards of the rest of society, and are characterised by problems such as addiction, worklessness or chaotic home and personal lives.

Activity 112 - Make sure you understand the ways in which social strata are hierarchical.

Social class is not as straightforward to define as it may seem. As an indicator of social stratification and differentiation a number of characteristics and features need to be taken into account such as income, occupation, wealth, status and power, lifestyle, norms and values, level of education etc.

Findings presented to the British Sociological Association following a BBC and academic collaboration entitled, 'The Great British Class Survey' of more than 160,000 people, suggests that rather than class categories being limited to the 3 classes used in the past (working, middle and upper class), there are now 7 classes that can be identified, when factors such as assets, occupation, education, cultural capital, economic capital, social activities and so on are taken into account. What is the same, however, in terms of categorisation is that those at the top of the class hierarchy are still fewer in numbers than those in the middle or bottom.

The seven classes are:

- Precariat – significantly deprived; low levels of socio-economic and cultural capital
- Traditional working class – not as deprived as the precariat in terms of economic and cultural capital but still when compared to the next group
- Emergent service class – low economic capital but aspirational social and cultural capital
- Technical middle class – small in numbers, high economic capital but low social and cultural capital
- New affluent workers – medium levels of all forms of capital, but not as high as the Elite
- Elite – extremely high levels of all three forms of capital – economic, cultural and social

Activity 113 -
Article from the Independent on the seven social classes in Britain:
http://www.independent.co.uk/news/uk/home-news/britain-now-has-7-social-classes--and-working-class-is-a-dwindling-breed-8557894.html

Article from the Financial Times = 'Social advantages still shape life chances'
http://www.ft.com/cms/s/0/72110f9e-0ab1-11df-b35f-00144feabdc0.html

The social class categorisations that are used by governmental departments are much more specific. The two systems of class definition that you should be aware of are the RG Scale, or Registrar's General Scale, introduced in 1913 and used up until 2000, as well as the currently-used NS-SEC, or National Statistics Socioeconomic Classification system.

Activity 114 –

You can find details of the NS-SEC scale here:
http://www.ons.gov.uk/ons/guide-method/classifications/current-standard-classifications/soc2010/soc2010-volume-3-ns-sec--rebased-on-soc2010--user-manual/index.html
What do you think are some of the weaknesses of the NS-SEC Scale?

It is this form of classification that is used in socio-economic research and analysis. The classes are as follows:

1	Higher managerial, administrative and professional occupations[47]
1.1	Large employers and higher managerial and administrative occupations
1.2	Higher professional occupations
2	Lower managerial, administrative and professional occupations
3	Intermediate occupations
4	Small employers and own account workers
5	Lower supervisory and technical occupations
6	Semi-routine occupations
7	Routine occupations
8	Never worked and long-term unemployed

---

[47] Note that this class has two sub-classes (1.1 and 1.2)

Power, influence and choice

Income and occupation (understood as class) are not the only factors that influence one's life chances. People exercise varying degrees of professional, economic and/or personal power over their daily environments, which can have a profound impact on individual experiences and opportunities.

Changes in structure of inequality

Changing patterns of social mobility

In the previous section, we looked at the 'classic' studies of social mobility. Now, it is time to examine how changes in income distribution and working patterns have influenced social mobility.

Changes in the Twentieth century

In the twentieth century, there was a huge increase in the number of professional and non-manual jobs. Participation in manual labour industries dropped from approximately 80 per cent to 44 per cent, and the coal mining industry especially declined, with rapid closures that brought the number of employed down from 750,000 at the industry's peak to 8,500 in 1994.

Gender roles also underwent a massive transformation, with over 70 per cent of women now in paid employment compared to the time when the majority of women left their paid jobs on marriage.

Activity 115 –
Make sure you can describe the major social and economic changes in the twentieth century and how these had an impact on social mobility.

You may like to review some of your earlier notes where relevant.

Following the war and throughout the rest of the twentieth century, the population grew wealthier; however, there remain significant gaps between the rich and the poor. One method of addressing this inequality is progressive taxation, which taxes the rich at higher rates, thus redistributing wealth across the different income groups.

Traditionally, it is Labour governments that push for progressive taxation and similar such equalising measures. Conservative governments tend to preserve the interests of capitalism by rewarding economic success. One way of doing this is through regressive taxation, which benefits the wealthiest members of society and disadvantages the poorest. When New Labour took over, rather than reverting to progressive taxation, they opted to protect capitalism with regressive taxation policies. Many would say that this was to make the British economy more competitive globally, thus attracting more investments. Some critics note that the government is dependent on capitalism to survive, and it is thus in their best interest to tax the public accordingly.

Changes to the working class

There has been much debate over the way in which the working class should be defined and about whether or not there remains a clearly defined gap between the working class and the middle class. As manual labour jobs decrease due to technological advancements, so do the employment prospects for what, traditionally, researchers and society-at-large would have labelled the 'working class'. However, some researchers argue that people of working class backgrounds do take up non-manual work. As service industry jobs have been on the rise, there would thus seem to be employment prospects for people of working class backgrounds.

On the other hand, a study by Marshall et al (1988) indicated that manual workers tend to define themselves as 'working class', and non-manual workers tend to describe themselves as 'middle-class' despite the fact that the former group can earn more than the latter. Because of the decrease in manual labour jobs, as well as the uncertainty surrounding social class definitions and self-categorisations, many sociologists feel that the working class is dividing and in danger of disappearing.

Formation of an underclass?

Sociologists are also debating about the existence of a distinct and separate underclass. Some think that there are simply 'lower levels' of the working class, in which unemployment and poverty is common; others argue that an underclass indeed exists: that members of this segment of society behave differently than members of the working class, thus separating themselves from the rest of the stratification system. Members of the underclass are often out of work for extended periods of time and depend on the welfare state for survival.

Activity 116 - Do you think that there a separate underclass in UK society?

Changes to the middle class

The question that many social researchers currently face: is there still a distinct middle class, or rather, are we faced with several smaller groups that experience varying degrees of social mobility and differing life chances?

The middle class has been divided and reconfigured by several social researchers. It used to be widely understood that routine clerical workers comprised the 'lower middle class', whilst professionals and civil servants comprised the 'upper middle class'.

However, more recently, researchers such as Savage *et al* (1992) argue that middle class lifestyles vary greatly depending on whether someone is employed in the public sector (less lucrative) or the private sector (more lucrative).

Giddens, on the other hand states that the middle class is still distinct and different from the working class because middle class workers use brainpower and specialised skills whereas working class labourers use physical strength.

Changes to the upper class

The Marxist notion of the 'ruling class' (that is, the people who own the means of production) does not directly apply to British society as the importance of the service and financial industries now supersede that of production.

Some researchers claim that the upper class consists of the remaining owners of production, as well as company directors and higher professionals that invest in the private sector. Overall, some would say that the upper class is shrinking in size and influence.

Theories of change

Changes in the working class

Marx famously prophesised that the proletariat would continuously expand to include all of the intermediate classes until ultimately they would revolt and overthrow the bourgeoisie. Clearly, this has not been the case in the UK. Conversely, the middle class has grown in size, some would argue by subsuming members of the working class through a process known as embourgeoisement. This means that, due to an increasing demand for their skills, manual labourers have entered the middle classes.

Several researchers have challenged this notion. Goldthrope *et al* (1969), for example, researched the attitudes and opinions of white collar and manual workers in Luton, Bedfordshire. They found that the two groups had differing opinions on the purpose of their work: manual labourers saw work as a means to an end whereas white-collar workers expressed levels of job satisfaction. The two different groups tended not to mix with one another socially; however, overall each group shared a similar look on family life, viewing their homes and familial relations as central to their social existence. This departs from past research on working class labourers who tended to live more communally and exhibited high levels of social solidarity.

Lastly, the political allegiances of the manual labourers interviewed exhibited neither strong affiliations with middle-class views, nor with the Labour party or trade unions. Goldthorpe et al concluded that this was due to an increase in the emphasis on work as a means to an end among manual labourers. This new, privatised lifestyle had surpassed any allegiances to former, traditional working class values of social solidarity.

Though these manual labourers exhibited more capitalistic values, they showed no signs of social integration with white-collar workers; as such, there was no evidence to support the theory of embourgeosiement.

Activity 117 –

Imagine that you are conducting research on whether embourgeoisement has occurred among manual labourers in Manchester.

Do you think that the social attitudes of manual labourers in Manchester today might differ from those of manual labourers in Luton in 1969?

To what degree could a small-scale study, such as Goldthorpe's, be useful to you in your research? What other types of information would you try to gather before conducting your study?

Think about the research methods you would use to collect this kind of information and how you would go about devising a research project to do this.

Changes in the middle class

Savage et al (1992) worked from a neo-Marxist perspective, claiming that members of the middle class did not necessarily exhibit similar lifestyles; rather, they possessed one or more of the following assets, which made it possible for them to exploit others:

- They owned property
- They possessed positions of power in organisations
- They gained specific cultural assets through middle class education/social networking
- Members of the middle class could exploit others to differing degrees, depending on which assets they possessed

Savage *et al* claimed that because public service workers, due to government policies, are less able to exploit others, they experience different lifestyles than members of the private sector, who tend to earn higher incomes.

Are class structures disappearing?

Many researchers would say that yes, they are. Here are some reasons as to why:

- People are turning to religious and cultural values, as well as ethnic and gender identities, to define themselves. These factors are becoming more influential and important than social class identity
- People are taking increasing interest in more universal issues, such as ecology and equality which can cut across class boundaries
- Social change is occurring more rapidly; people are recognising and accepting a variety of different values
- People now define their lifestyles based on the goods that they choose to consume. Patterns of consumption define people more than their social classes do

Patterns of Social Mobility

Over the past 50 years, Britain has seen an increase in social mobility, meaning that people are increasingly moving between social classes, rather than remaining in the ones that they were born into. Sociologists are very interested in changing patterns in social mobility because they indicate much about the ways in which social classes, and class identities, are formed. By researching social mobility, sociologists can gauge the extent to which people experience equality of opportunity. You should be able to apply concepts related to social mobility to your own personal life and to your friends of different cultural and economic backgrounds. Presumably, you know of someone who has experienced intergenerational mobility or have experienced or observed either ascribed or achieved status. What follows is a list of key terms that you need to be able to understand and apply:

- Closed societies
- Open societies
- Ascribed status
- Achieved status
- Absolute mobility
- Relative mobility
- Intergenerational mobility
- Intragenerational mobility
- Social closure
- Meritocratic society

Activity 118 -
You may like to use the following sociological glossary for your research into these key terms:
http://www.sociologyguide.com/basic-concepts/index.php
Now reflect on these terms and try to apply to your personal life and experience.

It is important that you have a working understanding of these forms of social experience and understand them in real-world contexts.
Explanations

Social mobility is rare in pre-industrial societies; status is usually ascribed and social class is fixed at birth, with the exception of people who married into different social classes. In modern, meritocratic, industrial societies, status is achieved, and absolute mobility is greater.

The 'classic' studies of social mobility

Glass's study of social mobility

A pioneering study of social mobility was conducted by David Glass in 1954. He examined social class differences between fathers and sons, concluding that there was evidence of short-range social mobility, equally upward and downward. Long-range social mobility was rare as the upper classes tended to engage in social closure, recruiting sons that were born into the same career structure.

Glass's study has been criticised for its lack of focus on the growing middle class occupations (he mainly focused on working-class and professional men). Also, his classification system was destroyed and thus it is impossible to compare his results to those of later studies. Nonetheless, his study certainly stimulated further research on social mobility.

Oxford mobility studies

Goldthorpe conducted a study of social mobility in the 1980s, which, like Glass's study, compared fathers to sons. Goldthorpe devised a seven-class scheme and found that 50 per cent of the sons experienced upward mobility. He also concluded that there were greater chances of long-range social mobility than there were in the 1940s. Part of the reason for this was that there were more jobs available in what Goldthorpe called the service (upper 2) classes.

4.3: Crime and Deviance with Theory and Methods

4.3.1: Crime and Deviance

Key Areas:

- Crime, deviance, social order and social control
- The social distribution of crime and deviance by age, ethnicity, gender, locality and social class, including recent patterns and trends in crime
- Globalisation and crime in contemporary society; the mass media and crime; green crime; human rights and state crimes
- Crime control, prevention and punishment, victims, and the role of the criminal justice system and other agencies

4.3.2 Theory and Methods

Key Areas:

- Quantitative and Qualitative Methods
- Sources of Data
- Primary and Secondary Data
- Positivism, Interpretivism, and Sociological Methodology
- Theoretical, Practical and Ethical Considerations
- Consensus, Conflict, Structural and Social Action Theories
- Modernity and Post Modernity
- The Relationship between Theory and Methods
- Subjectivity, Objectivity and Value Freedom
- The relationship between Sociology and Social Policy

4.3.1: Crime and Deviance

Introduction

We have previously discussed social norms, and hopefully you will recall the 'library scenario' at the start of this course, in which you were to imagine your peers engaging in, what you might consider to be rather 'odd' behaviour. In case you have forgotten, here is the scenario:

Now imagine that you are sitting in a quiet university library, revising for a difficult exam. Without realising it, you are upholding a widely held value in contemporary society: that of the importance of working hard at school. Opposite you, a fellow student stands up on her chair and begins to sing; to your left, an acquaintance enters the room wearing nothing but a pair of boxers: he takes a seat and begins to read silently.

Both the singing girl and the nearly naked boy are challenging social norms and thus engaging in deviant behaviour. It is important to realise that deviant behaviour is not always 'dangerous' or 'violent' or even, with a passive glance, noticeable. In fact, you have probably displayed deviance, perhaps without even realising it, at some point in the past month. Crossing the road where there is no marked zebra crossing is an example of deviance, as is standing on the left side of a crowded escalator on the London underground, though both of these are minor examples. They are, however, examples of behaviour which is against the norm, standard or expected behaviour in those particular circumstances.

However, on many occasions, deviant behaviours can be classified as criminal behaviours that break laws and can cause harm to the victims involved. Criminology is a branch of sociology that focuses on forms of behaviour that are sanctioned by criminal law. Law refers to the written 'rules' of a society. The law of any democratic country are the rules and regulations which govern society, and which have been made by the democratically elected body (the government) of that country. In an authoritarian regime, the law is more arbitrary: often, the dictator makes laws or changes rules as he wants. There is no democratic element, and the people often fear laws which may take away their liberty.

Law breaking is behaviour that goes against the law of a country. Often, this is criminalised: there is a penalty or punishment attached (such as a fine or jail sentence) for breaking the law.

Criminologists, unlike, say, behavioural psychologists, study broad trends in crime rates as well as policies that are aimed at reducing criminal behaviours in communities. For example, a criminologist might analyse the growing problem of knife crime in the UK, focusing on the effectiveness of government policies that have been created in response to this issue. Specifically, he or she might compare the Criminal Justice Act of 1988, which banned the sale of knives to persons under 16, to the Violent Crime Reduction Act of 2006, which raised the legal knife-purchasing age to 18. This researcher might then try to gauge how a recent government amendment has (or has not) had an impact on knife crime rates in a given community.

Let's say that the community in question is Doncaster, South Yorkshire. I read an article a about two young boys in Doncaster, aged 9 and 11, who were beaten nearly to death by two other boys, aged 10 and 11, apparently for their refusal to part with their mobile phones and trainers to the aggressors. The victims were found covered in blood from knife slashes. Here is the link to the article:

http://news.bbc.co.uk/1/hi/england/south_yorkshire/7984392.stm

Upon learning of this particular case, a criminologist or sociologist would probably question the effectiveness of the legal amendments brought on by the Violent Crime Reduction Act of 2006. Do the new buying-age laws really make a difference if children are stabbing one another in Doncaster?

Like most readers, you will no doubt agree that their behaviour was shocking, horrific, and inhumane. You might even agree with the passer-by who first discovered the brutally injured boys and referred to their aggressors as 'absolute animals' (see above article). In reacting as such, we have placed these boys in a realm that is not only external to society but also external to humanity. It is as if, in our gut reactions, we decide that these violent behaviours are so far beyond our comfort zones that they are 'animalistic' in natural: rooted in some sort of biological 'otherness'.

However, common sense tells us that criminal behaviour has nothing to do with an individual's physical makeup (biological theories of criminality were abandoned decades ago). That is, there is nothing actually 'animal-like' about the biology of the perpetrators. Psychology is another story. It is, of course, possible that these young boys both suffer from chemical imbalances which incite criminal behaviour; we do not know for sure. But we must remember that knife crime is a widespread problem in the UK. If the sole cause of knife crime is, indeed, aberrant psychoses, that would mean that our nation is overrun with weapon-wielding psychopaths. Surely this is not the case; surely there are broader, social influences that influence individual, criminal behaviour. This is where we turn to the sociology of deviance. The sociology of deviance incorporates criminological research whilst investigating conduct that lies beyond the realm of criminal law. Researchers of deviant behaviour are concerned with why certain behaviours are regarded as deviant and how these notions of deviance are applied differentially to people within society. Further, they often consider the influence of factors such as social class, social power and divisions between rich and poor. So then back to the Doncaster case: clearly the criminal acts of the young boys in Doncaster were deviant; the boys broke the law (thus choosing not to conform to a sanctioned norm) by essentially attempting murder; but what other social scenarios led up to this horrific act? How were these boys treated in school? Did they even attend school? Were they among a group of rebellious, anti-education 'lads', and, if so, were their behaviours in the classroom regarded by their teachers as 'deviant'? Were they punished for deviant behaviours in their classrooms, or were their behaviours tolerated? What sort of class and family backgrounds do these boys come from? Were they monitored closely by their parents or guardians in their homes? Do members of their families hold criminal records? These are the types of questions that a sociologist of deviant behaviour would investigate, bearing in mind criminological statistics, whilst probing for other social influences. One final note before we move on to theory: it is important to realise that crime and deviance are both socially constructed. Society's definitions of what behaviours are 'unacceptable' or 'criminal' change over time in line with changes to the legal system and with social changes in general. For example, until 1961, it was considered a criminal act to commit suicide. Also, homosexuality was decriminalised in 1967 for men aged over 21, showing that what society considers unacceptable or acceptable is certainly a social fact rather than an unchanging or biological norm.

Crime, deviance, social order and social control

Theories:

- Functionalism - We return, once again, to functionalism, which is one of the foundational schools of thought used to study crime and deviance. Sociologists of this school think that acts of crime and deviance arise when individual aspirations can no longer be fulfilled at a societal level; essentially, when people want or need certain things, which simply cannot be made available to them. To give an extreme example: one of the root causes of the Humanitarian Crisis in Darfur was a conflict over natural resources. In the 1980s and 1990s, drought and desertification, combined with rapid population growth, led to a lack of arable land for crop farming and thus widespread starvation. People needed to compete for the valuable, usable land that was left and this led to conflict

- Durkheim - Emile Durkheim stated that crime and deviance are social facts of the modern age, which is characterised by a greater sense of flexibility and more room for individual choice. Thus, there is bound to be some non-conformity. Durkheim felt that deviance actually serves an important, necessary purpose in society: When people challenge social norms, they introduce new ideas—deviance thus has an adaptive function. Additionally, deviance serves to uphold boundary maintenance between 'good' and 'bad' behaviours in society. Durkheim also claimed that crime has four key characteristics. It is inevitable, universal, relative and functional

- Merton - Robert K. Merton constructed another functionalist theory of deviance which stated that in American society and likewise in other industrial societies, there is a strong emphasis placed on material success. As such, people who wish to achieve high standards of living (or the 'American Dream') but cannot do so through conventional forms of work, resort to deviant and criminal modes of 'work' in order to generate income. These people are known as innovators. Innovators are unlike conformists, who can and do abide by social conventions to achieve widely understood cultural values. Of course, not all people adhere to social norms: those that reject societal values, often responding in radical ways, are known as rebels. Other responses to the social norm of material success are ritualism and retreatism

Criticisms of Merton:

Subcultural theory

Albert Cohen later expanded upon Merton's ideas, agreeing that crime in American society was a result of the contradictions between cultural values and actual states of material wealth. However, he felt that, rather than responding to cultural norms individually, people actually banded together in subcultural groups in order to make (often bold) social statements. Collectively, subcultures will, for example, reject middle class values, sometimes engaging in violent, criminal behaviours. For example, Cohen explained that boys in the lower working class who are frustrated with their lots in life - or suffering from status frustration - may come together, forming delinquent subcultures, such as gangs, and engage in delinquent behaviour (Cohen 1955).

Delinquent behaviour can be defined as 'antisocial and criminal behaviour committed by children and teenagers'. Cohen felt that working class boys were the most likely to partake in delinquent behaviour. Cloward and Ohlin (1961) expanded on Cohen's ideas.

Miller (1962) took a slightly different subcultural perspective. He felt that working class boys actually operated within their own, separate set of cultural norms and values. Their social lives centre on the 'focal concerns' of trouble, toughness and excitement. Thus, when they break the law, they are actually adhering to the norms of their subcultural group.

Gangs

Activity 119 -
Research UK gang culture a little further; you may like to use this document as a starting point:
http://www.sociology.ox.ac.uk/documents/graduate-research/life-cycle.pdf
What is the social structure and hierarchy of UK gangs? Do you think that there should be more social research on gangs in the UK? Why or why not?

Marxist Subcultural theory

Marxist sociologists argue that working-class boys join gangs as a reaction to capitalism. With fewer unskilled labour jobs available, their futures become seemingly bleak. Gangs provide a social outlet for them to rebel against society with like-minded peers.

Criticisms of Subcultural theory:

Activity 120 –

Research David Matza's perspective, as well as the perspective of social action theorists, in your evaluation of subcultural theory.

You may like to read this article in order to do this:
http://www.criminology.fsu.edu/crimtheory/matza.htm

Environmental theory

Environmental theory focuses on urban areas, linking people's living, work and leisure environments to patterns of crime.

Shaw and McKay

Shaw and McKay conducted research on crime rates in Chicago, dividing the city into concentric zones (a series of circles within a circle, each circle representing a zone of the city). They found that in zone 2, the zone closest to the city centre, there were higher rates of crime. They hypothesised that this was due to a high rate of population turnover; zone 2 provided the cheapest housing in the city, so people would move their first and make their way to the nicer, outer regions of the city. The 'unsettled', transient nature of zone 2 thus led to social unrest, causing higher rates of crime.

Sutherland and Cressey

Sutherland and Cressey came up with the concept of differential association. They argued that the more that people are exposed to others who are not law-abiding, the more likely they are to engage in criminal behaviour themselves. Certain people (e.g., family members) are more influential than others; the amount of time spent together is also a key factor.

Children are more likely to be influenced than adults. There is a higher concentration of people with criminal attitudes in inner city areas; thus people will influence each other more frequently to engage in criminal activity. One major criticism of this perspective is that it does not account for individual agency; e.g. people can think for themselves and can avoid getting caught up in criminal activities.

British studies

Early British studies did not find clear, measurable patterns like those that Shaw and McKay found in their Chicago study. They also did not build upon the concept of differential association; however, Bottoms (1976) did examine the process of tipping. Tipping occurs when areas of a city are noticeably, visibly going downhill. As such, respectable and law-abiding people leave the area, and friends and family of the existing problem families move in. When the problem families outnumber the respectable families, the area has 'tipped': it has become a problem estate. Wilson and Kelling conducted a similar study, introducing the (now fairly famous) broken windows theory. This theory states that when a single broken window is left unmended in a neighbourhood, the number of broken windows in this area will increase. More unmended windows lead to more broken windows—the cycle continues as the area continues to go downhill.

Privatisation of public space

This argument discusses the privatisation of security and the police force in public places, which has led to strict, often biased policing that excludes certain members of the public, relegating them to the streets. Some shopping centres, for example, have specific dress codes; teenagers who are not dressed in a certain way, therefore, turn back to their estates, where they are more likely to engage in deviant behaviour.

Nocturnal economy

Studies indicate that 75 per cent of all violent incidents in urban areas occur between 9pm and 3am on the weekend; as such, sociologists are increasingly linking time to crime. Hobbs and Lister (2000), argue that the increase in bar and nightclub activity in urban areas causes drunken teenagers to enter the streets in the early hours of Friday and Saturday morning; this leads to increased crime and disturbance.

Criticisms of environmental theory

Many people argue that environmental theory relies too heavily on statistics. Gill (1977), for example, took a social interactionist approach to measuring the Luke Street council housing area in Liverpool. He found that Luke Street did not develop into a delinquent area because all of the people living there were inherently 'bad', but rather, because people labelled Luke Street residents as 'delinquent'. As a consequence, people from Luke Street (law-abiding or not) faced problems and misjudgements in the public sphere because of where their homes were located. Luke Street residents thus built up feelings of resentment, which led to more fighting with the police. This created a snowball affect, first drawing the attention of police, and then the media (who sensationalised stories of crime), and then more police and more media, and so on.

Social action theory and crime

Supporters of social action theory point out that most people have broken the law in one way or another; however, only a small population is actually publicly considered to be 'deviant' or 'criminal'. Whereas the functionalist, subcultural and environmental perspectives tend to rely on official statistics, social action theorists challenge them. They think that 'crime' and 'deviance' are socially constructed; they are more concerned with how and why certain groups (e.g. poor, minority, working class, and men) are labelled as 'criminal' or 'deviant' to begin with.

Labelling theory (Symbolic Interactionism)

The broad topic of labelling theory technically falls under the theoretical umbrella of symbolic interactionism. However, Howard Becker's studies of labelling theory are sometimes discussed under the title of 'Social action theory and crime'. We know that this is confusing. For the purposes of your examination, understand that Becker is a social action theorist who conducted a well-known study of labelling theory as it relates to deviance. However, when answering more general questions on theory you should understand labelling theory as part of symbolic interactionism.
Now, onto the actual theory...

Like social action theorists, labelling theorists argue that behaviours are not inherently 'deviant': some people are just labelled negatively by others. Howard Becker (1963) discusses how deviance is a relative term; it only exists when figures of authority decide that something is deviant and start to apply this label to others. Whether or not an activity receives the 'deviant' label depends on who was participating in the activity, where they were doing it, and whether or not a person in a position of greater power or authority witnessed the incident.

You may recall the earlier example on labelling theory: law enforcers label boisterous working class boys who play on other people's property as deviant. Yet what of the middle class girl who steals berries from her neighbour's garden and makes her mum a pie? The latter type of behaviour might be labelled as 'playful' or 'mischievous' as a commonplace pastime to joke about, whereas the 'deviant' boys who do not actually steal anything but just play similar games, might be punished. Clearly, both gender and class are factors at work here.

Once someone is labelled as deviant, he or she can unfortunately come to accept this categorisation and thus see him or herself in this light. As such, he or she will continue to engage in behaviours that will warrant punishment. This is known as self-fulfilling prophecy.

Activity 121 - Research Becker's concept of the 'master label' and attempt to apply this idea to real-life scenario that you have encountered (or perhaps a scenario that a friend or family member has encountered).

You may like to start your research here:
http://www.criminology.fsu.edu/crimtheory/becker.htm

Jock Young ('hippie drug users'):

Jock Young (1971) applied Becker's ideas to his studies of marijuana use by 'hippies' in Notting Hill, London. He noted that marijuana use was once only a minor part of the daily lives of hippies living in this area. However, once the police labelled and treated the 'hippies' negatively, they banded together and took part in more exaggerated behaviour as a mechanism of self-defence. To use Becker's terminologies, they would have accepted the 'master label' of 'hippie drug user'. Thus, in this instance, according to Young, the police would have actually caused the criminal behaviour; this process is known as deviancy amplification.

W.J. Chambliss ('Saints and Roughnecks' and 'The RDU'):

W.J. Chambliss conducted another, relevant study in America of two different groups of high school boys: the Saints, a group comprised of eight, middle-class boys, along with the Roughnecks, a group comprising six, working-class boys. Both groups engaged in the same types of anti-social, or 'delinquent', behaviour and in roughly the same capacity. The Roughnecks, however, received the most attention and punishment from the local police. This happened for several reasons.

Firstly, the Saints conducted most of their activities outside of town, whereas the Roughnecks displayed 'delinquent' behaviour in public places. On the rare occasion that the Saints did encounter the police, they used their cultural capital to talk themselves out of trouble. The Roughnecks, on the other hand, eventually accepted the deviant label that they were given, engaging in even more delinquent behaviour. The Saints all graduated from high school, went to college and got middle-class jobs. In contrast, two of the Roughnecks became serious criminal offenders.

Chambliss also conducted research on the Rapid Development Unit (RDU) in Washington DC. He argued that police officers focused much more aggressively on 'black' areas than they did 'white' areas, stopping more cars driven by blacks than they did whites. Reportedly, some police officers imparted derogatory remarks to black men who they suspected to be drug dealers.

Braithwaite (labelling and disintegrative shaming):

Braithwaite adds an interesting notion to Becker's concept of the master label. He discusses how, beyond applying master labels, law enforcers and communities also shame offenders in order to induce feelings of remorse and guilt; this process (known as disintegrative shaming) causes offenders to view themselves as outsiders. They feel that they do not have a chance at being integrated into mainstream society and are thus more likely to return to criminal subcultures after completing their sentences. Through re-integrative shaming, on the other hand, communities express disapproval but do not completely cast out offenders.

Activity 122 – Apply Braithwaite's ideas on shaming to the above case study of the Doncaster offenders.

Do you think that the young offenders will be reintegrated into society? Why or why not?

What kind of sociological study could be devised in order to assess the extent of the offenders' reintegration into society?

Criticisms of social action theory:

Social action theory has been criticised for being too sympathetic towards criminal offenders, rather than victims. Also, many think that they do not focus enough on the initial causes of criminal behaviour, but rather overemphasise the labelling process and its deterministic impact on individuals' self-perspectives. Lastly, Marxists argue that social action theorists focus too much on the working class and should incorporate more studies of corporate crime.

What are the modern patterns of crime in the UK?

The Home Office is the government department in the UK with responsibility for issues related to crime and justice. It is the source of official, government statistics on crime.

Activity 123 –
Investigate some of the crime statistics in the UK.
For example, find out what kinds of crimes are committed, how often or how common they are and how these are spread across the country. Are all crimes committed at the same frequencies in the same places? Who are usually the victims of crime? Who are the perpetrators or criminals?
You may like to use the Home Office crime statistics as your starting point:
http://www.homeoffice.gov.uk/crime/

Interpretation of crime statistics

In the UK, since the mid-1990s, the level of crime has actually been in decline. However, some forms of crime, in particular youth crime, have been on the rise, and this is a form of crime that can create a great deal of fear among other people.

When we interpret official statistics, we have to remember good sociological methods: statistics can be reliable, but may not always be valid. As sociologists, we therefore have to look carefully at the method by which the data was collected.

Official crime statistics can actually fail to reflect the true levels of crime. There could be a lot of crime that goes unreported, and this kind of crime is very hard to evaluate, for the obvious reason that there is no official data to analyse.

Why does some crime go unreported?

Some victims of crime may fear further crime if they go to the police. They may have been intimidated by the criminals, and so fear attack if they speak out.

There may be a belief (which could be justified) that the police are ineffective, and so there's no point reporting a crime. There could also be a feeling that criminals only ever receive light sentences, so even if they are caught then justice won't be done.

Some victims of small-scale crime (such as petty theft) may feel that the crime is too insignificant to report to the police and that there won't be any follow up or any point in doing so.

Some victims of sensitive crimes such as sexual assault or domestic violence may feel shame talking about the crime and so avoid going to the police because they feel unable to do so.

If these factors influence victims not to report crime, then sociologists need to think about different methods to collect more accurate and valid crime data.

So how can sociologists do this?

One possibility is to select a sample and then to survey those people about their experience of crime. It is likely that most of these people will not have been a victim of crime, but many may have been victims of petty theft which they did not report. If the sociologist then investigates the levels of petty theft by asking people questions about crime they have experienced but they did not report, then they can try and gain a more reliable and valid picture of the levels of crime.

Activity 124 –
The social dimension of crime is clearly a huge issue, and one that is important to sociologists since (like education) it has a clear link to social deprivation.

Many sociologists of crime advocate ways in which society can be improved and made more equal through better prevention and understanding of crime and the nature of criminal behaviour.

One such body that seeks this aim is the Centre for Crime and Justice Studies. Their website contains a great deal of interesting and useful information on many different aspects of crime. If you have found the sociology of crime an interesting topic, then you may wish to research further:
http://www.crimeandjustice.org.uk/index.html

Social action theory and deviance: mental illness

In the UK, people with mental illness are heavily stigmatised. Though they are not considered to be criminals, they are often regarded as deviant. Here are some different social action views on mental illness:

Medical/psychiatric model:

Followers of the medical or psychiatric model think that mental illness is a very real condition that is caused by either disturbing childhood experiences or chemical or hormonal imbalances. This is the most dominant perspective in the Western world, calling for either antidepressant drugs, psychological treatment or other forms of behavioural therapy.

Labelling model of mental illness:

The labelling model of mental illness, in line with our discussion in the topic on Health, argues that 'mental illness' is a social construct, a label that is applied to social outcasts and those who behave in 'abnormal' ways by people that are in more powerful positions. Most labelling theorists argue that there is no such thing as 'mental illness': people just go through periods in their lives in which they are miserable and lonely. To label what is a natural occurrence in one's lifetime (sadness) as 'clinical depression' and to treat this with drugs and expensive therapy is morally wrong.[48]

Once people are labelled as mentally ill, it is difficult for them to protest against this label because they might be seen as aggressive, and it can also fuel the cycle of depression and become a self-fulfilling prophecy.

Activity 125 -
Research Rosenhan's famous 1973 study of American psychiatric hospitals. You may like to start your research here:
http://en.wikipedia.org/wiki/Rosenhan_experiment

---

[48] Some researchers might cite the current over-diagnosis of Attention Deficit and Hyperactivity Disorder (ADHD) which, in the opinion of many, reflects the fact that society has become more complex and distracting, as evidence that 'mental illnesses' are socially created.

How does his study support labelling theory?

What are some strengths and weaknesses of his research method? Do you think that Rosenhan's 'undercover' approach' was ethical? Why or why not?

Criticisms of the labelling model:

Many are critical of labelling theory, claiming that mental illness is a very serious issue that must be addressed carefully. As such, the majority of western medical and psychological practitioners would probably see labelling theory as naïve or even as dangerous.

Traditional Marxist views on crime:

Traditional Marxists argue that capitalism itself is a crime of exploitation in which the proletariat work for the bourgeoisie and make profit for them. They claim that the relationship between the two groups is unbalanced and unfair: the only reason it is not viewed as criminal is because all of the laws in capitalist societies are created to serve the needs of the bourgeoisie. Furthermore, capitalism itself is a cause of criminal behaviours ('criminal' in the sense that we have previously discussed) in that it is a system based on cut-throat competition and greed. With communism, traditional Marxists believe that crime would cease to exist.

Corporate, white-collar and state crime:

Marxists are also interested in corporate crimes, which can be defined as crimes committed by corporations (or for corporations) to further their own interests. Corporate crimes can be divided into financial crimes and negligence. White-collar crimes are usually committed by individuals who are independently wealthy or of middle class backgrounds, and usually within and against their own corporate environments. White-collar criminals therefore take advantage of their professional status to commit crimes such as fraud, tax evasion or embezzlement.

State crimes are crimes committed by the government against society such as genocide, terrorism, war crimes and corruption.

Sociological views on corporate crimes:

Box (1981) argues that so many people get away with corporate crimes because they use 'mystification' to convince politicians, the media and the general public that corporate crimes are much less harmful than street crime and other types of crime. It is likely that most corporate and white-collar crimes are left undocumented; this creates an inbuilt statistical bias, leaving people to think that most crimes are committed by the working class who by definition would find it hard or impossible to commit white collar crime since they lack insider status within professional or corporate environments.

Criticisms of traditional Marxism:

Many are critical of these traditional Marxist views. For example, some point out communist countries such as Cuba, China and Russia experience crime. Also, they argue that people are much more concerned with crimes such as mugging and burglary than they are financial crimes. Lastly, most victims of crime are working-class.

The Social Distribution of Crime and Deviance

The New Criminology and New Left Realism

The New Criminology:

It is important that you are aware of some more contemporary Marxist views on crime. The New Criminology is a book by Taylor et al (1973) that presents a new theory on crime in deviance which calls for researchers to consider a multitude of factors surrounding a given criminal act. These include:

- Reasons behind the crime
- The roles played by law enforcers
- The role of mass media
- The role of the courts
- Politics
- Capitalism

Hall (1978) draws upon this research by examining the moral panic which surrounded the crime of mugging in Britain in the 1970s when Afro-Caribbean men were wrongly scapegoated by the public and aggressively pursued by law enforcers. Hall claims that moral panic developed because British capitalism was experiencing two crises: an economic crisis due to underemployment and strikes, as well as a political crisis over authority. The public had lost faith in the government and authorities, and law enforcers conveniently attempted to mask their shortcomings, diverting the public's attention by scapegoating Afro-Caribbean men as criminals. The media caught on, the public took to similar scapegoating, and moral panic ensued (this is a good example of deviancy amplification).

Gilroy (1982) similarly discusses how Afro-Caribbean men are unfairly treated and unfairly labelled. In the 1980s, there were such high unemployment rates amongst this section of society that authorities diverted attention from their problems e.g., their failure to ensure employment by creating a 'myth' of black crime.

Hall and Gilroy would both argue that Afro-Caribbean men are victims of a racist society. They are no more criminal than white men but are, unfortunately, labelled as such, and so a self-fulfilling prophecy is put into action.

Criticisms:

Hall and Gilroy actually contradict themselves. They both say, at some stage in their arguments, that the rise in black crime rates was inevitable due to the high unemployment rates. Critics of New Criminology would say something like this: 'if criminal acts by black men did actually happen—it must not have been a moral panic after all.'

New Left realism

New Left realists are critical of traditional Marxist and New Criminology views: they think that these theories are too politically charged e.g. not everyone is 'fighting back' against exploitative capitalist forces.

Some key elements of the New Left approach:

- Researchers need to pay more attention to victims
- Crime is a very serious problem that is growing, and not just due to labelling, scapegoating, racist policing, etc.
- Researchers need to pay attention to urban areas that are becoming increasingly dangerous, particularly for women
- Official statistics are not social constructs, as argued by traditional Marxists and new criminologists. They are actually pretty accurate
- White men are more likely to commit burglary; Afro-Caribbean men are more likely to commit street crimes, such as mugging, than are whites
- Researchers should pay more attention the relationship between crime and ethnicity

New Left theorists do to a certain degree accept that police forces may exaggerate the crime rates of ethnic minorities. However, they also criticise the new criminology assumption that police are targeting and labelling all Afro-Caribbean men as criminals. They point out that the majority of crimes are actually identified and reported by the public before the police would have a chance to make such judgement calls. They also think that there has, in fact, been an increase in street crimes committed by ethnic minorities, the majority of which are committed by Afro-Caribbeans against Afro-Caribbeans.

Young and Lea (1984) think that the reasons for this increase in black street crime are: relative deprivation, subculture, and marginalisation.

Evaluation of New Left realism:

Perspectives from the Right

The conservative sociological perspectives on crime all agree on the following:

- Criminals have made rational, intentional choices to break the law
- The government is supposed to punish criminals, not eliminate the 'root causes' of crime (which they think probably do not exist)
- If humans are poorly socialised, crime is inevitable as all humans are naturally greedy
- Crime can never be eliminated: it can only be reduced

Right realism

Right realists argue that crime does not result from social conditions such as poverty: there are plenty of old people living in poverty, and they are not engaging in criminal behaviour. Instead, right realists target issues such as the disintegration of the nuclear family; children and teenagers who are raised in single-parent families (which, according to right realists, comprise what is known as the underclass) and thus are not properly socialised, are the ones that commit crimes. They also point to the breakdown of communities as a cause of crime. Lastly, they think that police forces are not strong enough: they need to adopt 'zero tolerance' policies.

Rational choice and administrative criminology

Rational choice theorists apply a 'cost-benefit analysis' mentality to crime. They think that people who engage in criminal activity make a logical choice, weighing the costs (punishment) and benefits (financial reward, excitement, peer group acceptance) before committing a crime. As such, it is the police force's job to make sure that the costs always outweigh the benefits! In the UK, these ideas have been applied to administrative criminology, which includes the implementation of Neighbourhood Watch schemes and CCTV.

Postmodernity

Postmodernists argue that we live in a society which is dictated by individual choice and a plurality of options. There is no single theoretical perspective that can summarise or predict the way in which people will behave. This mindset can be applied to crime. Postmodernists would say that all acts of crime should be examined as unique, individual instances and that different policing styles may be needed for different areas. Some postmodernists would say that in a postmodern era, in which we pick and choose from a variety of ways to express ourselves, that crime should be considered as a part of an individual's self-expression.

Social Competition – Ethnicity

The basic issue regarding ethnicity that several criminologists are interested in is this: Why is the number of imprisoned, Afro-Caribbean men disproportionately high? In the UK, 2 per cent of the general population is Afro-Caribbean in comparison to 15 per cent of the prison population. (The statistics in the US are markedly more shocking: approximately 13 per cent of the general population is black, and 50 per cent of the prison population is black). What accounts for these incongruences? Some think that the legal system is biased; others feel that Afro-Caribbean men simply commit more crimes so what we need to do is figure out why and try to stop them.

Biased legal system?

You will recall Chambliss's study of the RDU in Washington DC in which he concluded that black men were unfairly pursued by the police. Several similar studies have followed suit in the UK. Phillips and Bowling, for example, argue that the UK criminal justice system is racist, pointing to the following factors:

- Over-policing of inner-city areas
- High number of stop and searches of black men (5-8 per cent higher than whites)
- High number of arrests
- Use of racially abusive language by police
- High imprisonment rate for blacks

Regarding the 'stop and search' figures, some people argue that there are simply more Afro-Caribbean men out at night in inner-city areas. The police are targeting everyone in high-crime areas but have no control over which segments of the populations choose to roam the streets.

Reasons for high crime rates among Afro-Caribbeans:

Many researchers think that the high crime rates are simply due to the fact that Afro-Caribbean men commit more crimes. Here are some reasons that have been put forth:

- Lea and Young (New Left realists): relative deprivation, subcultures and marginalisation
- Hall and Gilroy (though they thought high black crime rates were just moral panics, contradicted themselves): poverty, unemployment and poor housing
- Lack of educational success
- Family structure: 60 per cent of young black children live in single-parent families = possible lack of male role model and more likely to be poor
- Influence of mass media, especially a youth culture which glamorises crime through the gangster lifestyle

Social competition – Gender

You may have noticed that we have not really touched upon the subject of female criminals up until this point. The majority of sociological theories on crime and deviance do, indeed, focus on men. This even includes recent theories.

Statistics indicate that only 8 per cent of prison inmates in the UK are female. Most researchers assume that women simply commit less crime; however, some do propose that in fact women get away with more than men. For example, some argue that police officers and court officials give lower sentences to women compared to men, even for the same crimes. Of course, this is itself a sociological issue.

Theories:

Some feminists examined the current theories on crime to see if they are applicable to women. Here is what they found:

- Merton – Merton discussed how American society is dominated by the cultural value of material success. Those who cannot achieve the 'American Dream' through legal or straightforward work become 'innovators', often breaking the law. Does this theory apply to women? Should women not be 'innovating' to achieve material success, just like men? Some argue that women's goals are different than men's in that women are more focused on families than they are on wealth

- Sub-cultural theory and environmental theory - The thought that women might be gang members was never really incorporated into sub-cultural research. Environmental studies focused on social class but not really on gender, meaning that there is perhaps a lack of research into women and criminality

- Labelling theory – Again, labelling theory focuses on social class but not gender. Many feminists think that labelling theory could be usefully applied to the differential treatment of men and women by law enforcers

- Marxist theories – Traditional Marxist, the new criminology, and New Left realism theories all ignored women

Feminist views on why women commit crime:

Adler (1975) discusses how western women have taken to an increasing amount of criminal activity since women's liberation in the 1960s. Women engage in more 'masculine' behaviour in order to be competitive in job markets; this translates to other areas of their lives, e.g., smoking, drinking, more sexual activity and crime. Most people agree with Adler that women's behaviour has changed since the 1960s; however, many are sceptical of her claim that this change has included an increase in criminal activity. Statistics indicate that most female criminals are working class, and it was the middle class that was more affected by women's liberation as an intellectual and cultural movement, though all women have been affected by changes such as the right to vote and legislation such as the 1970 Equal Pay Act and the 1975 Sex Discrimination Act.

Carlen (1988) conducted research on a group of working class female criminals in London, rejecting Adler's liberation argument and, instead, applying rational choice theory. She claimed that when working class women resorted to criminal behaviour when they could not access the 'class deal' e.g. reasonably paid work, and the 'gender deal' e.g. decent relationships with men and the ability to have children. Both of these deals had previously dictated working class women's lives, giving them a sense of security. When the class deal became unattainable, women turned to crime for financial security. The gender deal, on the other hand, gave them the necessary emotional support to counterbalance their troublesome childhoods. Without this, they would turn to crime.

Some criticise Carlen's study for being too small scale (only 39 women). Also, many women who experience a breakdown in class and gender deals do not turn to crime.

On a final note, some feminists have reasons for why it is that most women do not turn to crime. These include: differential socialisation, fewer opportunities due to an abundance of household duties, preference for lower risk activities, and less knowledge of or ability to commit crimes (though this applies only to some forms of crime, such as violent crimes which typically require greater strength than the assailant).

Social class and age

Statistics indicate that young people are more likely to commit crimes than older people, and that people of working-class backgrounds are more likely to commit crimes than people of middle or upper class backgrounds.

Different theories explain this pattern in different ways.

Activity 126 - Ensure that you can explain the relationship between crime and social class according to the following theoretical perspectives:

- **Functionalists**
- **Early sub-cultural theorists**
- **Environmental theorists**
- **Right theorists**
- **Social action theorists**
- **Traditional Marxists**

- **New criminologists**
- **New Left realists**

Victims and crime

Victimology is the study of victims and is a fairly new addition to criminological research. The Home Office began publishing the Crime Survey for England and Wales (CSEW),[49] which is a large-scale social survey that asks people whether they have been victims of crime.

Gender and victimisation

Statistics indicate that young men aged 16-24 are the most at risk when it comes to violent crime. Men are generally more likely than women to become victims of street crime; however, women are more likely to be victims of rape and domestic violence.

Percentage of victims once or more		
All violent crimes[50]	Women	Men
Age	%	%
16-24	5.7	11.0
25-34	3.2	5.6
35-44	2.1	3.0
45-54	1.6	2.4
55-64	1.0	1.1
65-74	0.3	0.6
75+	0.2	0.2

CSEW 2001/2012

[49] Formally known as the British Crime Survey (BCS)
[50] 1 'All violence' includes wounding, assault with minor injury, assault without injury and robbery

Ethnicity and victimisation

The CSEW indicates that minority ethnics are more likely to be victims of most crimes, particularly burglary and vehicle theft, than whites. Blacks and Indians are specifically more likely to be victims of robbery; blacks are most likely to be assaulted or murdered. Proposed reasons for these trends: areas that minority ethnics live in, higher rates of unemployment, and increases in gang activity.

2012/2013: Percentage victimised once or more[51]	
White	5.0
Black or Black British	7.2
Asian or Asian British	6.4
Mixed	11.1
Chinese or other	4.2

Age and victimisation

An obvious shortcoming of the CSEW is that it only includes people aged 16 and older. As such, different types of victimisation surveys have been administered to youths with varying results. One problem with surveying children is that of defining what a 'crime' entails e.g. taking someone's lunchbox, mixing up gym clothes, etc.

Globalisation and crime

Ian Taylor (1997) discusses how the spread of global capitalism has led to financial strain (and thus criminal activity) in many areas of the world. As multinational corporations move from place to place in search of cheaper labour, working class labourers experience job shortages and often turn to crime. Taylor argues that in American and British cities material deprivation and job insecurity lead to increased crime rates.

---

[51] Source: Crime Survey for England and Wales

Globalisation has also had an impact on crime rates through the following means:

- Drug trafficking from South American and Middle Eastern countries to the UK and US. Globalisation has made drug trafficking faster and easier
- People trafficking has become much easier. People can be moved around for forced labour, prostitution and the removal of organs; children can be trafficked for illegal adoption and forced marriage
- Cybercrime, e.g. computer hacking, virus attacks, financial scams, email stalking, identity theft, websites that promote racial or religious hatred

Green/Environmental crime

Environmental crimes, or green crimes, are simply crimes that harm the environment. These crimes can be very small-scale such as an individual littering, or large-scale and disastrous such as nuclear disasters, and can be committed by individuals, banks and governments:

- Individual green crime – includes littering, the illegal dumping of waste (fly-tipping), picking of protected flora, disturbing endangered fauna. Individual green crime is unlike the other types of crime that we have discussed thus far in that people who commit green crimes usually do not consider themselves to be criminals. In response to global environmental concerns, the UK Environment Agency has cracked down on making people more environmentally aware in recent years
- Green crimes committed by businesses – include pollution and fly tipping
- Government green crime – include the transportation and dumping of waste material and pollution. Other government-related issues which have caused much controversy are the building and use of nuclear power stations or nuclear weapons, as well as whaling

State Crime

State crimes are crimes committed by the government, including breaches of human rights which can be evident from war crimes and genocide.

Genocide

Genocide is the systematic killing of an entire national, religious, ethnic or racial group. The most well known case of genocide is that which was committed by the Nazis against the Jews during the Second World War (the term 'genocide' was actually first used to describe this event). More recent examples are the mass killing of the Tutsis by the Hutus in Rwanda in 1994, as well as in Darfur in which a group of Janjaweed militants, armed and supported by the Sudanese government, has killed over 2 million black Africans since 1983.

War crimes

War crimes committed by the state include the torture of prisoners, the taking and holding of hostages, attacks on civilians, the use of child soldiers, the use of civilians as a shield, and the settling of an occupied territory. War crimes can also be committed by individuals and small groups. Perhaps the most famous series of war crime trials were those that were held in Nuremburg to prosecute prominent Nazi leaders and soldiers following the Second World War.

It is often difficult to identify whether or not something constitutes a war crime. For example, some commentators would say that George W. Bush and Tony Blair should be tried for war crimes, arguing that the war in Iraq was illegal.

Mass Media and crime

The mass media often sensationalise criminal activity and deviant behaviour to a degree that causes moral panic. If you recall, we looked at moral panic in the media and the work of Cohen who suggests that an act does not become criminal or deviant until it has been labelled as such, and that the media can be used as a instrument to perpetuate negatively certain actions by presenting people associated with such actions as folk devils. This can lead to widespread stereotyping of ethnic, racial or sub-cultural groups, which results in aggressive policing and even more exaggerated press.

Crime control

In this section, we will discuss measures taken by the government and competing political parties to prevent and control criminal behaviour.

Crime control, prevention and punishment

New Labour:

When elected in 1997, the New Labour party set out to tackle crime and the causes thereof. They report that factors contributing to crime, such as poverty, poor housing, and unemployment had gone down since 1997, as had the overall crime rate (though members of other parties, of course, think differently).

Here are some of the measures taken by New Labour:

ASBOs[52] – 'Antisocial behaviour orders', which tackle antisocial behaviour—e.g. vandalism, theft, harassment, begging, illegal raves—that which causes alarm or distress to the public. These civil orders are sought by local councils and issued by magistrates' courts. ASBOs are criticised for targeting vulnerable youths and unnecessarily labelling them as troublemakers; police warnings are, in many instances, much more effective. Also, ASBOs can have a reverse effect—some young people seek these labels as proud indicators of their deviance.

ABCs[53] – or voluntary 'acceptable behaviour contracts'. ABCs have no specific statutory basis - they are an informal, voluntary agreement between an individual who has committed anti-social behaviour, and a local agency whose role includes protecting victims and communities from such behaviour. These are created on an individual basis, forcing a person to confront and amend their destructive behaviours. Should an ABC be broken, the next step will be decided upon by the police, social workers and the local council (sometimes this could be an ASBO).

---

[52] https://www.gov.uk/asbo
[53] https://www.gov.uk/government/publications/acceptable-behaviour-contracts

Parenting contracts and orders – target parents of children that engage in antisocial behaviour. Contracts, which encourage parents to re-examine their responsibilities and parenting skills, can be followed by orders, which are sometimes issued by magistrates' courts and can require parents to attend classes.

Curfew and dispersal orders – these are orders issued by local councils, and enforced by the police, to ban children under the age of 16 from certain areas after certain hours (usually after 9 o' clock). Curfew and dispersal orders have raised much controversy. For example, they have been criticised for breaching human rights and for unnecessarily labelling young people as dangerous 'animals' that need be locked up indoors.

The role of the criminal justice system

There are varying sociological perspectives on what roles the police, courts and the prison currently play in UK society.

The role of the police and the courts

The official role of the police is to catch criminals, thereby enforcing the law, whereas the courts are to determine whether people are guilty and give appropriate sentences. Sociologists, depending on their perspectives, may view these roles differently, as follows:

- Functionalists, sub-cultural theorists and right-wing perspectives – the police and the courts are to target, catch and punish criminals—usually male criminals of working class backgrounds, as most crimes are committed by this group
- Social action theorists – the police and courts label some people as more criminal than others; usually, they target working class males; because of this, the working class falsely appears more criminal than other sectors of society
- Marxists – the police and courts target people with less power, ignoring business crime and state crime
- Feminists – the police and courts do not treat men and women equally and fairly

Activity 127 –

Ensure that you understand how the Criminal Justice System works and its role in crime prevention and punishment.

You may like to start your research here:

http://open.justice.gov.uk/

The role of prisons

Imprisonment is the most common form of punishment in the world; in the UK, 140 in 100,000 people are sent to prison each year (in the US, the figure is far higher at 700 in 100,000). Prisons aim to do the following:

- Punish criminal behaviour
- Protect the public
- Reform criminals
- Deter people from crime

It is difficult to measure the efficiency of prisons; for example, while prisons might protect the public from the most dangerous of criminals by keeping them jailed for life, about 70 per cent of prisoners that are released will re-offend.

Activity 128 - Do you think that prisons are the best form of punishment or deterrent for criminal behaviour?

To consider this question fully, you may like to think about alternative or newer forms of justice. One of these is Restorative Justice:
http://www.restorativejustice.org.uk/

4.3.2 Theory and Methods

Research methods in context: Official crime statistics and self-report studies

Official crime statistics are gathered in several different ways: through the reporting of crime (to the police), the recording of crime (by the police), and the Crime Survey for England and Wales - CSEW (formally known as the British Crime Survey (BCS)). Self-report studies are another way of acquiring information about illegal activities.

The former two collection methods are inherently problematic in that not all crimes are reported by public witnesses (or even by victims, for that matter); also, the police do not record every single crime that occurs. Instead, they use their discretion on a case-by-case basis and may issue warnings etc. before arresting individuals for criminal activity.

The CSEW is a large-scale questionnaire issued by the Home Office, which questions a representative sample of over 40,000 people aged 16+ on whether they have been victims of criminal activity.

Activity 129 - What do you think are the advantages and disadvantages of using the BCS to measure crime in the UK?

To think about:
Self-report studies involve questioning individuals on their own past criminal behaviour. These studies actually show higher rates of criminal activity than the official statistics.

What do you think are the advantages and disadvantages of using self-report studies versus official statistics to measure crime?

What do sociologists say about the use of crime statistics?

Functionalists, sub-cultural theorists, environmental criminology theorists and most right-wing perspectives view official crime statistics as social facts, or absolute truths. Later perspectives, such as Marxist theories and social action theories, see official crime statistics as social constructs, or as interpretations rather than facts. They use explanations such as labelling theory and deviancy amplification to explain crime.

Other ways to study deviance

Sociologists can employ several other methods to study deviance, including participant observation, informal interviews, field experiments and secondary sources.

Activity 130 - Complete the following chart, referring back to your earlier notes if necessary.

Method + Description	Quantitative or Qualitative?	Advantages	Disadvantages
Participant Observation			
Informal Interviews:			
Field Experiments:			
Social Surveys:			
Secondary Sources:			

Conclusion

Like education, crime and deviance is a hot topic for sociologists who are concerned with social exclusion. Can you see any links between social stratification and inequality and how they permeate through the education system and the legal justice system?

Just to re-iterate, data can be collected first-hand by the researcher, as primary data or from other printed sources (official statistics, historical information, etc.) as secondary data. There are advantages and disadvantages to both approaches; it is your job as a researcher to decide what types of data are most suited to your research project.

Research Methods in general

Surveys:

Sociologists often use surveys to collect primary data, asking members of the public specific questions about, for example, class, education and occupation. Researchers may also use information gathered by government-conducted surveys as secondary data.

Interviews:

Unstructured interviews are a qualitative method of primary data collection, often employed by researchers particularly when looking into areas of differentiation.

Activity 131 -

Evaluate the advantages and disadvantages of using unstructured interviews. What do interviews provide that surveys do not?

Is it possible that information collected in interviews could reflect the interests of the researcher rather than the primary concerns of the interviewee?

How would you, as a researcher, prevent your interviews from producing subjective results?

Participant observation

Sociologists also use the qualitative approach of participant observation in stratification research; they may immerse themselves in specific groups of society in order to learn more about their perspectives. This type of research tends to provide rich, detailed information but can pose many ethical problems.

Types of data: quantitative vs. qualitative

To review what you should already know (and what you will be asked to describe, once again, in the following section on theory and method), sociological data can be collected in either qualitative or quantitative forms.

Quantitative data:

- Numerical
- Used to provide statistical evidence
- Often covers large-scale segments of society
- Often accounts for broad cross-sections of society
- Gathered through surveys, structured interviews, official statistics, experiments

Qualitative data:

- Descriptive
- Based on people's personal experiences and feelings
- Gathered through interviews—usually informal and often unstructured
- Gathered through participant observation

Activity 132 - Evaluate the strengths and weaknesses of quantitative research
What types of researchers tend to prefer quantitative data?
Give an example of how quantitative data could be useful in studies of social class and stratification
Evaluate the strengths and weaknesses of qualitative research
What types of researchers tend to prefer qualitative data?
Give an example of how qualitative data could be useful in studies of social class and stratification

Primary vs. secondary:

Both primary and secondary data can be either qualitative or quantitative in nature. For example, unstructured interviews provide primary, qualitative data, whereas structured interviews can additionally provide primary, quantitative data.

Is society like a web? How can sociologists find this out?

Sociological studies

Secondary sources

Activity 133 -
How can secondary data produce different results when analysed by different researchers?

You may like to investigate the example of the National Child Development survey as an example of the importance of interpretation:
http://www.esds.ac.uk/longitudinal/access/ncds/l33004.asp

Primary resources

Methods in triangulation

Activity 134 - What is triangulation? What are some important cautions to take when using sociological methods in triangulation?

Action research

Action research aims for social change, and is usually driven by personal political and social motives. Whilst this type of research can be very rich and informative because the person conducting it is usually heavily-invested in the topic, it also has the potential to be biased and politically charged.

Activity 135 –

Describe a social issue that you are passionate about.

Should you ever choose to conduct research on this issue, what precautions would you take to ensure that your results and observations were as reliable and valid as possible?

Theory

Introduction

In this final section of the A-level sociology course, you should endeavour to work from, and expand upon, the knowledge of theory and methodology that you have gained throughout this course.

Essentially, this section will discuss, through various theoretical approaches, how individuals have an impact on society, and vice versa. You will also explore further the social factors and broad patterns that keep society 'together'.

Positivism

One question that is often asked is:

Is sociology a science?

In order to address this question we have to be quite clear as to what constitutes a science and from there see if sociology has all or any of the characteristics associated with the sciences.

The sciences, like Sociology will start with a theory or hypothesis and from there conduct experiments, observations and measurements in order to establish and test the theory or hypothesis. One of the key features favoured by science is that of objectivity, therefore, personal opinions and points of views are not encouraged or valued, and as such the results generated from scientific experiments are seen as more credible and valid. Note, however, some thinkers such as Lyotard (1984), a post modernist, argue that it is not possible to be completely objective even in science. Some areas of Sociology have tried to replicate and take on board certain characteristics of the science, and this group of sociologists are referred to as Positivists. They believe that Sociology should be objective and therefore scientific in its approach to looking at social facts, and any findings should be value-free. They are therefore more likely to be in favour of methodologies that can provide correlative and quantifiable data.

Interpretivist approach

This approach is very much in contrast to the Positivist approach in that as far as Interpretivist are concerned it is not possible for anyone to be completely objective or value free. By virtue of being social beings we have values and opinions that inevitably have an impact upon how we interpret things, even those things that may seem beyond our control and detached.

From this perspective, in order to understand the many facets of society, we have to understand the meanings and reasons behind social interaction. As Weber suggests, we need to understand why people do what they do (empathy).[54]

Modernity and postmodernity

The classical sociological approaches were developed during modernity; contemporary theories are shaped by postmodernity. You must be able to define, compare and contrast these terms and understand which sociological concepts these two periods influenced.

Sociological theory, consensus and conflict: Society as a functional unit

A recap: a functionalist sociologist is one who understands society in terms of a system. A society is a complex system: one with many parts, but one which essentially works together. In other words, a functionalist sociologist would see all the parts of society (such as the different economic classes) as working together to produce a solid and cohesive whole.

When it comes to analysis of social class, therefore, it is important to look at the relationships between the classes to see how this maintains cohesion, stability or the ability of the whole society to function.

---

[54] Weber referred to this as 'verstehen'

Durkheim and social facts

You may recall that Durkheim felt that broader patterns in society shaped individual actions; he argued that society consists of objective, measurable social facts e.g. law, language or money, which exist externally to individual actions; these social facts also possess collective, cultural values, which influence, or 'constrain', individual actions.

Durkheim demonstrated this perspective in his research findings on suicide; he concluded that, when people are too integrated, or not integrated enough, in society e.g. over-influenced or under-influenced by external constraints, they are more likely to commit suicide.

Parsons and society as a social system

Parsons viewed society as a series of interlinked systems, of which the social system is the most influential. The social system contains a variety of social institutions (education, religion, family, etc.) which play a huge role in the socialisation process. For example, the institution of education aims to socialise students into becoming obedient, hard-working contributors to the economy. Ideally, people will internalise the values and social roles projected by the institution of education, thus absorbing them into what Parsons calls the personality system. It is the job of the social system to fulfil functional prerequisites, or specific societal needs so that people may transfer over into the other systems, thus allowing society to function effectively. (Parsons also identified the community sub-system, the political sub-system and the economic sub-system, for example.)

However, Parsons did account for the fact that not all people would internalise social norms and values in the same way, leading to people with varied goals and outlooks on life. He discussed pattern variables, which are dilemmas that people face that may change their course of action.

Evaluation of Parsons

The structural functionalism of Parsons is a variation of systems theory, and so the focus is on the cohesion of the whole rather than on the disagreements or discord that may exist between individuals or between individuals and social structures. The key question of day-to-day social interactions and how these add up to make society was not part of Parsons's model, and so Merton looked at this in his revision of Parsons.

Activity 136 – What do you think of Parsons's model as a way to explain how society works?

Merton

The last functionalist theorist that we will consider in this section is Merton who placed more emphasis on individual actions than Parsons. He argued that people will respond to the goals of society in one of five different ways; for example, people who wish to achieve material wealth in American society but cannot do so through traditional means, may become innovators, achieving wealth through a non-traditional, possibly illegal, means. He also discussed how disadvantages relating to particular social institutions could influence individual behaviour.

Merton challenged what he considered to be the rigid views of early functionalism, questioning three key notions.

How did Merton question early functionalism?

Merton felt that the focus on the large-scale or the small-scale (either big social institutions or everyday interactions between individuals) failed to account for how these two levels joined.

Therefore, Merton argued instead for a middle point, moving nearer to conflict theory in doing so.

To find a middle ground, Merton developed the concepts of manifest function and latent function. The manifest function is the intended or observable function of an action, and the latent function is the unintended or unspoken outcome.

For example, the manifest function of the Olympic Games is to award medals for sporting excellence, but one latent function of the Olympic Games held in London 2012 could be the romantic relationship between two spectators who met while watching an event, the friendship between two stewards that started at the event or a prize-winning photo that a spectator took while at the Games. All of these latter outcomes were never the stated, official ones of the Olympic Games, and yet a large sporting event of this kind will have the effect of bringing people together and stimulating creativity in this way as well.

Problems with functionalism in general

The main issue that many researchers have with functionalism is that it tends to overlook individual contributions to society. Also, some would argue that it lacks a thorough account of social conflict and fails to see dysfunction in big social institutions such as education, the legal system or government because by definition it views them as functional.

Ideology, capitalism and domination

Marx

Marx argued that the base, or economy, possesses inequalities that are masked by dominant ideologies, which are spread by institutions in the superstructure. This projection of ideologies by the superstructure onto the base economy allowed the relationship of exploitation to exist in capitalist societies.

Activity 127 –

Marxism has been a hugely influential school of thought. You may wish to research the life and thought of Marx further. You can start your research here: http://plato.stanford.edu/entries/marx/

Marx's solution to the exploitative nature of capitalist society was communism: He felt that communism would resolve issues of social inequality in a class-divided society.

Analysis of Marx:

Clearly, as we previously discussed, there has not yet been a working class 'revolution' as predicted by Marx's theory. However, Marx made important, pioneering contributions to research on inequality and power relationships in society.

Althusser (Structural Marxism)

Althusser differed from Marx in that he focused on how social structure, and thus capitalist society, regenerates itself to remain stable over time. He thought that society consisted of three different, autonomous 'levels': the economic level, the political level and ideological the level. Any contradictions that arose between these three different aspects of society could bring about social disorder and/or social change. Althusser claimed that the ideological state apparatus (ISA) transmits ideologies, which prevent such changes and conflicts from occurring.

Analysis of Althusser:

Researchers have criticised structural Marxism for its over-emphasis on abstract social structures and its failure to account for individual agency.

Gramsci (Humanist Marxism)

Gramsci argued that hegemony makes capitalism possible. Hegemony is the ideological control that the ruling class has over the masses; it enables the former to exploit the latter. However, Gramsci believed that members of the lower classes have minds of their own. The masses are perfectly capable, under the leadership of intellectuals, of fighting exploitation through collective action, which will ultimately lead to radical social change.

The Frankfurt school

The Frankfurt school argued that the values which defined Marx's early capitalist society had disappeared. They claimed that late capitalist societies are centred on human fulfilment, which is achieved through instrumental reason. People who think in terms of instrumental reason view people and money as strategic pawns, both of which will allow them to achieve their self-serving goals (as opposed to relationships with people being sources of genuine fulfilment). For example, an actor might befriend a director so that she has a better chance at being cast in his future films; a boss might see her employees as exploitable 'investments', rather than as friends.

The Frankfurt school also carried out much research into the dominance of mass media. They argued that the media dictates the way that people carry out their daily lives, generating false needs through means such as advertising, which as a result create weak, self-absorbed personalities that can be further manipulated.
Problems with Marxism in general.

In common with other theorists who laid the foundations for sociology (such as Durkheim or Weber), Marx did not make extensive comment on gender as a social category. For him, the key to ending oppression in society was through revolution: class warfare. Women's oppression in society would end when social stratification by class was overthrown, because then the concept of woman-as-male property would have to end.

For Marx, social problems are always in essence about class, but this leads us to an on-going problem with current and future sociological research:

- To what extent can one social category (e.g., gender) be best understood by reference to others (such as ethnicity, class or age)?
- In other words, is there a 'basic' or 'master key' social category that explains and is at the root of all others, and if so, what is this?

Feminism, patriarchy and identity

By now, you should understand the basic underlying currents of feminism: patriarchy causes women to hold a subordinate position in society; people are treated differently and hold different positions in work, educational and domestic environments based on their gender.

There are five different approaches to feminism: liberal feminism, radical feminism, Marxist feminism, Black feminism, and postmodern feminism that you should understand from AS.

Walby on patriarchy: private and public

The feminist Sylvia Walby is a sociologist who argues that the concept of patriarchy is fundamental in understanding gender and gender inequality. She formulated two concepts:

- Private patriarchy - This is the patriarchy that occurs inside the household where each individual woman is oppressed by a patriarch: a man who holds power over her in some form or another, such as a husband or a father
- Public patriarchy - This is the patriarchy that occurs in the public sphere, such as government, the workplace or in the education system. Here, women are excluded from the real centres of power and decision-making and are instead relegated to lower-status and lower-paid positions within these structures

According to Walby, each of the following structures perpetuates patriarchal values (either private or public):

- Housework – because women take on a disproportionate role in childcare and housework, and this unpaid labour is used to the advantage of her husband, father or male companion, who benefits from this care but does not return the same
- Paid work – women are relegated to lower-status, lower-paid positions, and so are excluded from the top positions which accrue the best pay and authority; these are only available for men. In this stereotype, women experience a 'glass ceiling' and can only ever become secretaries, whereas men are the managers, bosses and CEOs
- The state – it is largely men who make up 'the state' in the form of elected representatives and governmental officials and so they perpetuate sexism and discrimination against women
- Male violence – the threat and the experience of domestic and sexual violence works to limit and curtail women's activity and their ability to speak out against the forms of oppression they suffer
- Cultural institutions – such as the media or cultural heritage. These write women out of history and culture and perpetuate unequal gender roles in the present

Understanding gender relations

Gender order is a term used by sociologists to refer to the pattern or network of (unequal) relationships between men and women.

Gender regime is a term used by sociologists (from the sociologist R W Connell's comprehensive analysis of gender) to refer to how gender order plays itself out in a specific setting, such as an institution like a school or hospital, or even just one particular household or family.

Activity 128 - How do you think that feminism has made a useful contribution to sociological theory?
To answer this question you may wish to reflect on the notes you have made on feminism so far in units 1-3.

Sociological Research's impact on Social Policy

Sociological research can provide the basis for reforms following identification of a particular social issue or an area of social concern. It can be the basis upon which policy changes and alterations try to remedy possible social problems. Bauman, who is a postmodernist thinker, argues that sociological research is valuable in that it can provide an insight into potential social issues, if, not taken on board can lead to greater social problems. From a Marxist perspective, despite the findings of any sociological research, any policy changes implemented or made will still only benefit the ruling classes who are the ones that make the final policy decisions anyway.

Examples of policy and social changes can be seen in changes in the law and welfare state following numerous pieces of research over the years regarding poverty and causes and extent of it. Sociological research has been instrumental in other changes in the law such as, The Disability Discrimination Act, Race Equality legislation, Sex Discrimination legislation

Overall, according to thinkers such as Giddens, Sociology is about:

- Understanding society
- Awareness of cultural difference
- Increased self-knowledge and awareness
- Assessment of government policies.

BV - #0014 - 210520 - C0 - 297/210/24 - PB - 9781326424350